From Awareness to Funding

A study of library support in America

A Report to the OCLC Membership

OCLC

From Awareness to Funding
A study of library support in America

A Report to the OCLC Membership

Principal contributors
Cathy De Rosa, Vice President for the Americas and Global Vice President of Marketing
Jenny Johnson, Executive Director, Branding and Marketing Services

Graphics, layout and editing
Brad Gauder, Creative Services Writer
Rick Limes, Art Director
Sam Smith, Art Director

Research partner
Leo Burnett USA

OCLC would like to thank:
The Bill & Melinda Gates Foundation for funding the advocacy research presented in this report and for making the research findings broadly available to the library community.

Members of the Advocacy Research Working Group, for giving time, support and insightful feedback throughout the project:

Bruce Astrein, Executive Director, Libraries for the Future

Mary Baykan, Director, Washington County Free Library

Mamie Bittner, Deputy Director for Policy, Planning, Research, and Communications, Institute of Museum and Library Services

Denise Davis, Director, ALA Office for Research & Statistics, American Library Association

Martín Gómez, President, Urban Libraries Council

Herb Landau, Director, Milanof-Schock Library

Greta Southard, Executive Director, Public Library Association

Larry Tramutola, President and CEO, Tramutola, LLC

OCLC
Dublin, Ohio USA

Copyright © 2008, OCLC Online Computer Library Center, Inc.
6565 Kilgour Place
Dublin, Ohio 43017-3395

ALL RIGHTS RESERVED. No part of this publication may be reproduced, stored in a retrieval system or transmitted, in any form or by any means, electronic, mechanical, photocopying or otherwise, without prior written permission of the copyright holder.

The following are trademarks and/or service marks of OCLC: OCLC, the OCLC logo, WebJunction, WorldCat and WorldCat.org.

Third-party product, service, business and other proprietary names are trademarks and/or service marks of their respective owners.

Printed in the United States of America

Cataloged in WorldCat on June 20, 2008
OCLC Control Number: 232357947

ISBN: 1-55653-400-0

13 12 11 10 09 08   1 2 3 4 5 6

Table of Contents

	Chapter/Page
Introduction: Funding the mission	**vii**
Methodology	xi
From awareness to funding	**1-1**
Who are the library's financial supporters?	**2-1**
Elected officials and library funding	**3-1**
Library funding support is an attitude, not a demographic	**4-1**
Motivating Probable and Super Supporters—testing the facts in the field	**5-1**
Mobilizing Probable and Super Supporters—what makes the difference	**6-1**
Conclusion	**7-1**
Appendices	**8-1**
A: Glossary	A-1
B: About the Bill & Melinda Gates Foundation and Leo Burnett USA	B-1
C: About OCLC	C-1

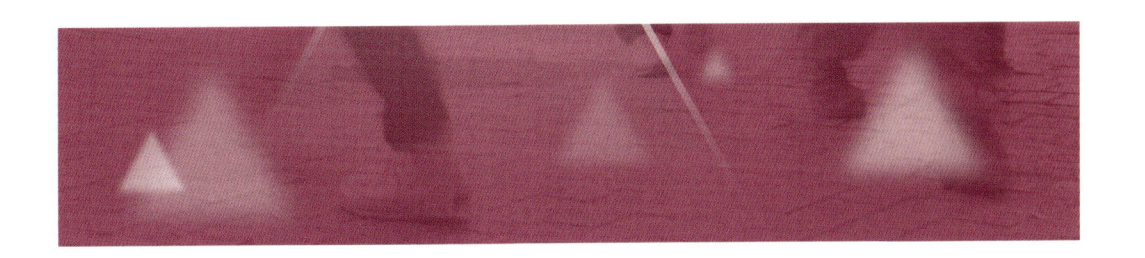

Introduction: Funding the mission

Each of the 9,000 public library systems in the United States[1] has a unique mission, a mission crafted to meet the unique needs of the community it supports. But together these libraries also share a collective mission: *to provide every resident of the United States the opportunity to thrive through access to information and lifelong learning.* The importance of this collective mission has been strengthened by decades and generations of experiences that confirm that free and open access to information transforms; it transforms lives, it transforms communities and it transforms societies.

> *"The library is a great promoter of equality and democracy. Anyone can go, anyone can read what they want and make whatever use they want of it for whatever they want to pursue."*
> (Research participant, Minneapolis, Minnesota)

Free access transforms, but transformation is not free.

While the majority of residents of the United States have visited their public library and have used its services, most cannot describe how their library is funded. Over 80% of funding for U.S. public library operations comes from local tax receipts. State and federal taxes provide a relatively small portion of public library operating funds in most states. Together, state and federal funds accounted for approximately 10% of total annual operating budgets of U.S. public libraries in 2005[2], down from 14% of operating budgets in 2000. Dependence on the local purse for public library funding is high, and increasing.

Local taxpayers provided over $9 billion in 2004 to support the operations of their public libraries. U.S. taxpayers also provided $800 billion in local taxes for other community services including fire, police, schools, health and parks.[3] All of these vital community services demand time, attention and tax support from citizens and their elected officials. There is growing pressure and increasing competition for the community mindshare.

Public libraries funding represents roughly 1% of total local community operating expenditures.

Source: U.S. Census Bureau, 2004

For many public libraries, the need to grow awareness and mindshare is intensifying as library annual operating funds are not keeping pace with the services and resources needed to meet their mission. Analysis of 2005 data collected by the National Center for Education Statistics highlights that over a third of U.S. public libraries are operating with budgets that are declining. Many more are operating with budgets that are level or slightly ahead of inflation, but significantly behind the current inflation rates for employee benefits, energy and materials. As a result, many libraries are being forced to reduce staff, cut hours and reduce community services.

Introduction: Funding the mission

The longer term public library funding picture is also challenging. Library levies, referenda and bond measures have been failing at an increasing rate over the past decade. And the number of library levies placed on a ballot for voter consideration is also in decline.[4]

If residents are not aware of how their libraries are funded, are they aware of the growing financial pressures on libraries? Are the service reductions or trade-offs that occur as library budgets decline debated sufficiently within local communities? And is the collective library voice strong enough to attract the mindshare necessary to ensure future funding? These critical questions now face many U.S. public libraries.

We live in a country, and a world, blanketed by marketing messages and appeals for consumers' and voters' time, money, endorsements and mindshare. It is estimated that total advertising spend in the United States will reach nearly $300 billion this year.[5] The marketing techniques deployed by organizations to reach their sales or advocacy goals are becoming increasingly sophisticated and effective. Indeed, the number and effectiveness of library marketing and advocacy campaigns are also growing. These campaigns have been successful at increasing awareness and library use. Library visits are up 19% from 2000 to 2005. Circulation of library materials is up 20%. Access to public computers is up 86%.[6] But funding is not keeping pace with this demand. While successful in raising demand, the majority of library campaigns have been aimed at promoting library services and driving library use, not increasing library funding.

Funding the collective library mission is a growing problem and without proactive and large-scale action, we can see no economic, social or political factors or events that will reverse the trends in library funding. So, in 2007, funded by a generous grant from the Bill & Melinda Gates Foundation, we set out to ask the question: is it possible to apply the latest marketing and advocacy techniques that are being so successfully used in other venues to create funding awareness, drive action and *ultimately increase funding for public libraries?* Is it possible to reverse the downward trend in library levy passage rates? Can libraries be more effectively positioned alongside other critical local services like fire, police, schools and public health? And could a national library support campaign make a difference in the ability of public libraries to fund their collective mission?

Our hypothesis:

> U.S. public libraries are facing marketing and advocacy challenges that have been faced by other 'super brands.' Lessons learned and successes achieved can be applied to increase library funding. Utilizing marketing and advocacy techniques targeted to the right community segments with the right messages and community programs, we can improve the state of public library funding.

OCLC partnered with Leo Burnett, a national research and advertising agency, to conduct the research and exercise this hypothesis, utilizing the most current marketing techniques and practices. We also worked with a distinguished group of librarians and community leaders who guided and advised us throughout the project.

> *We set out to ask the question: is it possible to apply the latest marketing and advocacy techniques that are being so successfully used in other venues to create funding awareness, drive action and ultimately increase funding for public libraries?*

Introduction: Funding the mission

There is sufficient, but latent, support for increased library funding among the voting population.

I am pleased to report the results are promising. Findings suggest that there is sufficient, but latent, support for increased library funding among the voting population. There is evidence that a large-scale library support campaign could make a difference. Working together with librarians, local communities, library consortia and association leaders and other partners, we believe that it is indeed possible for a library support campaign to increase, and sustain, public library funding in the United States.

This report summarizes our findings. We look forward to your comments, your feedback and the opportunity to work together to put this research into action. You can post ideas, observations and suggestions at www.community.oclc.org/funding. You can contact me directly at derosac@oclc.org.

Again, our thanks to the Bill & Melinda Gates Foundation for its support of this research and for the opportunity to partner on library advocacy initiatives.

Cathy De Rosa
Vice President for the Americas and
Global Vice President of Marketing
OCLC

---

1. Chute, A. and P.E. Kroe, *Public Libraries in the United States: Fiscal Year 2005* (NCES 2008-301), Table 1, p.6, National Center for Education Statistics, Institute of Education Sciences, U.S. Department of Education, Washington, DC, 2007.

2. Ibid., Table 9, p. 22; and Chute, A., P. Garner, M. Polcari and C.J. Ramsey, *Public Libraries in the United States: Fiscal Year 2000* (NCES 2002-344), Table 12, National Center for Education Statistics, Institute of Education Sciences, U.S. Department of Education, Washington, DC, 2002.

3. U.S. Census Bureau, "State and Local Government Finances by Level of Government and by State: 2003–04," http://ftp2.census.gov/govs/estimate/04slsstab1a.xls.

4. Freeman, Christopher, "Library Referenda 2007: A Mixed Bag," Library Journal, March 15, 2008, p. 39; and Gold, Anne Marie, "Library Referenda 2006: Thumbs Up, and Down," *Library Journal*, March 15, 2007, http://www.libraryjournal.com/article/CA6422277.html.

5. *eMarketeer*, "Where Is Ad Spending Headed?" May 2, 2008, http://www.emarketer.com/Article.aspx?id=1006250.

6. Chute, A. and P.E. Kroe, *Public Libraries in the United States: Fiscal Year 2005* (NCES 2008-301), Table 1, p.6 and Table 9, p. 22, National Center for Education Statistics, Institute of Education Sciences, U.S. Department of Education, Washington, DC, 2007; and Chute, A., P. Garner, M. Polcari and C.J. Ramsey, *Public Libraries in the United States: Fiscal Year 2000* (NCES 2002-344), Table 12, National Center for Education Statistics, Institute of Education Sciences, U.S. Department of Education, Washington, DC, 2002.

Introduction: Funding the mission

Methodology

OCLC received a grant from the Bill & Melinda Gates Foundation to conduct research, develop strategies, create materials and evaluate the potential of marketing and communications programs to sustain and increase funding for U.S. public libraries.

OCLC engaged Leo Burnett to field an advocacy research program that included both quantitative and qualitative research.

Quantitative research

The quantitative study targeted two audiences: residents in U.S. communities of populations less than 200,000 and elected officials in the United States. More than 90% of all U.S. public libraries serve communities with populations of 200,000 or less. The study was intentionally designed to capture and analyze the attitudes, behaviors and opinions of residents in these communities.

The objectives of the quantitative research survey were twofold:

- To create a market segmentation analysis of the U.S. voting population that identifies which segments of voters are the most likely to generate increased support for U.S. public libraries. The segmentation study was designed to help uncover the underlying motivations and attitudes toward libraries that are indicative and predictive of their level of support for library funding.

- To understand the attitudes and behaviors of elected and appointed officials about libraries in general, the library's importance to the community and how those attitudes impact the officials' willingness to support local library funding.

Voter survey

The survey measured over a dozen parameters, including demographics, library usage, perceptions of the local public library and librarian, attitudes toward taxation, voting behavior, community involvement, perceptions of local tax-supported services and willingness to vote for increased library funding.

The questionnaire was administered in two phases to an online panel of respondents and supplemented with phone interviews to account for people without Internet access. All interviews were conducted in cities, towns or suburbs with populations of less than 200,000 with residents ages 18–69. The survey did not include residents younger than 18 because they are not eligible to vote. The survey did not include

Methodology

residents older than 69 because they are typically difficult to recruit for participation in market research; to capture a sample that would have been representative of people in the age group over 69, alternative research methodologies would have been required.

A 25-minute, online survey of more than 8,000 adults was fielded in January 2007. Twenty-seven percent (26.6%) of respondents self-identified as 'Chronic Non Voters' (i.e., they weren't registered to vote or they were registered but never voted) and were excluded from the sample. A second 60-minute online questionnaire was fielded to the remaining respondents in February 2007 and 1,901 adults completed the second survey. Results were weighted to be nationally representative of adults ages 18–69 in populations of less than 200,000. Together, both phases provided 85 minutes of data across a sample of 1,901 adults. The survey data for the total sample have a statistical margin of error of +/− 2.4 percentage points at the 95% confidence level for the U.S. population ages 18–69 in communities of less than 200,000 people. Subsamples will have a larger margin of error.

BrandProspect™ segmentation

The trademarked segmentation methodology employed by OCLC's research partner, Leo Burnett, has been used successfully to help the world's leading brands be more effective. This is what Leo Burnett says about this trademarked approach:

"Not everyone is alike and different people want different things from the category. They also evaluate, perceive and use brands differently. No brand has 'universal appeal' and the more brands there are in a category, the more this is true.

For every brand, there is greater chance to build business among some segments of consumers than others. If these segments can be identified, the brand has a 'roadmap for growth' and can customize marketing efforts to the most likely prospects. By identifying and prioritizing groups of consumers, valuable segments become brand targets and other segments can be ignored, deferred or given lower priority. This in turn maximizes the impact of limited marketing dollars.

There are lots of ways to segment: behavior, attitudes, need states, perceptions, benefits, demography, lifestyle, life attitudes, etc. Most segmentation studies are based on a single approach imposed at the outset and the interaction of other category and brand dynamics often goes unnoticed. Brands lose sight of constructs that really matter and the findings from the study are frequently not linked to brand growth.

Leo Burnett developed BrandProspect™ to overcome this. It's different from other segmentation studies because it's grounded in the reality of brand growth dynamics, built around hypotheses—not around an approach—based on a multimeasure segmentation, constructed hierarchically and held to a behavioral standard."

Methodology

Segmentation results

The BrandProspect™ segmentation analysis resulted in the development of a Library Supporter Segmentation Pyramid representing U.S. residents ages 18–69 in communities of 200,000 residents or less. The Library Supporter Segmentation Pyramid is made up of four tiers: Super Supporters, Probable Supporters, Barriers to Support and Chronic Non Voters. The Barriers to Support and Probable Supporters tiers are further segmented: Financially Strapped, Detached, The Web Wins, Just for Fun, Kid Driven, Library as Office, Look to Librarians and Greater Good. The chart below provides a summary of key data relating to the tiers and segments that comprise the Library Supporter Segmentation Pyramid.

Segmentation data summary

Tier/Segment	Percentage of total population	Percentage of voting respondents (excluding Chronic Non Voters)	Percentage of the segment that would definitely vote yes*	Percentage of all definite yes voters*	Number of annual library visits	Percentage of all reported annual library visits	Library Support Index**	Library Use Index***
Super Supporters	7.1%	9.7%	80%	21.0%	15.9	9.4%	295	132
Probable Supporters	32.3%	44.0%	47%	55.6%	19.9	59.6%	172	186
Just for Fun	7.1%	9.7%	37%	9.7%	36.3	23.9%	136	336
Kid Driven	6.6%	9.0%	48%	11.5%	19.0	11.6%	176	177
Library as Office	3.4%	4.6%	49%	6.0%	18.0	5.7%	176	167
Look to Librarians	6.5%	8.9%	50%	12.2%	24.5	14.8%	187	227
Greater Good	8.7%	11.8%	50%	16.2%	4.5	3.6%	188	42
Barriers to Support	34.0%	46.3%	19%	23.4%	6.4	20.1%	69	76
Financially Strapped	10.6%	14.4%	11%	4.4%	10.6	10.4%	42	98
Detached	16.0%	21.8%	21%	12.4%	3.7	5.5%	77	34
The Web Wins	7.4%	10.1%	24%	6.6%	6.2	4.2%	90	57
Chronic Non Voters	26.6%	0%	0%	0%	7.4	10.9%	0	41
TOTAL	100%	100%	N/A	100%	N/A	100%		

*In response to survey question: "If there was a referendum, ballot initiative or bond measure for your local public library on the ballot, how do you think you would vote?"

**The Library Support Index is a measure of a segment's relative willingness to definitely support a library referendum, ballot initiative or bond measure.

$$\text{Library Support Index} = \frac{\text{\% Definite Library Supporters}}{\text{\% population ages 18-69 in communities < 200,000}} \times 100$$

***The Library Use Index is a measure of a segment's relative frequency of library visitation.

$$\text{Library Use Index} = \frac{\text{\% Library Visits}}{\text{\% population ages 18-69 in communities < 200,000}} \times 100$$

From Awareness to Funding: A study of library support in America

Methodology

Elected officials survey

Elected officials who self-identified as having some level of responsibility for local library funding were surveyed using a 30-minute online questionnaire that was a shorter version of the voter survey. Survey participation was solicited via an e-mail sent to subscribers of *Governing* magazine, a monthly magazine whose primary audience is state and local government officials. Elected officials who self-identified as part of the voter study were also invited to complete the elected official questionnaire. Eighty-four elected officials completed the online survey. Due to the process by which respondents were recruited, they represent a convenience sample that is quantitative but not statistically representative of all local elected officials in the United States.

Qualitative research

Two rounds of qualitative research were conducted to understand the attitudes and perceptions of the voters identified during the quantitative research as the most likely supporters—Probable Supporters and Super Supporters. The qualitative research was also used to test messaging for a potential library support campaign.

Qualitative round one

The objective of the first round of qualitative research was to gain an in-depth understanding of the factors influencing the willingness of Probable Supporters and Super Supporters to vote for an increase in taxes for public library funding. Research aimed to develop a deeper understanding of the barriers and motivations to supporting library funding, including prioritization of library funding versus other publicly funded services. The initial qualitative research also aimed to inform potential brand strategies and messaging platforms for a potential library support campaign. The screening criteria were developed based on an algorithm that was created from the market segmentation analysis. The algorithm provided a pared-down set of questions that was used to identify and recruit voters who fell into the desired market segments.

Ten focus groups were conducted in April 2007 with two groups in each of five markets: Huntsville, Alabama; McPherson, Kansas; Medford, Oregon; Minneapolis, Minnesota; and Pittsburgh, Pennsylvania. The five U.S. cities were chosen to represent a continuum of size, geography and situational context of library funding (e.g., communities where a levy had recently passed or failed or where there was no recent levy activity). Unlike the quantitative survey research that was conducted in towns and cities with populations of less than 200,000, the qualitative research was broadened to include two larger urban markets (Minneapolis and Pittsburgh) to evaluate whether perceptions and attitudes differed significantly across community population size.

Participants were taken through a series of exercises in order to provide insights into:

- **Early memories:** Past associations were explored through a 'first memory of the library' exercise
- **Current perceptions of the library:** Current associations were explored through the development of individual collages
- **Life without the library:** To explore the role and importance of libraries in their communities today, participants were asked to imagine a scenario where the library had closed permanently and to recount what they perceived the impact would be on their community
- **Rallying support:** Participants were asked to develop individual arguments and respond to written concepts that represent compelling reasons for supporting funding for the local library.

Qualitative round two

The second round of qualitative research tested potential marketing and advocacy campaign concepts with Probable Supporters, Super Supporters and elected officials. The concepts were developed based on the insights provided by the quantitative survey and the first round of qualitative focus groups.

Six focus groups were conducted in June 2007 in three of the five cities chosen for the first round of qualitative research: McPherson, Kansas; Huntsville, Alabama; and Minneapolis, Minnesota. Phone interviews with elected officials were conducted in June and July 2007.

Participants were exposed to five potential campaign concepts and asked questions regarding their interpretations and reactions without any previous discussion about their perceptions or usage of the library. Concepts were rotated to avoid order bias. The goal was not to reach group consensus about the 'best' creative direction, but instead to evaluate each concept against a set of creative evaluation criteria.

For each campaign concept, participants were asked what they perceived the concept was asking them to do (i.e., use the library, support the library, etc.). After all concepts had been presented, participants were asked a number of 'compare and contrast' questions to gauge the effectiveness of each concept:

- Which concept makes you see the library differently?
- Which concept makes the library seem more important to your community?
- Which concept would you talk about with your friends, family and neighbors?
- Which concept would incite you to take some sort of action to support the library?
- Which concept would motivate you to vote yes on a library levy?

The ability of a concept to generate conversation was both observed and asked directly.

Methodology

Report structure

The report presents the findings from the advocacy research:

- **Chapter 1: From awareness to funding**
  A brief overview of the research findings: an executive summary

- **Chapter 2: Who are the library's financial supporters?**
  A detailed overview of the market segmentation analysis

- **Chapter 3: Elected officials and library funding**
  A review of survey findings about elected local officials

- **Chapter 4: Library funding support is an attitude, not a demographic**
  Eight key insights from the quantitative survey that outline the factors most likely to influence a voter's willingness to support increased funding for libraries

- **Chapter 5: Motivating Probable and Super Supporters—testing the facts in the field**
  A review of the findings from qualitative focus groups that provide a deeper understanding of attitudes and perceptions of potential library supporters

- **Chapter 6: Mobilizing Probable and Super Supporters—what makes the difference**
  A review of the findings from qualitative focus groups that indicate what messages and approach would potentially increase voters' willingness to support the library

- **Chapter 7: Conclusion**
  Conclusions of the advocacy research and an overview of next steps toward a possible national library support campaign.

From awareness to funding

This report summarizes the research findings of an advocacy research grant awarded to OCLC by the Bill & Melinda Gates Foundation. The grant was awarded to conduct research, develop strategies, create materials and evaluate the potential of marketing and communications programs aimed at increasing and sustaining library funding for U.S. public libraries.

The problem:

Public library use in the United States is growing. Circulation and visits to U.S. libraries are increasing and a wide range of services, such as literacy classes, teen programs and public access computing, are also experiencing strong demand. But the public funding required to sustain the variety, use and appetite for library services is not keeping pace with demand. For many public libraries, particularly those in smaller rural communities, funding is a growing concern.

Federal and state funding for public libraries has flattened or declined, and the ability to raise funds from local sources, which represent 81% of all library funding, has also become more difficult.

Library levies and referenda are being placed on election ballots less frequently in recent years and passage rates of the library levies that make it to the ballot have steadily declined over the past decade.

Public library funding

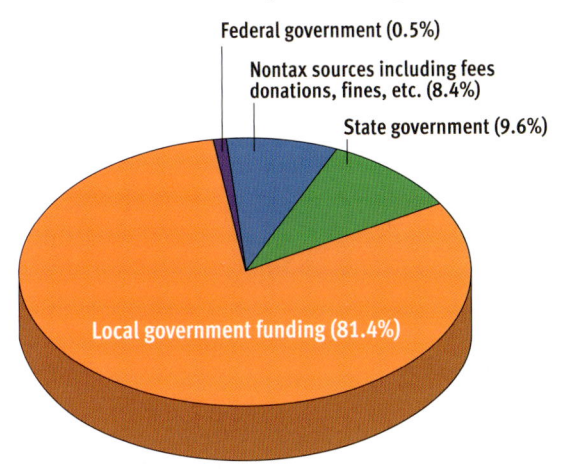

- Federal government (0.5%)
- Nontax sources including fees donations, fines, etc. (8.4%)
- State government (9.6%)
- Local government funding (81.4%)

Source: National Center for Education Statistics, 2007

As a result, for many U.S. libraries, operating expense increases are now outstripping funding.

Rate of success of library levies

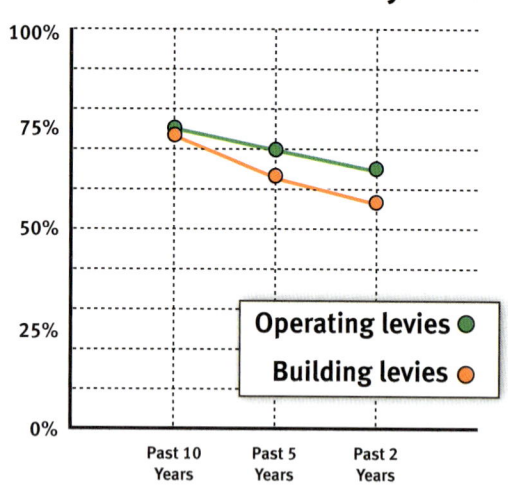

Source: *Library Journal* Public Library Referenda, 2006

Without some action, this funding problem will not self-correct and is likely to worsen. Public library budgets face significant economic strains with increased energy and healthcare costs and declining property values, leading to a reduction in local property taxes, the source of most local library funding. The cost of employee benefits increased 62% between 2000 and 2005, just one factor that has resulted in a 12% reduction in spending on collections and programs (source: National Center for Education Statistics; figures not adjusted for inflation).

Public libraries are not alone in facing these economic challenges. As the economic factors that impact libraries also impact other locally funded services such as police, fire service and education, there will be heightened competition for a share of the community purse. The research findings will show that voters do not necessarily trade-off funding support to one public service for another, and those who vote for increased funding do so across all services. However, libraries must effectively communicate their value to local voters and funding bodies to ensure that they are included for consideration. Most voters are unaware of the source and status of library funding in their communities, and many rural and suburban libraries lack the resources to create the library advocacy and marketing programs required to increase awareness.

The advocacy research goal:

The goal of the research project was twofold: first, to understand the factors that both drive, and limit, local library funding support; second, to ascertain whether a national library support campaign could be effective at increasing and sustaining funding for U.S. public libraries by reaching and influencing the segments of the voting population that have the most potential to become committed library supporters.

The project was designed to test the application of traditional market research, segmentation and targeting techniques to the library funding problem. Could marketing segmentation methods, targeted campaigns, tailored messaging and grassroots advocacy activities create a positive difference for library funding?

Our research findings suggest that the answer to this important question is 'yes.' This conclusion was reached after the evaluation of findings from five market research activities:

1. **Market segmentation analysis** to identify the most likely, and least likely, library funding supporters
2. **Quantitative research** to identify the most important library funding drivers for voters and elected officials
3. **Qualitative research** to learn more about the most likely library funding supporters, their attitudes about their library, their attitudes about their community and their willingness to actively support increased library funding
4. **Campaign strategy development** to create messaging and approach for a national library support campaign to target the most likely library funding supporters and increase their commitment
5. **Creative concept field tests** to test messaging and approach for a national library support campaign with target segments of the voting population and elected officials.

Detailed findings from the quantitative research, market segmentation and qualitative research are presented in this report. The report concludes with an overview of creative concept development, field test findings and potential next steps.

What we learned:
1. Building market segmentation

A primary goal of the advocacy research project was to create a segmentation and targeting framework of U.S. residents ages 18 to 69 in cities, towns and suburbs with populations of less than 200,000. More than 90% of all U.S. public libraries serve communities of this size.

The survey results provided important high-level understandings about commitment to library funding among the U.S. voting population. For example, survey results show that 74% of respondents would *probably* or *definitely* support a library referendum if there was one on the ballot at the next local election. While this appears to be a positive finding, it is not consistent with the results many libraries are experiencing at the voting booth in their local communities. If 74% of U.S. residents were consistently voting 'yes' for library referenda, ballot initiatives and bond measures, the public library community would be better-funded, and the rate and margin of success for library levies would be much higher than has been the case for the last several years. Therefore, a 'probably vote yes' answer on voting intent does not always translate to actual favorable voting behavior.

While 74% of respondents indicate that they would either *probably* or *definitely* vote in favor of a levy, that support is evenly split. Only 37% of respondents indicated they would *definitely* vote in favor of a library levy, too few to pass a library referendum in any state. Understanding which voters are most likely to provide *definite* library funding support, which voters will provide limited or no library funding support, and which voters represent *probable* support for increased library funding was a primary goal of the quantitative research.

Using a robust market segmentation methodology developed by OCLC's research partner, Leo Burnett, the survey data were analyzed to create a Library Supporter Segmentation framework that categorizes and profiles segments of the voting population in relation to their level of commitment to public library funding support.

The segmentation analysis identified six constructs that are the key drivers of library funding attitudes and behaviors: residents' likelihood of voting favorably if a library referendum is on the ballot; residents' general voting behavior; their stated barriers to using or supporting the library; the library services they use; their overall attitudes toward the library; and finally, their perceptions of librarians.

Significantly and surprisingly, library funding support is not driven by demographics, i.e., income, age, gender, race, political affiliation, etc. Voters' attitudes, perceptions and behaviors, not their demographic profiles, are the most important determinants of willingness to support increases in library funding. Library support is more about a mindset or an attitude than a traditional demographic profile.

A Library Supporter Segmentation Pyramid was constructed based on the six identified constructs. Library supporters were categorized from those least likely to fund libraries at the ballot box (those at the bottom of the pyramid) to those most likely to vote 'yes' for a library referendum (those at the top of the pyramid).

The segmentation pyramid identified four distinct tiers:

Super Supporters: Voters at the top tier of the segmentation pyramid. These are people who are most firmly committed to supporting a library funding initiative.

Probable Supporters: Voters who are likely to support library funding initiatives but are not fully committed.

Barriers to Support: Voters who, for a variety of factors, have significant barriers to voting in favor of increased library funding.

Chronic Non Voters: People who are not registered to vote or have a track record of choosing not to vote in presidential and local elections. They also indicate they are not likely to vote in the future, and are therefore unlikely to provide support for library funding initiatives.

Library Supporter Segmentation Pyramid
Total Respondents

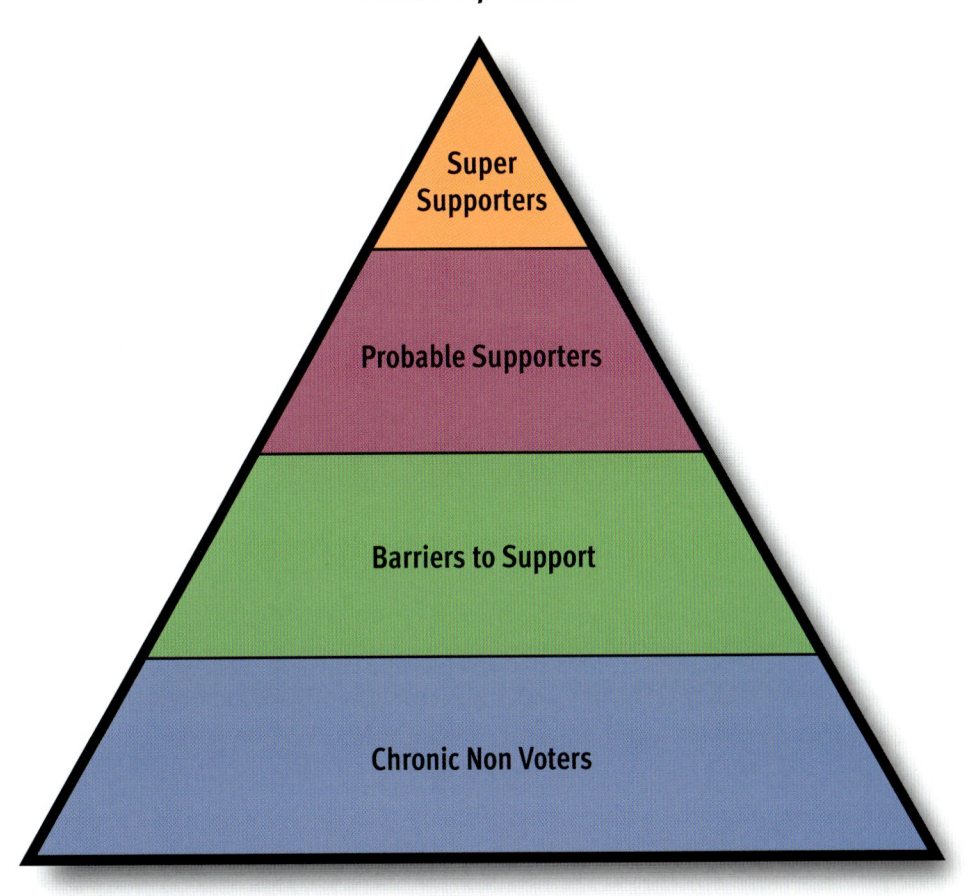

- Super Supporters
- Probable Supporters
- Barriers to Support
- Chronic Non Voters

Population ages 18–69 living in communities of less than 200,000 residents
Source: *From Awareness to Funding*, OCLC, 2008

Profiles of the voter segments that make up the Library Supporter Segmentation Pyramid provide valuable insights about how to most effectively identify, select and influence individuals who support library funding. "Chapter 2: Who are the library's financial supporters?" provides a detailed review of the segmentation pyramid with a review of each tier and each of the 10 segments that make up those tiers.

While many U.S. libraries are funded at least in part by local library referenda, ballot initiatives and bond measures, not all communities fund their public libraries using library levies. Many communities fund libraries through resource allocation from general community funds. Local elected officials work with their constituents to allocate funding to libraries and other public services.

Quantitative research was also conducted to better understand the attitudes and opinions local elected officials hold about libraries and local library funding. Elected official respondents are higher-than-average users of the library and believe that the library is an important community resource. Surprisingly though, given their involvement with the library, the majority of local elected officials feel that their libraries have sufficient funds to meet their day-to-day operational needs.

When asked to indicate which of a number of public services they would agree to fund through an increase in local taxes, most elected officials indicated a higher likelihood to support funding initiatives for the fire department, public schools and police department than for the public library. "Chapter 3: Elected officials and library funding" provides a detailed review of the research findings relating to elected officials.

2. Quantitative research—identifying the drivers of library funding

The quantitative survey provided significant detailed information about the factors that drive, and limit, funding support of U.S. public libraries. These include information about the attitudes and behaviors of the respondents relating to libraries, librarians, the library's role in the community and respondents' willingness to increase taxes to support an increase in funding for libraries and other locally funded public services. There were eight important findings derived from the quantitative research:

1. **Most people claim they would support the library at the ballot box—fewer are firmly committed to it.**

2. **There is a lot that people don't know about their public library.**

3. **Library support is only marginally related to visitation. Advocating for library support to library users focuses effort and energy on the wrong target group.**

4. **Perceptions of the librarian are highly related to support. 'Passionate librarians' who are involved in the community make a difference.**

5. **The library occupies a very clear position in people's minds as a provider of practical answers and information. This is a very crowded space, and to remain relevant in today's information landscape, repositioning will be required.**

6. **Belief that the library is a transformational force in people's lives is directly related to their level of funding support.**

7. **Increasing support for libraries may not necessarily mean a trade-off of financial support for other public services.**

8. **Elected officials are supportive of the library—but not fully committed to increasing funding. Engaging Probable Supporters and Super Supporters to help elevate library funding needs is required.**

More detail about the key drivers of library funding can be found in "Chapter 4: Library funding support is an attitude, not a demographic."

3. Qualitative research—understanding attitudes toward libraries and library funding among the most likely supporters

The findings of the quantitative research were further informed by qualitative research. The objective of the qualitative research was to gain a more in-depth understanding of two key market segments, the Probable Supporters and the Super Supporters, and their perceptions of the local library today.

Ten focus groups were conducted in April 2007, including one group of Super Supporters and one group of Probable Supporters each in: Huntsville, Alabama; McPherson, Kansas; Medford, Oregon; Minneapolis, Minnesota; and Pittsburgh, Pennsylvania.

The findings of the qualitative research reinforced the quantitative research results. Respondents have rich and detailed memories of their first experiences at the library and strong, positive current perceptions of the library. Respondents who have the strongest beliefs that the library is a source of transformation are those who are most passionate about the need to protect, support and fund the library.

However, the focus groups also showed that even the most avid supporters of the library have concerns about the relevance of the public library in today's world and their favorable vote in support of library funding initiatives cannot be assumed. While Probable Supporters and Super Supporters have a strong emotional connection to the public library, that connection is latent and is exhibited fully only during the use of projective research techniques. Discussion during the focus groups about a potential tax increase in support of public library funding highlighted other issues that any library support marketing campaign would need to overcome. Voters have little or no awareness of how their local public libraries are funded and are also unaware of any funding problems.

It was clear that the positive emotional connections that Probable Supporters and Super Supporters have with libraries were not always sufficient to convince them to increase library funding. Instead, the research indicated a need to appeal to both the heart and mind of the potential voter, positioning the library as an important part of the community's infrastructure that plays a key role in providing equal access to resources vital for thriving in today's digital world. "Chapter 5: Motivating Probable and Super Supporters—testing the facts in the field" provides more in-depth information about the findings of the qualitative focus groups.

Telephone interviews with elected officials provided similar insights. Elected officials hold attitudes similar to those of Probable Supporters. While elected officials have strong positive associations with the library and believe it plays a key role in the community, pragmatic factors often temper their support for increasing taxes.

4. Campaign strategy development—creating messaging to motivate the most likely supporters to action

The problem a library support campaign strategy must consider is how to turn the tide of dwindling library funding support in an environment where people think libraries are becoming less relevant, where we can anticipate tougher tax choices and where market-specific conditions vary.

The proposed solution is to create and promote a brand—not a library product brand focused on marketing library consumption (i.e., usage) but a library *support* brand. The brand must do more than position the library as relevant—it must activate citizen participation and drive positive funding behavior.

Based on the research findings, the OCLC and Leo Burnett team developed a library support brand strategy and outlined options for messaging and specific marketing tactics for a library support campaign to move the most likely voters from *probable* support of library referenda to *definite* support.

The brand strategy and campaign messaging options are based on the following communications objectives:

Make the library relevant for the 21st century.

Instill a sense of urgency by putting the library in the consideration set for local funding with other public services, like police, parks and fire.

Activate a conversation about how the library is a vital part of the community's infrastructure and future.

Several creative concepts were developed based on these communications objectives. Each creative idea was embodied in the form of an image and a messaging narrative that could form the basis for a library support brand and associated campaign. "Chapter 6: Mobilizing Probable and Super Supporters—what makes the difference" provides details on the creation and testing of campaign strategies.

5. Creative concept field tests—evaluating the potential for a library support campaign to impact voters and elected officials

Creative concepts were developed specifically for the purposes of evaluative testing with Probable Supporters, Super Supporters and elected officials. The creative directions were evaluated by focus groups of Probable Supporters (five groups) and Super Supporters (one group) in McPherson, Kansas; Huntsville, Alabama; and Minneapolis, Minnesota. The concepts were also reviewed by elected officials during phone interviews. Qualitative research findings were analyzed to establish the creative direction for a potential library support campaign.

Responses from voters and elected officials were evaluated against a number of criteria:

- Can this creative direction effectively create a library support brand?
- Does the idea position the library as transformational?
- Is the message broad enough to resonate with all target audiences?
- Does the idea push people to think about the library differently?
- Is the idea compelling and motivating?
- Is the tone of voice appropriate for the 'universal' library brand?

Overall, the feedback from Probable Supporters, Super Supporters and elected officials about the concepts was positive. The concepts held the potential to achieve the communications objectives and met the evaluative criteria. Concepts resonated with the voters and elected officials and reflected an aspect of what they believed to be true about the library. When respondents were asked to compare and contrast concepts, each idea was selected as a favorite of one or more respondents. Respondents often wanted to combine concepts.

Probable Supporters and Super Supporters were easily prompted by the concepts to begin a discussion of the library support problem and they did not respond negatively to raising the issue of library funding. The response to the creative directions indicated that the right campaign can generate the desired response from our target segments, repositioning the library as relevant for the 21st century, instilling a sense of urgency to support the library in various ways, and activating conversation with their friends and families. The participants expressed a desire to find out more and specifically learn more about what their local elected officials thought about funding the library.

Local elected officials saw the potential for the concepts to provide them with a positive platform they could use to dialogue with their constituents. The platform also influenced them personally to give support to library funding initiatives. "Chapter 6: Mobilizing Probable and Super Supporters—what makes the difference" provides more detail about the potential impact of the creative concepts as part of a national library support campaign.

Chapter 2

Who are the library's financial supporters?

Library supporter segmentation

What factors drive local funding support of libraries?

A primary goal of the research project was to create a segmentation and targeting framework of U.S. residents ages 18 to 69 in cities, towns and suburbs with populations of less than 200,000 that identified:

- Which segments of the public are most interested in financially supporting their local libraries and what motivations drive their support
- Which segments are least likely to support libraries and what are their barriers to support
- Whether it is viable to use marketing and advocacy techniques to target interested segments and positively impact library funding.

The segmentation approach

Classic market segmentation techniques were employed to analyze the thousands of survey data points collected and create a market segmentation for library funding. The deployed segmentation methodology analyzed multiple constructs to determine the factors most likely to define a library supporter segmentation framework. The constructs included behavior, attitudes, need states, perceptions, benefits, demography and lifestyle. Each construct was independently evaluated to explore a possible relationship to library funding support.

The analysis identified that the most critical construct for the Library Supporter Segmentation framework was the intent to vote for any future library funding referendum, ballot initiative or bond measure. This was a clear and quantifiable indicator of the level of commitment to library funding and formed the basis for the segmentation framework hierarchy.

The remaining constructs were evaluated based on their relevance in predicting a favorable vote for a library funding measure. The constructs that had little or no relationship to the likelihood of voting favorably were set aside and constructs that did predict library voting intent became part of the library supporter segmentation framework.

Constructs that predicted favorable voting were then compared to assess interactions and determine which combination of constructs would most likely predict levels of intent to fund public libraries.

The segmentation analysis identified six constructs that are the key drivers of library funding attitudes and behavior and form the basis of a Library Supporter Segmentation framework. The constructs are:

1. Likelihood of voting favorably if a library referendum was on the ballot
2. General voting behavior
3. Barriers to using/supporting the library
4. Library services used
5. Library attitudes
6. Librarian perceptions.

Significantly and surprisingly, library funding support is not driven by demographics, i.e., income, age, gender, race, political affiliation, etc. A voter's attitudes, perceptions and behaviors, not his/her demographics, are the most important determinants of willingness to support increases in library funding. Library support is more about a mindset or an attitude than a traditional demographic profile.

Strength of library support—the most important market segmentation driver

Intent to vote in a library referendum is the critical construct in defining library funding support and the key driver in building a predictive Library Supporter Segmentation framework.

Respondents were asked about their intent to vote if there was a library referendum, ballot initiative or bond measure on the ballot at the next local election. The survey results indicate that a large percentage of respondents claim they would either *probably* vote yes or *definitely* vote yes to increase funding for their local public library. After eliminating the respondents who are not registered to vote or show a track record of not voting (identified as Chronic Non Voters), almost three quarters of the remaining voting respondents (74%) claim that they would either *probably* or *definitely* vote yes.

Nearly three quarters of voting respondents claim they would support a library referendum

Total Voting Respondents

If there was a referendum, ballot initiative or bond measure for your local public library on the ballot, how do you think you would vote?

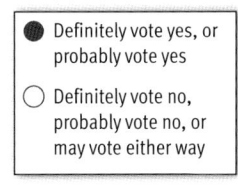

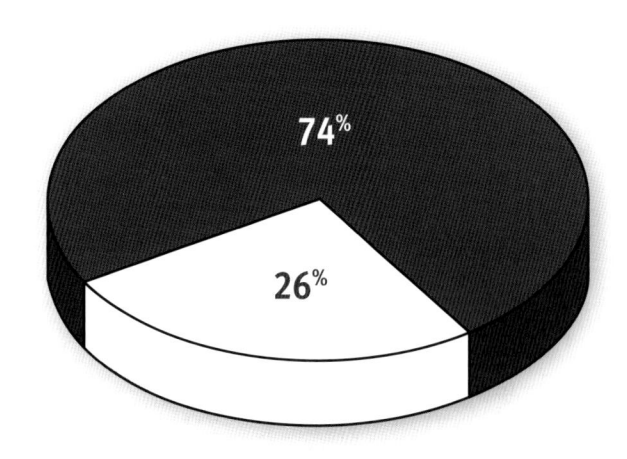

- Definitely vote yes, or probably vote yes: 74%
- Definitely vote no, probably vote no, or may vote either way: 26%

Source: *From Awareness to Funding*, OCLC, 2008

If 74% of all voters voted yes in support of public library referenda, ballot initiatives and bond measures in the United States, more library measures would be passing and the current pressure on library funding would likely be a much less urgent issue. This is not the case. Tracking studies show there has been a steady decline in the pass rate of library referenda over the past ten years and levies that do pass are often ratified by only a small number of votes. The 74% favorability among voters is not materializing at the voting booth. Depending on voters who say they would *probably* or *definitely* vote yes is not enough to be confident in a positive outcome for future library funding initiatives. A stronger determinant of funding commitment is needed.

Of the voting respondents who indicated that they would *probably* or *definitely* vote yes, the group is evenly split between those who say they would *probably* vote yes for a library referendum and those who say they would *definitely* vote yes. Thirty-seven percent (37%) would *probably* vote yes for a library referendum. Only 37% would *definitely* vote yes—a much smaller pool of committed library supporters.

Who are the library's financial supporters?

Only 37% of voters say that they will *definitely* support the library at the ballot box

Total Voting Respondents

Now we'd like you to think ahead to the next election and assume that you are at the ballot box and ready to cast your vote. If there was a referendum, ballot initiative or bond measure for your local public library on the ballot, how do you think you would vote?

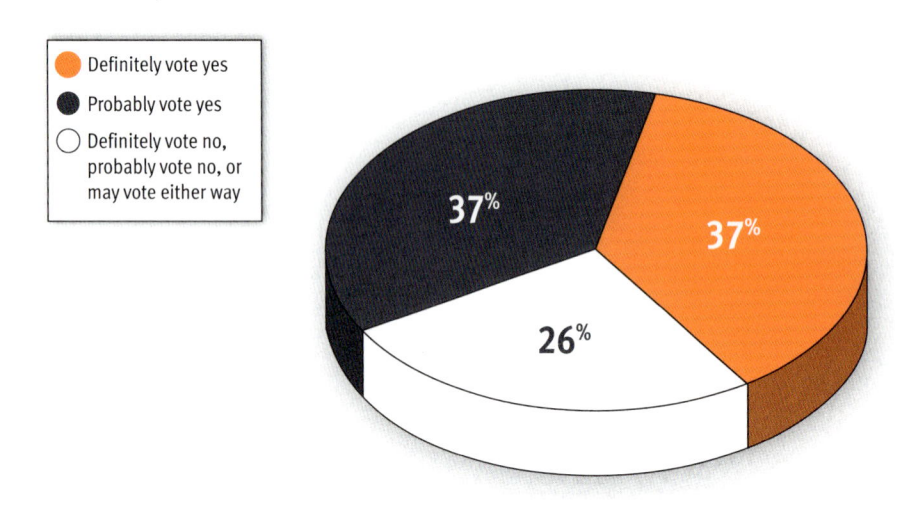

- Definitely vote yes
- Probably vote yes
- Definitely vote no, probably vote no, or may vote either way

37% / 37% / 26%

Source: *From Awareness to Funding*, OCLC, 2008

The Library Supporter Segmentation Pyramid

Four tiers of library support

Analysis of *probably* favorable and *definitely* favorable voting intent provides the hierarchy for the Library Supporter Segmentation framework. The pyramid has four tiers. The higher the tier is on the pyramid, the more likely respondents in that tier are to support an increase in library funding. The four tiers are:

- **Super Supporters:** People who are the most likely regular voters to be committed to vote yes for a library referendum, ballot initiative or bond measure. They represent the core of the libraries' current support base. This tier represents 7.1% of survey respondents.

- **Probable Supporters:** People who are regular voters and overall are in favor of supporting the libraries financially. This group has the potential to be persuaded to increase their commitment to voting favorably for a library referendum, bond measure or ballot initiative. This tier represents 32.3% of survey respondents.

Who are the library's financial supporters?

- **Barriers to Support:** People who say they vote in primary, presidential and local elections but have significant barriers to supporting the library financially. They are the least likely of the voting respondents to vote in favor of a library referendum. This tier represents 34.0% of survey respondents.

- **Chronic Non Voters:** People who are either not registered to vote or are registered but do not vote in primary elections, presidential elections or local elections. The people in this segment say that they are unlikely to be motivated to vote in the future. This tier represents 26.6% of survey respondents.

Library Supporter Segmentation Pyramid

Total Respondents

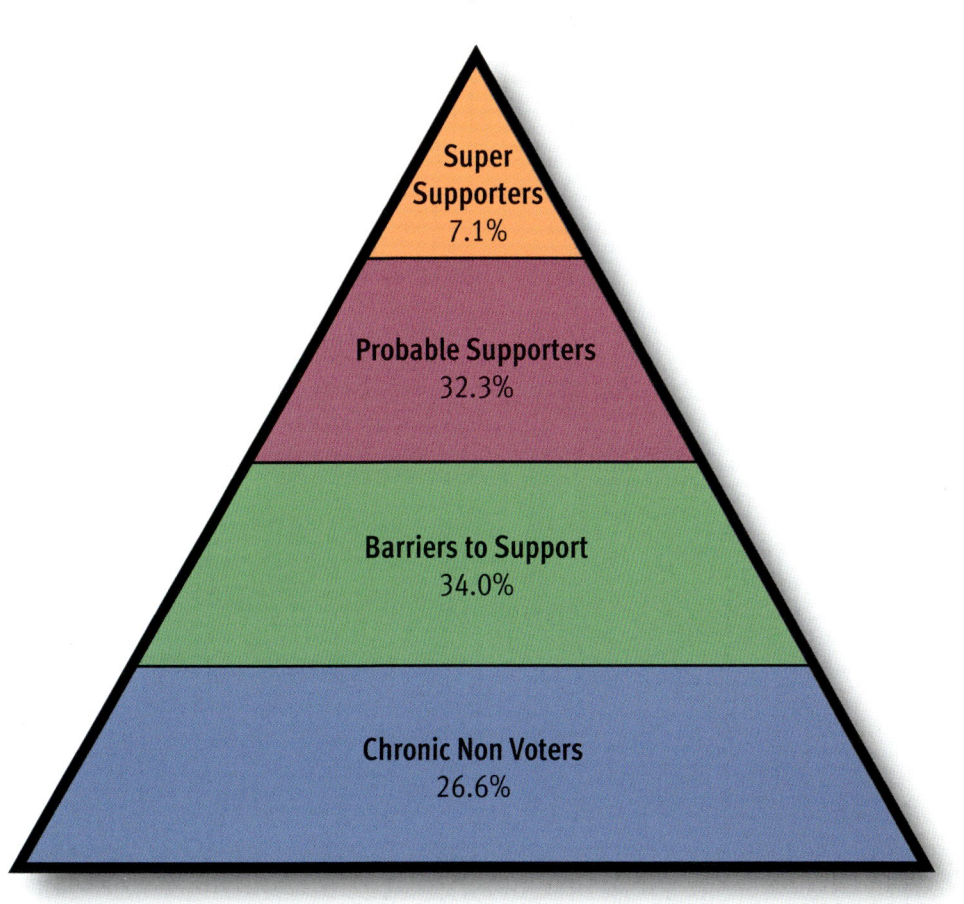

- Super Supporters 7.1%
- Probable Supporters 32.3%
- Barriers to Support 34.0%
- Chronic Non Voters 26.6%

Percentage of population ages 18–69 living in communities of less than 200,000 residents
Source: *From Awareness to Funding*, OCLC, 2008

Excluding Chronic Non Voters

Chronic Non Voters are residents who either are not registered to vote or are registered voters but show a track record of not voting in primary elections, presidential elections or local elections. To gain library funding support from this segment, any marketing exercise that initiative would first have to convince these residents to register to vote and to vote. Due to their significant barriers to supporting the library, Chronic Non Voters were excluded from further study.

Who are the library's financial supporters?

The results presented in this report will be referenced as follows: Findings that include information about all four tiers of the segmentation including Chronic Non Voters will be referenced as 'Total Respondents.' Findings that include data about only the top three tiers of the segmentation pyramid without the Chronic Non Voters will be referenced as 'Total Voting Respondents.'

The four segmentation tiers and voting intent

Analysis shows a measurable increase in the percentage of *probable* or *definite* yes votes for a library referendum in the Probable Supporters and Super Supporters segmentation tiers. Most important, the proportion of respondents who are *definitely* willing to vote yes for a library referendum increases significantly.

Fifty-nine percent (59%) of respondents in the Barriers to Support tier say they would either *probably* or *definitely* vote yes for a library referendum but only 19% say they would *definitely* vote yes.

The percentage of favorable voters increases in the Probable Supporters tier. Eighty-six percent (86%) of respondents say they would either *probably* or *definitely* vote yes for a library referendum. The percentage who would *definitely* vote yes increases to 47%.

The Super Supporters tier is the group most firmly committed to supporting the library financially with 94% of respondents indicating that they would *probably* or *definitely* vote yes for a library referendum. The majority, 80%, say they would *definitely* vote yes.

'Definitely vote yes' is a critical measure of which voters are truly committed to providing financial support to the library

Total Voting Respondents

If there was a referendum, ballot initiative or bond measure for your local public library on the ballot, how do you think you would vote?

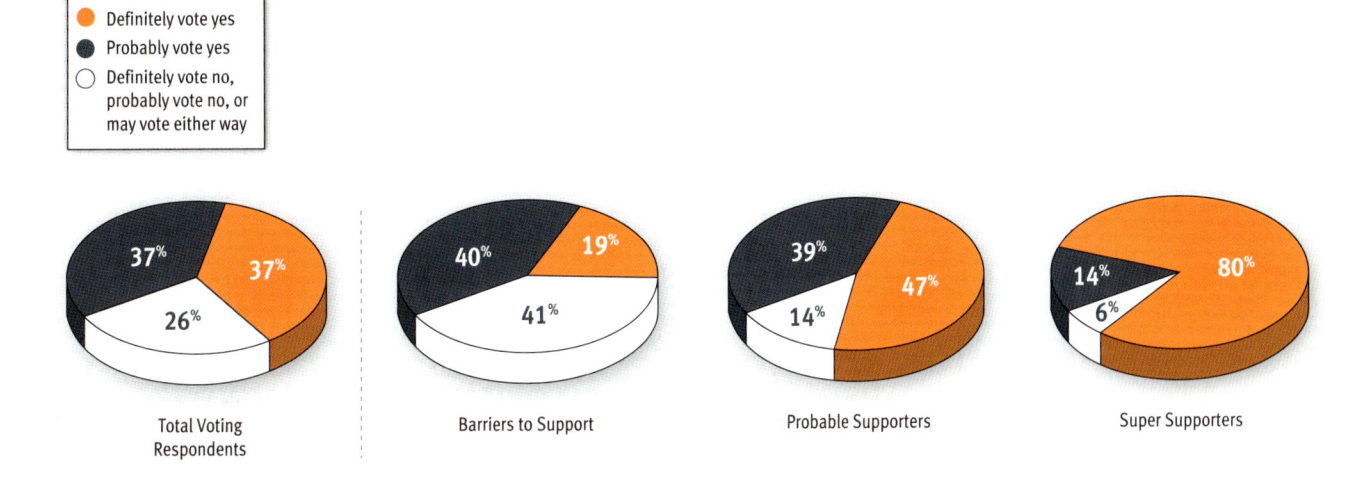

- Definitely vote yes
- Probably vote yes
- Definitely vote no, probably vote no, or may vote either way

Total Voting Respondents: 37% definitely vote yes, 37% probably vote yes, 26% other

Barriers to Support: 19% definitely vote yes, 40% probably vote yes, 41% other

Probable Supporters: 47% definitely vote yes, 39% probably vote yes, 14% other

Super Supporters: 80% definitely vote yes, 14% probably vote yes, 6% other

Source: *From Awareness to Funding*, OCLC, 2008

The ability to segment the U.S. population into distinct tiers based on a voter's willingness to *definitely* support a library referendum at the polls provides a new framework for analyzing library funding support. What are the behaviors, attitudes and perceptions that define voters as Probable Supporters or as Super Supporters— the two groups most likely to vote for an increase in taxes to support their local libraries? What are the distinctions or segments within each of these tiers and what do they tell us about library funding support? Is there a way to identify these important supporters within a community? And is there a way to use the information about what drives or limits their support to increase library funding?

Who are the library's financial supporters?

Understanding the segments of the Library Supporter Segmentation Pyramid

The Library Supporter Segmentation Pyramid contains 10 segments. Each distinct combination of the six constructs defines a segment. The pyramid is presented below, including the percentages of survey respondents that fall into each segment. Survey responses were weighted to be nationally representative, therefore these percentages represent residents ages 18 to 69 in U.S. communities of less than 200,000.

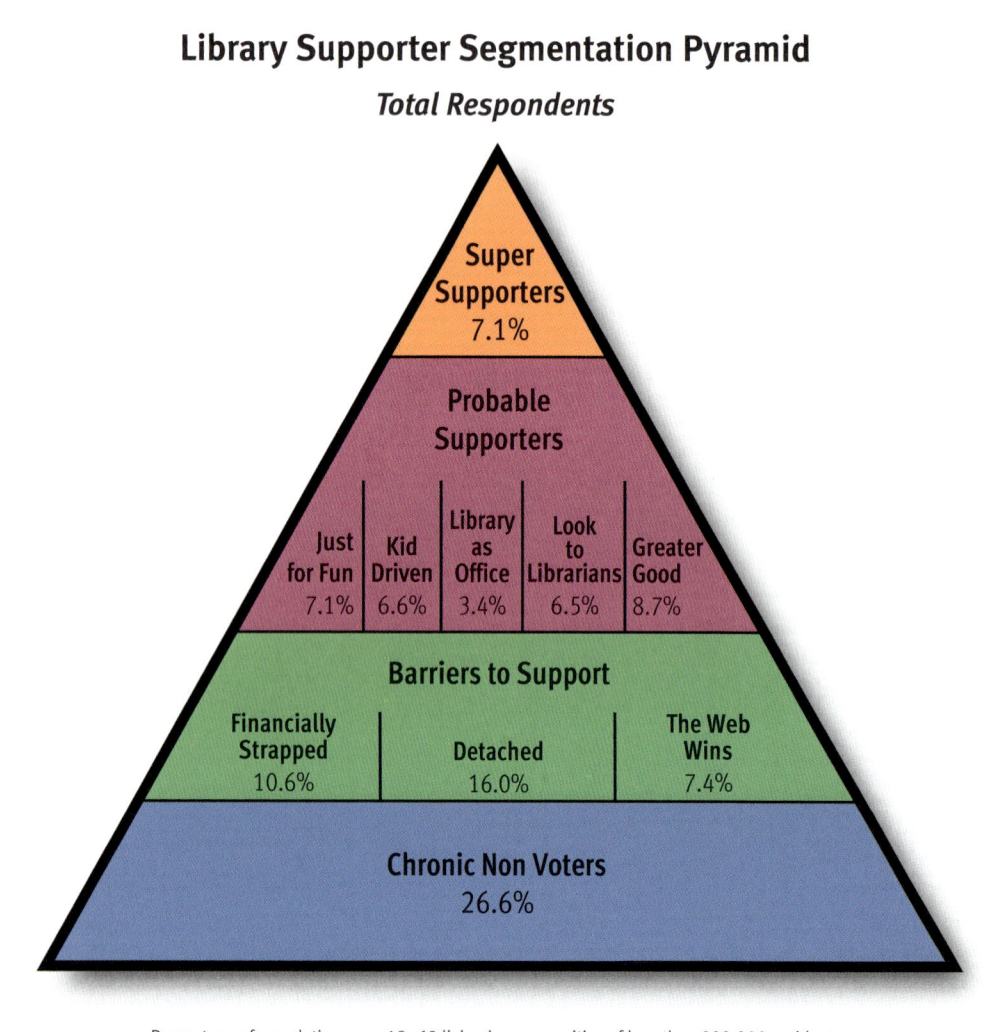

Library Supporter Segmentation Pyramid
Total Respondents

- Super Supporters — 7.1%
- Probable Supporters:
  - Just for Fun 7.1%
  - Kid Driven 6.6%
  - Library as Office 3.4%
  - Look to Librarians 6.5%
  - Greater Good 8.7%
- Barriers to Support:
  - Financially Strapped 10.6%
  - Detached 16.0%
  - The Web Wins 7.4%
- Chronic Non Voters — 26.6%

Percentage of population ages 18–69 living in communities of less than 200,000 residents
Source: *From Awareness to Funding*, OCLC, 2008

The top tier and the bottom tier of the pyramid, the Super Supporters and Chronic Non Voters, are each distinct segments, meaning that the characteristics that define each group are similar for all respondents in that tier. There are no other major factors among respondents within each of these tiers that drive or limit funding attitudes and behaviors.

Analysis of the middle two tiers identified variations and characteristics that were unique enough to merit further market segmentation. The Barriers to Support tier includes three segments described as Financially Strapped, Detached and The Web Wins. The Probable Supporter tier is made up of five segments: Just for Fun, Kid Driven, Library as Office, Look to Librarians and Greater Good.

Each segment differs in meaningful ways from the others along one or more market constructs. The segments are labeled to reflect the predominant mindset that defines the segment. The segments are organized within the pyramid according to library funding voting intent. The chart below outlines the percentage of each segment that would *definitely* vote yes for a library referendum.

Percentage of voters who would *definitely* vote yes for a library referendum within each segment
Total Respondents

If there was a referendum, ballot initiative or bond measure for your local public library on the ballot, how do you think you would vote?

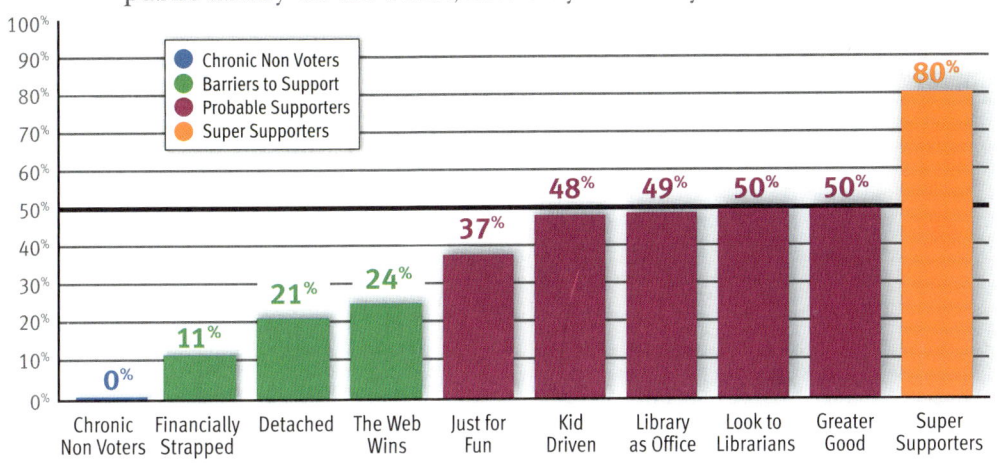

- Chronic Non Voters
- Barriers to Support
- Probable Supporters
- Super Supporters

Segment	%
Chronic Non Voters	0%
Financially Strapped	11%
Detached	21%
The Web Wins	24%
Just for Fun	37%
Kid Driven	48%
Library as Office	49%
Look to Librarians	50%
Greater Good	50%
Super Supporters	80%

Percentage of respondents who would *definitely* vote 'yes' for a library referendum
Source: *From Awareness to Funding*, OCLC, 2008

A detailed profile of each segment of the Library Supporter Segmentation Pyramid follows. Over 100,000 data points were captured in the quantitative research, therefore only the most pertinent data have been selected for discussion.

Five profile dimensions are presented for each segment:

1. Demographic profile
2. Library usage
3. Public service support
4. Library support compared to library usage
5. Attitudes toward libraries and funding.

Who are the library's financial supporters?

Five segment profile dimensions

Five profile dimensions are presented for each segment and are described below. The figures are illustrative only.

1. Demographic profile

Demographics were not a key factor in determining the Library Supporter Segmentation, yet some segments show unique or interesting demographic tendencies. A table is presented for each segment that outlines a standard set of demographic information including age, gender, household children and household income. The table also provides an overview of any demographic characteristics that are specific to the particular segment.

	Total Voting Respondents	Segment Name
Age	X%	X%
Gender	X%	X%
Children	X%	X%
Household income	X%	X%
Demographic tendencies		
Tendency 1	X%	X%
Tendency 2	X%	X%

Source: *From Awareness to Funding*, OCLC, 2008

3. Public service support

Respondents' willingness to increase taxes in support of seven public services, including the public library, fire department, police department, public health, public schools, road maintenance and park service are charted for each segment.

Public service support

For each service, please rate how much you agree with the phrase "I'd be willing to pay more in local taxes to better fund this service." Please use a 10-point scale, where a 10 means you 'Completely Agree' and a 1 means you 'Completely Disagree.'

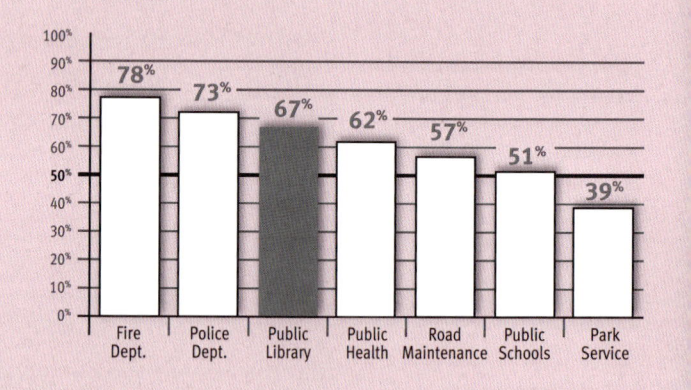

- Fire Dept.: 78%
- Police Dept.: 73%
- Public Library: 67%
- Public Health: 62%
- Road Maintenance: 57%
- Public Schools: 51%
- Park Service: 39%

2. Library usage

A chart is presented for each segment highlighting the segment's use of library services. The frequency of library visits is also presented.

Library usage

Below is a list of activities and services offered by public libraries. Please indicate how frequently you do each one at your local public library.

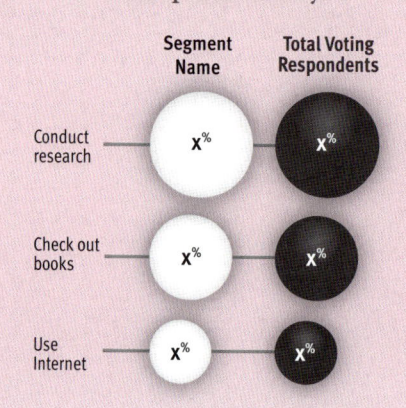

	Segment Name	Total Voting Respondents
Conduct research	x%	x%
Check out books	x%	x%
Use Internet	x%	x%

Annual Library Visits

Segment: 10.0

Total Voting Respondents: 13.2

2-10 From Awareness to Funding: A study of library support in America

4. Library support compared to library usage

Two indices were developed for each segment that illustrate the segment's relative frequency of library visitation and relative willingness to fund the library. In each case, an index of 100 is average.

Library support compared to library usage

If there was a referendum, ballot initiative or bond measure for your local public library on the ballot, how do you think you would vote?

How many times have you visited your local public library in the past 12 months?

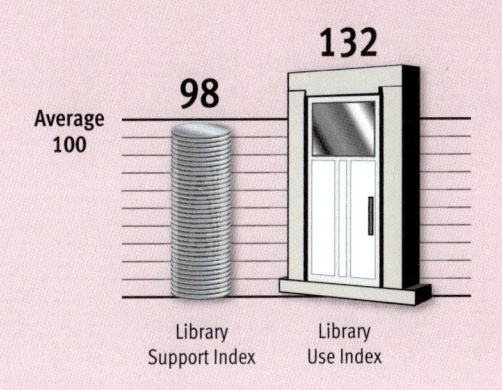

Average 100
Library Support Index: 98
Library Use Index: 132

Index definitions

$$\text{Library Support Index} = \frac{\text{\% Definite Library Supporters}}{\text{\% population ages 18–69 in communities < 200,000}} \times 100$$

$$\text{Library Use Index} = \frac{\text{\% Library Visits}}{\text{\% population ages 18–69 in communities < 200,000}} \times 100$$

5. Attitudes toward libraries and funding

An overview of the factors that are most helpful in defining the segment are presented and compared to attitudes held by total voting respondents.

Attitudes toward libraries and funding

For each statement below, please rate your level of agreement on a scale from 1 to 10, where a 10 means 'Agree Strongly' and a 1 means 'Disagree Strongly.'

	Total Voting Respondents	Segment Name
Attitude 1	X%	X%
Attitude 2	X%	X%
Behavior 1	X%	X%
Behavior 2	X%	X%

Source: *From Awareness to Funding*, OCLC, 2008

Who are the library's financial supporters?

Chronic Non Voter tier/segment

The Chronic Non Voters segment of the Library Supporter Segmentation Pyramid represents 26.6% of the survey respondents. Chronic Non Voters are the least likely group to increase funding support for libraries. Chronic Non Voters are not registered to vote, or they are registered to vote but report a track record of not voting in primary elections, presidential elections or local elections. Chronic Non Voters also indicated that they are unlikely to be motivated to vote in the future. This segment represents 0% of respondents who said they would *definitely* vote yes in a library referendum.

Library Supporter Segmentation Pyramid

Chronic Non Voters

Super Supporters

Probable Supporters

Just for Fun | Kid Driven | Library as Office | Look to Librarians | Greater Good

Barriers to Support

Financially Strapped | Detached | The Web Wins

Chronic Non Voters
26.6% | 0% | 0

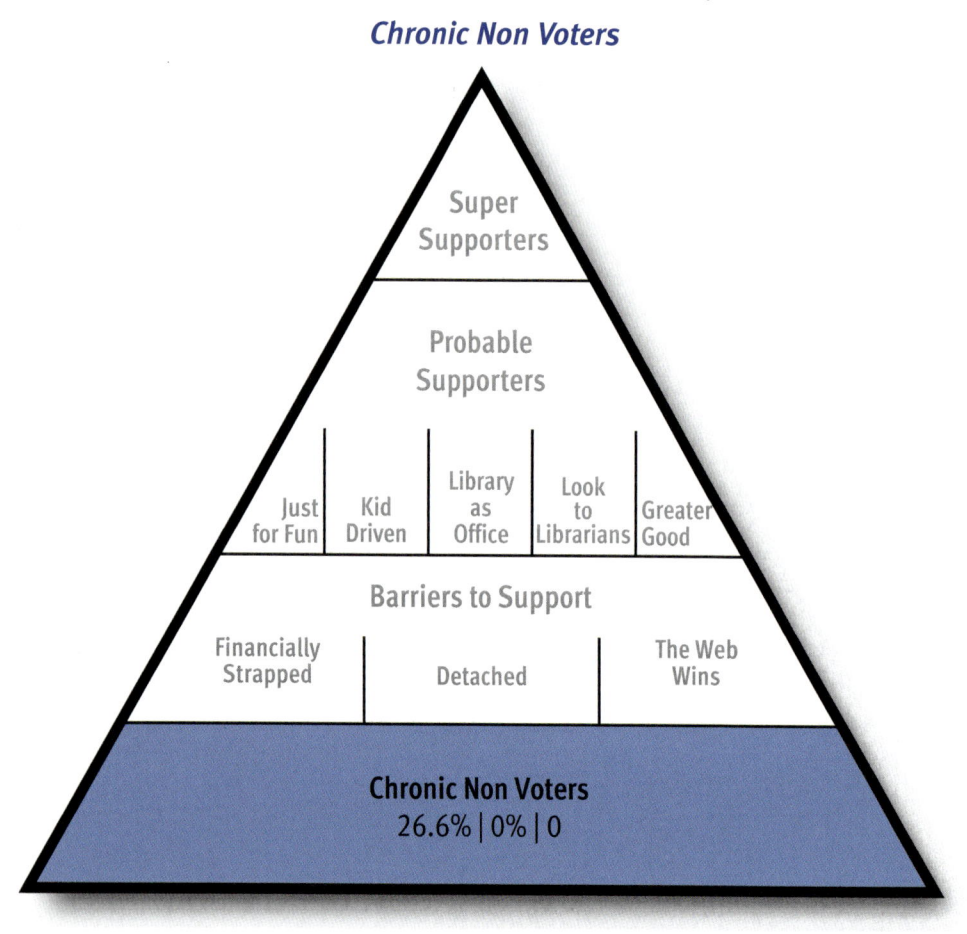

% Population ages 18–69 in communities < 200,000 | Definite Library Supporters | Library Support Index

$$\text{Library Support Index} = \frac{\text{\% Definite Library Supporters}}{\text{\% population ages 18–69 in communities < 200,000}} \times 100$$

Source: *From Awareness to Funding*, OCLC, 2008

To gain library voting support from this segment, Chronic Non Voters would first need to be persuaded to register to vote and to exercise that vote. Increasing voter registration and turnout is an important activity but not a goal for a potential library support campaign. As a result, the Chronic Non Voters were not included in subsequent reported findings.

Barriers to Support

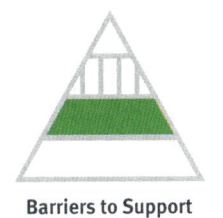

Barriers to Support tier

The Barriers to Support tier of the Library Support Segmentation Pyramid represents 34.0% of total survey respondents and just under half (45%) of the voting respondents. While this tier represents more than a third of all respondents and an even higher number of voters, it represents a relatively small number of library funders.

Less than a quarter (23%) of respondents who said they would *definitely* vote yes in a library referendum are represented in this tier of the market segmentation.

This tier has the largest population of any tier on the segmentation pyramid, and represents the most challenging group of voters to convince to support library tax funding. A calculation of relative library support value (the Library Support Index) shows that the Barriers to Support tier provides less than average funding support. This tier has a Library Support Index of 69, compared to an average index of 100.

The segmentation analysis identified three distinct segments within the Barriers to Support tier:

- **Financially Strapped**
  The Financially Strapped segment represents 10.6% of the total survey respondents, but only 4.4% of respondents who would *definitely* vote yes in a library referendum.

- **Detached**
  The Detached segment represents 16.0% of the survey respondents, the largest segment on the Barriers to Support tier. However, only 12.4% of *definite* library supporters are in the Detached segment.

- **The Web Wins**
  The Web Wins segment is the smallest segment on this tier and represents 7.4% of all survey respondents. Only 6.6% of respondents who said they would *definitely* support a library referendum are in this tier.

Each of these segments represents a group of voters with distinct barriers that limit financial support of libraries. We will review each segment across each of the five profile dimensions outlined earlier in this section.

Who are the library's financial supporters?

Library Supporter Segmentation Pyramid
Barriers to Support

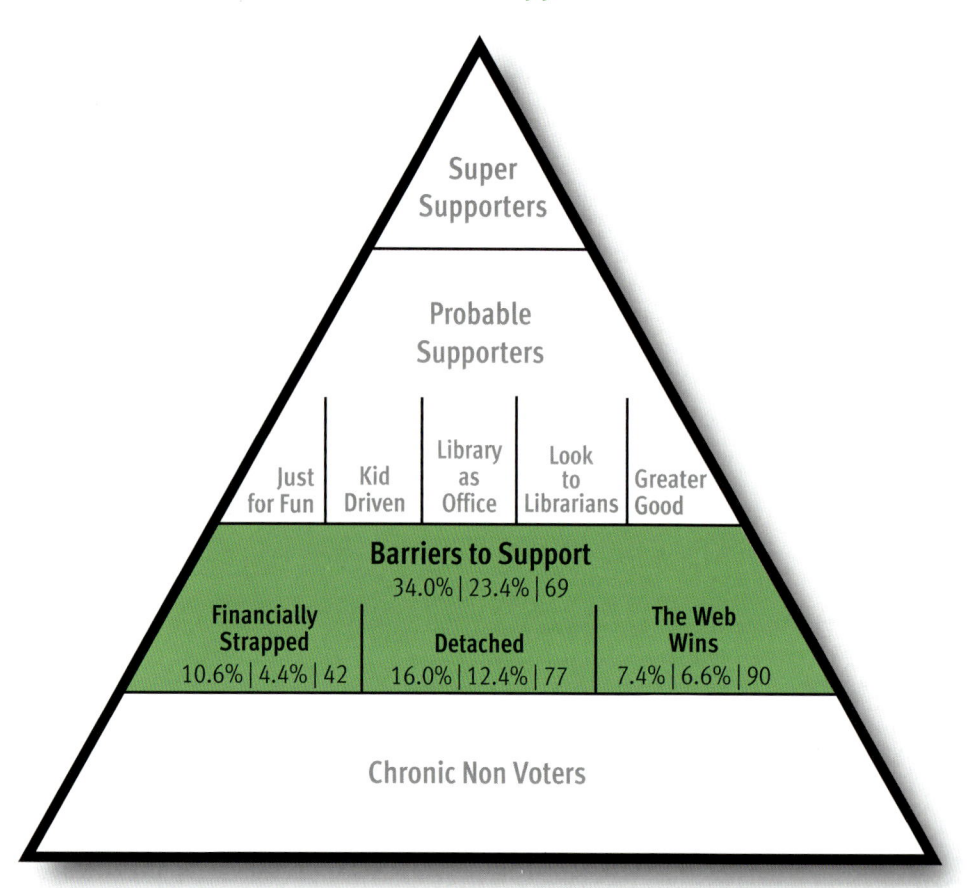

```
                    Super
                 Supporters
              ─────────────────
                  Probable
                 Supporters
          ┌──────┬──────┬──────┬──────┐
          │      │Library│ Look │      │
          │ Just │ Kid  │  as  │  to  │Greater│
          │for Fun│Driven│Office│Librar-│Good │
          │      │      │      │ians  │      │
          ├──────┴──────┴──────┴──────┤
              Barriers to Support
                34.0% | 23.4% | 69
          ┌──────────┬──────────┬──────────┐
          │Financially│          │ The Web  │
          │ Strapped │ Detached │   Wins   │
          │10.6%|4.4%│16.0%|12.4%│7.4%|6.6% │
          │   | 42   │   | 77   │   | 90   │
          ├──────────┴──────────┴──────────┤
                 Chronic Non Voters
```

% Population ages 18–69 in communities < 200,000 | Definite Library Supporters | Library Support Index

$$\text{Library Support Index} = \frac{\text{\% Definite Library Supporters}}{\text{\% population ages 18–69 in communities < 200,000}} \times 100$$

Source: *From Awareness to Funding*, OCLC, 2008

Calculating a Library Support Index

A Library Support Index was calculated for each segment of the pyramid. The index is a measure of a segment's willingness to definitely support a library referendum levy or bond measure relative to the overall size of the segment.

$$\text{Library Support Index} = \frac{\text{\% Definite Library Supporters}}{\text{\% population ages 18–69 in communities < 200,000}} \times 100$$

For example:

- The Barriers to Support tier has a Library Support Index of 69.
- 23.4% of definite library supporters are in the Barriers to Support market tier.
- 34.0 % of U.S. residents ages 18–69 are in the Barriers to Support market tier.
- Barriers to Support Library Support Index = (23.4% divided by 34.0%) X 100 = 69.

Barriers to Support—Financially Strapped

Barriers to Support tier

Financially Strapped segment

The Financially Strapped segment of the Barriers to Support tier represents 10.6% of the U.S. population ages 18–69. This group represents the smallest number of library funders. Only 4.4% of all *definite* voter support for library funding measures comes from this market segment.

As the name suggests, financial strains are this segment's chief barriers to committing to supporting an increase in funding for libraries. The Financially Strapped segment has a lower than average income and its members report that they struggle to make ends meet. These voters are not willing, and believe they are unable, to pay more in taxes.

While the research indicated that demographics were not a primary driver in determining the overall library supporter segmentation, most segments of the pyramid did show some demographic skews. The Financially Strapped segment has some identifying demographic tendencies. It is the youngest market segment with a higher number of college students than average for the total voting respondents. The Financially Strapped are less likely than other segments to have access to the Internet at home or work. They are also less likely to be married and more likely than average to live in urban communities.

The Financially Strapped also have a tendency to believe that the library is sufficiently funded. Given their financial barriers, they do not feel that they, or their financially strapped communities, should be asked to give more.

The Financially Strapped are the least likely of any market segment to recognize the importance of the library. This segment was the most strongly opposed to raising taxes to support the library. In fact, when asked if they would raise taxes in support of a variety of local public services, respondents were less likely to support a tax increase for libraries than for any local service.

A subset of the research findings is presented for each of the five profile dimensions:

1. Demographic profile
2. Library usage
3. Public service support
4. Library support compared to library usage
5. Attitudes toward libraries and funding.

Who are the library's financial supporters?

1. Demographic profile

Analysis of the Financially Strapped segment identified several demographic tendencies. It is the youngest segment with a higher percentage of students (21%) than average for the total voting respondents (8%). The Financially Strapped are less likely than other segments to have access to the Internet at home or work. They are also less likely to be married and more likely to live in urban communities.

Barriers to Support—
Financially Strapped

Demographic profile
Financially Strapped segment

	Total Voting Respondents	Financially Strapped
18–29	15%	26%
30–39	20%	17%
40–49	24%	23%
50–59	23%	19%
60–69	19%	14%
Female	50%	38%
Has at least one kid <18 years old	34%	22%
Less than $20,000	18%	24%
$20,000–$29,999	12%	12%
$30,000–$39,999	16%	23%
$40,000–$49,999	12%	15%
$50,000–$59,999	8%	6%
$60,000–$74,999	11%	7%
$75,000–$99,999	12%	8%
$100,000 or more	19%	7%
Demographic tendencies		
Full-time college student	8%	21%
Have Internet access at home or work	69%	50%
Married	52%	42%
Urban	19%	29%
Suburban	49%	52%
Rural	32%	19%

Source: *From Awareness to Funding*, OCLC, 2008

The Financially Strapped are less likely than other segments to have access to the Internet at home or work.

2-16 From Awareness to Funding: A study of library support in America

Who are the library's financial supporters?

Annual Library Visits

Financially Strapped
10.6

Total Voting Respondents
13.2

2. Library usage

The Financially Strapped are avid and frequent users of their public libraries. They report, on average, 10.6 library visits annually and account for 10.4% of all annual library visits reported by respondents. So, while funding support is relatively low, this group demonstrates close to average frequency of library visits.

The Financially Strapped use the library for a variety of activities, with higher than average use across most library services. They report heavier than average use of the library for research purposes. They are also more likely to use the computer and Internet at the library than other segments and are above average in their use of library literacy training programs.

The Financially Strapped use the library for research primarily

Financially Strapped segment

Below is a list of activities and services offered by public libraries. Please indicate how frequently you do each one at your local public library.

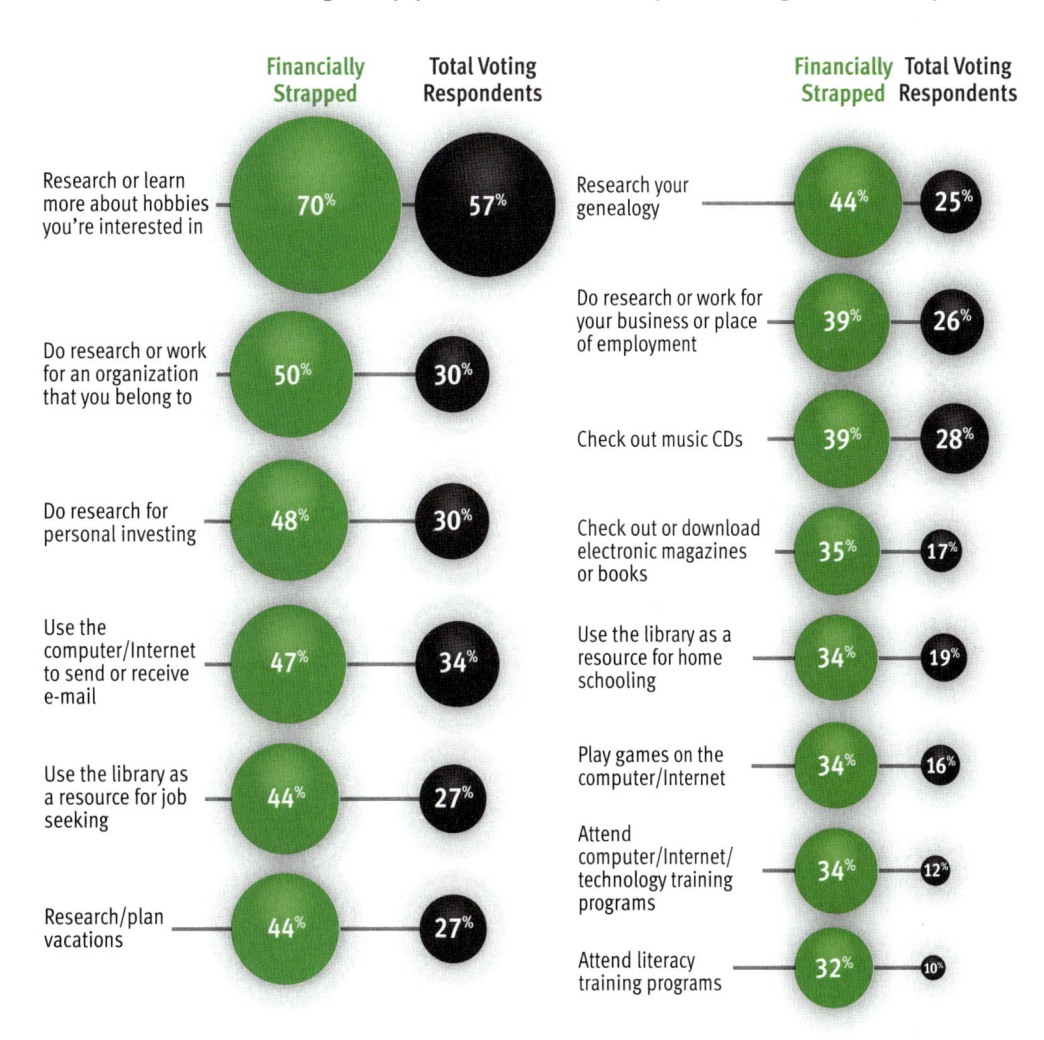

	Financially Strapped	Total Voting Respondents		Financially Strapped	Total Voting Respondents
Research or learn more about hobbies you're interested in	70%	57%	Research your genealogy	44%	25%
Do research or work for an organization that you belong to	50%	30%	Do research or work for your business or place of employment	39%	26%
Do research for personal investing	48%	30%	Check out music CDs	39%	28%
Use the computer/Internet to send or receive e-mail	47%	34%	Check out or download electronic magazines or books	35%	17%
Use the library as a resource for job seeking	44%	27%	Use the library as a resource for home schooling	34%	19%
Research/plan vacations	44%	27%	Play games on the computer/Internet	34%	16%
			Attend computer/Internet/technology training programs	34%	12%
			Attend literacy training programs	32%	10%

The chart shows *once a month or more* responses only
Source: *From Awareness to Funding*, OCLC, 2008

Who are the library's financial supporters?

3. Public service support

Survey respondents rated the degree to which they would be willing to pay more in local taxes to better fund a variety of public services.

The Financially Strapped are among the least likely of the voter segments to indicate that they would be willing to raise taxes to support public services. Less than half were willing to raise new taxes to support any of the seven services surveyed.

The fire department was the public service that received the highest level of support and garnered support for a tax increase from just 43% of this segment.

Even though the Financially Strapped are regular users of the public library, the public library receives the lowest level of funding support of any service from this segment. The public library ranked last with only 12% of the Financially Strapped voters agreeing they would be willing to pay more taxes to support the public library.

Barriers to Support—Financially Strapped

Even though the Financially Strapped are regular users of the public library, the public library receives the lowest level of funding support of any service.

Libraries rank last on the list of public services the Financially Strapped are willing to support

Financially Strapped segment

For each service, please rate how much you agree with the phrase "I'd be willing to pay more in local taxes to better fund this service." Please use a 10-point scale, where a 10 means you 'Completely Agree' and a 1 means you 'Completely Disagree.'

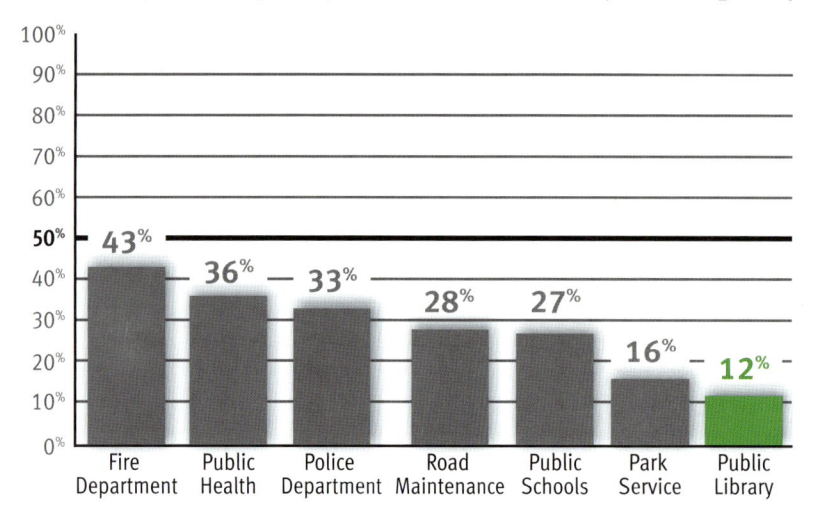

Service	%
Fire Department	43%
Public Health	36%
Police Department	33%
Road Maintenance	28%
Public Schools	27%
Park Service	16%
Public Library	12%

Percentage of voting respondents with an agreement rating of 8, 9 or 10
Source: *From Awareness to Funding*, OCLC, 2008

Who are the library's financial supporters?

4. Library support compared to library usage

Barriers to Support— Financially Strapped

The Financially Strapped segment represents 10.4% of all the library visits (Library Use Index = 98). This group visits the library at a frequency just under the average.

In contrast, the willingness of the Financially Strapped segment to vote favorably for a library referendum is well below average. They represent only 4.4% of respondents who said they would *definitely* vote in favor of a library referendum (Library Support Index = 42), the lowest rate for all market segments except Chronic Non Voters.

Despite average library usage compared to other segments, the Financially Strapped segment is the least likely to support the library at the ballot box

Financially Strapped segment

If there was a referendum, ballot initiative or bond measure for your local public library on the ballot, how do you think you would vote?

How many times have you visited your local public library in the past 12 months?

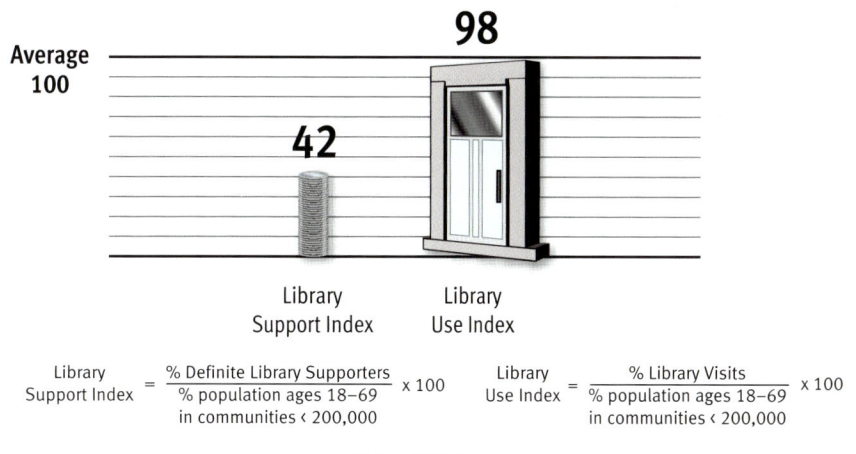

Average 100

98 — Library Use Index
42 — Library Support Index

$$\text{Library Support Index} = \frac{\text{\% Definite Library Supporters}}{\text{\% population ages 18–69 in communities < 200,000}} \times 100$$

$$\text{Library Use Index} = \frac{\text{\% Library Visits}}{\text{\% population ages 18–69 in communities < 200,000}} \times 100$$

An index of 100 is average
Source: *From Awareness to Funding*, OCLC, 2008

Calculating a Library Use Index

A Library Use Index was calculated for each segment of the pyramid. The index is a measure of a segment's use of the library relative to the size of the segment.

$$\text{Library Use Index} = \frac{\text{\% Library Visits}}{\text{\% population ages 18–69 in communities < 200,000}} \times 100$$

For example:

- The Financially Strapped segment has a Library Use Index of 98.
- 10.4% of library visits are made by the Financially Strapped market segment.
- 10.6% of U.S. residents ages 18–69 are in the Financially Strapped market segment.
- Financially Strapped Library Use Index = (10.4% divided by 10.6%) X 100 = 98.

Who are the library's financial supporters?

5. Attitudes toward libraries and funding

The attitudes most critical to defining the Financially Strapped segment are their attitudes toward money. This segment has a low income level in comparison to the total voting respondents. They struggle to make ends meet and believe they already pay enough in property taxes. As a result, they are the segment most likely to oppose tax increases.

Barriers to Support— Financially Strapped

The Financially Strapped live in communities characterized by financial concerns. Their communities are struggling financially and respondents in this segment believe that their communities have much bigger concerns than library funding, including unemployment, crime and safety.

The Financially Strapped generally believe that the public library already has sufficient funding. The Financially Strapped segment is more than twice as likely (53%) as the average for all voting respondents (23%) to believe the library should be able to operate on its current budget. This segment is not willing to increase taxes for library funding.

Attitudes toward libraries and funding
Financially Strapped segment

For each statement below, please rate your level of agreement on a scale from 1 to 10, where a 10 means 'Agree Strongly' and a 1 means 'Disagree Strongly.'

The Financially Strapped respondents feel they are unable to afford any tax increases

	Total Voting Respondents	Financially Strapped
I never seem to have enough money to make ends meet	36%	50%
I can't afford to pay more taxes	50%	74%
I feel like I pay too much in property taxes	41%	56%
I oppose tax increases across the board	35%	57%

Percentage of voting respondents with an agreement rating of 8, 9 or 10
Source: *From Awareness to Funding*, OCLC, 2008

The Financially Strapped respondents feel they are unable to afford any tax increases.

The Financially Strapped respondents are more likely to live in communities that are struggling financially

	Total Voting Respondents	Financially Strapped
People in my community can't afford to have their taxes raised	45%	55%
In recent years my community has really struggled economically	28%	39%
My community suffers from a high unemployment rate	25%	37%

Percentage of voting respondents with an agreement rating of 8, 9 or 10
Source: *From Awareness to Funding*, OCLC, 2008

2-20 From Awareness to Funding: A study of library support in America

Who are the library's financial supporters?

Barriers to Support—Financially Strapped

The Financially Strapped respondents believe their communities have bigger concerns than library funding

	Total Voting Respondents	Financially Strapped
My community has much more important issues to worry about than funding the public library	13%	24%
My community suffers from crime and gang-related violence	18%	34%
I worry about safety at the public library since it's a public place that everyone has access to, including homeless people and criminals	15%	33%

Percentage of voting respondents with an agreement rating of 8, 9 or 10
Source: *From Awareness to Funding*, OCLC, 2008

The Financially Strapped respondents believe that the library already has sufficient funding.

The Financially Strapped respondents believe that the library already has sufficient funding

	Total Voting Respondents	Financially Strapped
I think the local government provides adequate funding for the public library	27%	57%
Between donations, fund-raising and government funding, I feel like the local public library is well-funded	30%	54%
The public library should be able to operate on its current budget with no increase	23%	53%
My local public library receives enough funding to keep up with the technology needs of the community	28%	51%

Percentage of voting respondents with an agreement rating of 8, 9 or 10
Source: *From Awareness to Funding*, OCLC, 2008

The Financially Strapped segment is strongly opposed to library tax increases

	Total Voting Respondents	Financially Strapped
I would not be willing to pay higher taxes in order to fund the local public library	23%	53%
I don't support tax increases that fund services I don't use or benefit from	26%	50%
I think raising taxes to fund the public library would be a waste of the public's money	16%	40%

Percentage of voting respondents with an agreement rating of 8, 9 or 10
Source: *From Awareness to Funding*, OCLC, 2008

Who are the library's financial supporters?

Barriers to Support tier
Detached segment

The Detached segment of the Barriers to Support tier represents 16.0% of the total U.S. population ages 18–69. A relatively small number of *definite* supporters of library referenda, ballot initiatives or bond measures (12.4%) are from the Detached segment.

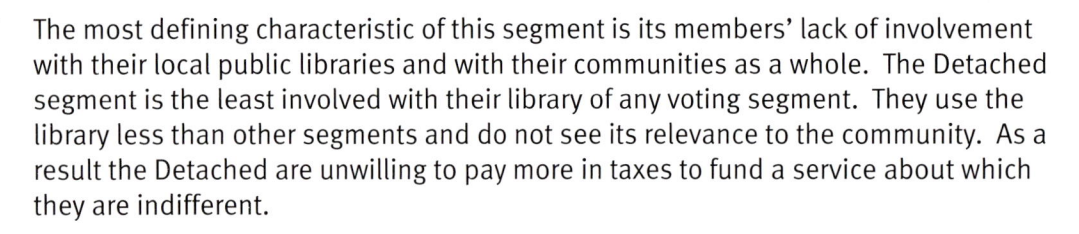

The most defining characteristic of this segment is its members' lack of involvement with their local public libraries and with their communities as a whole. The Detached segment is the least involved with their library of any voting segment. They use the library less than other segments and do not see its relevance to the community. As a result the Detached are unwilling to pay more in taxes to fund a service about which they are indifferent.

Although demographics were not a key construct in the definition of the library supporter segmentation, the Detached segment shows some demographic tendencies. The Detached segment tends to have higher household incomes than average, with 29% having an annual household income of $100,000 or more, compared to 19% of the total voting respondents.

The Detached segment is the segment whose members are least likely to have a library card and are the least aware of what the library has to offer. They are more likely to have Internet access at home than other voting respondents and think that the information provided by the Internet is as good as that provided by the library. They see the library as outdated technologically and do not see the library as relevant to their families or their communities.

Not only are the Detached respondents uninvolved with their local libraries, they are uninvolved with their communities. They pay less attention than average to issues around local politics and the local economy, and are less-frequent consumers of local media. The Detached segment tends to believe that everyone in their communities has Internet access. They fail to recognize the library's role in providing equal access to technology for community residents.

With higher than average income, the Detached segment is better able to afford an increase in taxes to support public services than many other segments. But lack of connection to or interest in the library and their communities make them unlikely to support tax increases to fund the library.

A subset of the research findings is presented for the five profile dimensions.

Barriers to Support—
Detached

The most defining characteristic of the Detached segment is its members' lack of involvement with their local public libraries and with their communities as a whole.

Who are the library's financial supporters?

1. Demographic profile

Only one demographic measure, household income, was noteworthy for the Detached segment. This group tends to have higher household incomes than other voting respondents (19%) surveyed with 29% earning more than $100,000 annually.

Barriers to Support—Detached

The Detached segment tends to have higher household incomes than other respondents.

Demographic profile
Detached segment

	Total Voting Respondents	Detached
18–29	15%	11%
30–39	20%	21%
40–49	24%	22%
50–59	23%	22%
60–69	19%	24%
Female	50%	46%
Has at least one kid <18 years old	34%	29%
Less than $20,000	18%	12%
$20,000–$29,999	12%	9%
$30,000–$39,999	16%	12%
$40,000–$49,999	12%	13%
$50,000–$59,999	8%	12%
$60,000–$74,999	11%	11%
$75,000–$99,999	12%	17%
$100,000 or more	19%	29%
Demographic tendencies		
$75,000–$99,999	12%	17%
$100,000 or more	19%	29%

Source: *From Awareness to Funding*, OCLC, 2008

Who are the library's financial supporters?

2. Library usage

The Detached segment has the lowest frequency of library usage of all voting respondents, reporting an average of 3.7 visits annually, compared to an average of 13.2 for all voting segments.

The frequency of use for most library resources and services is also below average. The Detached segment does take advantage of access to best-seller and nonfiction reading materials and a third of its members regularly use the library to research hobbies and interests or use print reference materials.

Annual Library Visits
Detached ● 3.7
Total Voting Respondents 13.2

The Detached use library services less than other segments
Detached segment

Below is a list of activities and services offered by public libraries. Please indicate how frequently you do each one at your local public library.

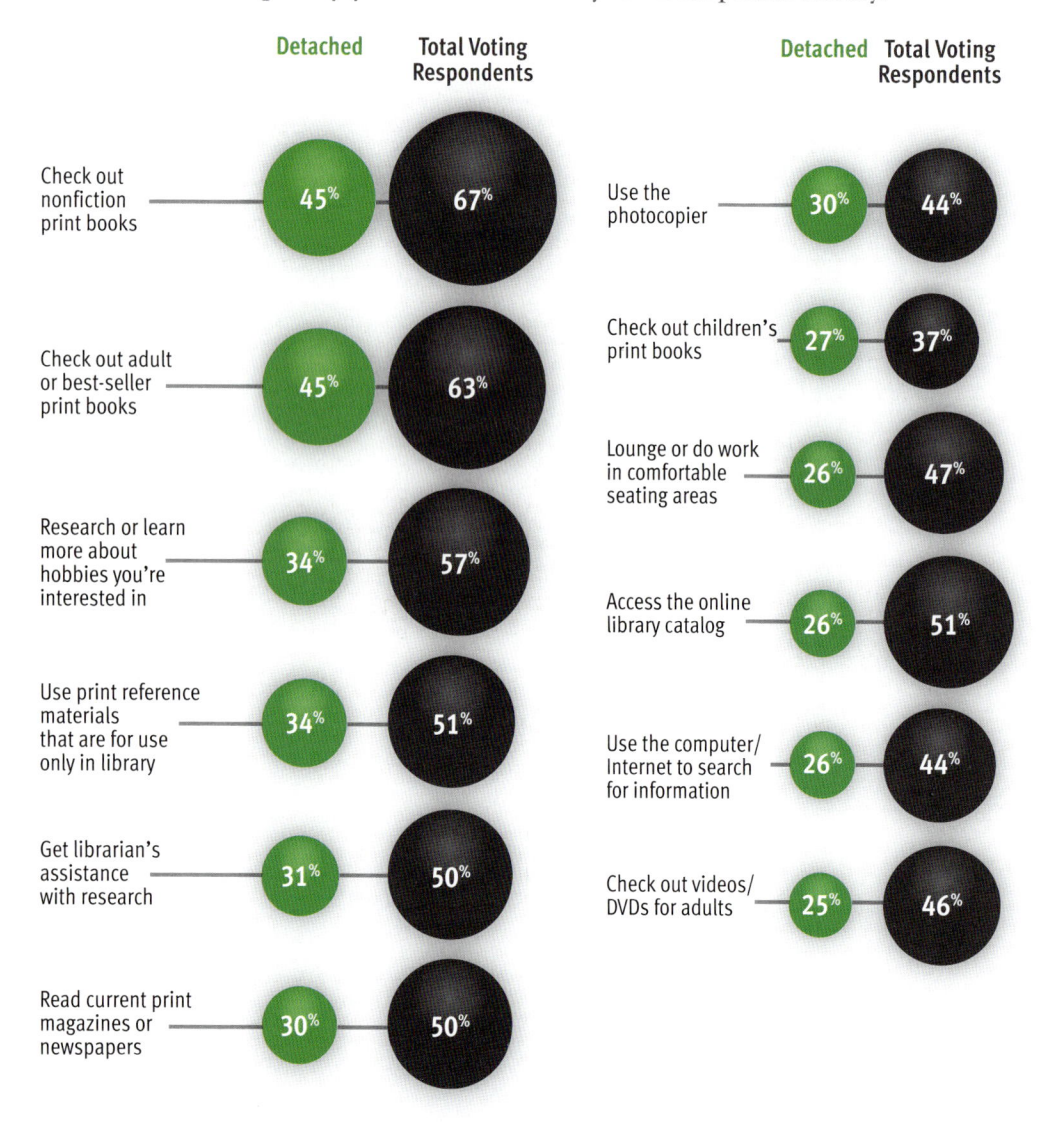

Activity	Detached	Total Voting Respondents
Check out nonfiction print books	45%	67%
Check out adult or best-seller print books	45%	63%
Research or learn more about hobbies you're interested in	34%	57%
Use print reference materials that are for use only in library	34%	51%
Get librarian's assistance with research	31%	50%
Read current print magazines or newspapers	30%	50%
Use the photocopier	30%	44%
Check out children's print books	27%	37%
Lounge or do work in comfortable seating areas	26%	47%
Access the online library catalog	26%	51%
Use the computer/Internet to search for information	26%	44%
Check out videos/DVDs for adults	25%	46%

The chart shows *once a month or more* responses only
Source: *From Awareness to Funding*, OCLC, 2008

2-24 From Awareness to Funding: A study of library support in America

Barriers to Support— Detached

3. Public service support

Members of the Detached segment are generally uninvolved with their local communities and are not inclined to vote for tax increases to fund local services. Only one public service, the fire department, has majority support from this segment. Fifty-one percent (51%) agree they would be willing to pay more taxes for the fire department. The police department (45%) and public schools (43%) rank second and third.

The public library ranks sixth of seven public services for financial support from the Detached segment, with only 20% of respondents willing to increase tax funding. Only the park service (17%) receives a lower level of support.

The park service is the only public service that gets less support from the Detached segment than the library

Detached segment

For each service, please rate how much you agree with the phrase "I'd be willing to pay more in local taxes to better fund this service." Please use a 10-point scale, where a 10 means you 'Completely Agree' and a 1 means you 'Completely Disagree.'

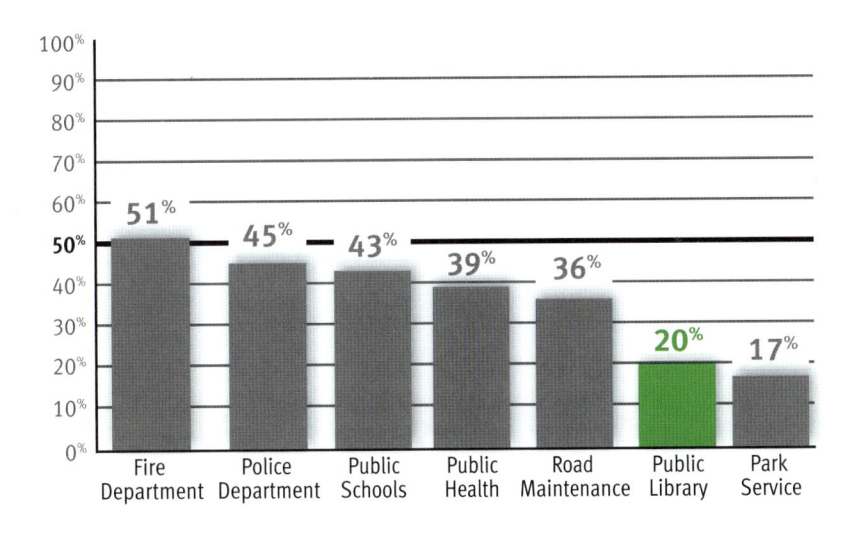

Service	Percentage
Fire Department	51%
Police Department	45%
Public Schools	43%
Public Health	39%
Road Maintenance	36%
Public Library	20%
Park Service	17%

Percentage of voting respondents with an agreement rating of 8, 9 or 10
Source: *From Awareness to Funding*, OCLC, 2008

Who are the library's financial supporters?

4. Library support compared to library usage

The members of the Detached segment are lower than average financial supporters of the library and represent significantly lower than average frequency of library visits.

The Detached segment represents only 5.5% of annual library visits reported by all respondents. They visit the library less than four times a year. Their Library Use Index is just 34.

The Detached segment represents 12.4% of people *definitely* willing to vote in favor of a referendum, ballot initiative or bond measure, resulting in a less than average Library Support Index score of 77. The Detached segment is unlikely to support or use library services.

Barriers to Support—Detached

The Detached segment is less likely than average to support the library at the ballot box and rarely uses its services

Detached segment

If there was a referendum, ballot initiative or bond measure for your local public library on the ballot, how do you think you would vote?

How many times have you visited your local public library in the past 12 months?

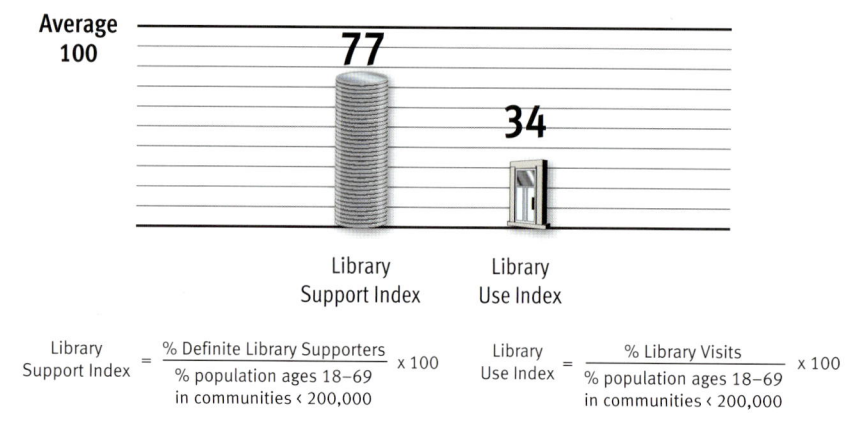

Average 100

Library Support Index: 77
Library Use Index: 34

$$\text{Library Support Index} = \frac{\text{\% Definite Library Supporters}}{\text{\% population ages 18–69 in communities < 200,000}} \times 100$$

$$\text{Library Use Index} = \frac{\text{\% Library Visits}}{\text{\% population ages 18–69 in communities < 200,000}} \times 100$$

An index of 100 is average
Source: *From Awareness to Funding*, OCLC, 2008

**Barriers to Support—
Detached**

5. Attitudes toward libraries and funding

The Detached segment is most strongly differentiated from other market segments by a lack of involvement with the community in general and its public libraries in particular. The Detached are the least likely group to have a library card and are unaware of the services that the library has to offer. In contrast, the Detached are most likely to have Internet access at home. They believe the Internet is a source of information at least as good as the public library, which they consider to be outdated technologically.

The Detached are disconnected from their communities. They devote little time and energy to keeping up with the community's economic or political issues. They are less likely than other voters to read the local newspaper or watch the local news and do not see the importance of the role that the library plays in the community. They believe others in their communities have access to information through the Internet at home and don't consider that the library offers unique access to information resources.

The Detached are the least likely group to have a library card and are unaware of the services that the library has to offer.

Due to their lack of involvement with their library and their community, the Detached respondents are less likely than other segments to see a need to support tax increases for the library.

Attitudes toward libraries and funding

Detached segment

For each statement below, please rate your level of agreement on a scale from 1 to 10, where a 10 means 'Agree Strongly' and a 1 means 'Disagree Strongly.'

The Detached are the least likely segment to have a library card and to frequent the library

	Total Voting Respondents	Detached
Have a library card	77%	55%
I don't go to the library in my community often	36%	76%

Percentage of voting respondents with an agreement rating of 8, 9 or 10
Source: *From Awareness to Funding*, OCLC, 2008

Who are the library's financial supporters?

The Detached admit they are not involved with the library and do not consider it relevant to them

	Total Voting Respondents	Detached
My library is not top of mind—I just don't think to go there	24%	60%
I don't pay much attention to what's going on at the library	24%	59%
It's been so long since I've been to the library that I'm not even sure what it has to offer anymore	19%	43%
The librarians at my local public library know me by name	24%	10%
I spend a lot of time in the library in my community	24%	8%

Percentage of voting respondents with an agreement rating of 8, 9 or 10
Source: *From Awareness to Funding*, OCLC, 2008

Barriers to Support—Detached

The Detached segment is more likely than other segments to have Internet access at home.

The Detached segment is more likely than other voting respondents to have Internet access at home

	Total Voting Respondents	Detached
Have Internet access at home	68%	78%
Have Internet access at work	27%	32%

Percentage of voting respondents with an agreement rating of 8, 9 or 10
Source: *From Awareness to Funding*, OCLC, 2008

The Detached think that everyone else has Internet access also and therefore do not recognize the library's role in providing equal access to all

	Total Voting Respondents	Detached
Almost everyone today has access to the Internet at home or work	42%	51%
A lot of people who use the library in my community don't have Internet access at home	44%	33%
The local public library provides essential resources that people couldn't otherwise afford	68%	53%
The local library levels the playing field by providing access to books, technology and special classes for everyone	49%	32%

Percentage of voting respondents with an agreement rating of 8, 9 or 10
Source: *From Awareness to Funding*, OCLC, 2008

Who are the library's financial supporters?

Barriers to Support—Detached

The Detached perceive the Internet as a good source of information, equal to or better than the public library

	Total Voting Respondents	Detached
It's easier to do research on the Internet using search engines like Google and Yahoo! than in the local library	37%	53%
All the information in the library I could just as easily get on the Internet	26%	43%
The information you can find yourself using search engines like Google or Yahoo! is every bit as good as the library	30%	43%
It's just easier to buy books from a bookstore/online bookstore than to borrow them from the library	15%	23%

Percentage of voting respondents with an agreement rating of 8, 9 or 10
Source: *From Awareness to Funding*, OCLC, 2008

The Detached do not believe the library is technologically relevant to them, their children or their community

	Total Voting Respondents	Detached
The public library has done a good job of keeping up with changing technology	60%	41%
The public library in my town is one of the best places to go to learn computer skills	26%	17%
The library is one of the first places I would go if I wanted to engage my child with computers and technology	30%	16%

Percentage of voting respondents with an agreement rating of 8, 9 or 10
Source: *From Awareness to Funding*, OCLC, 2008

The Detached do not believe the library is technologically relevant to them, their children or their community.

This segment is detached from the library, and also from the community

	Total Voting Respondents	Detached
Do you read the local newspaper on a regular basis?		
Yes	80%	69%
No	17%	27%
How often do you watch local news on TV?		
Every day	57%	47%
Do you access community information online on a regular basis?		
Yes	42%	29%
No	54%	65%
How interested are you in public policy/economics in your community?		
Very interested	32%	20%
How closely do you follow local politics?		
Very closely	31%	19%
Not too closely	18%	27%

Source: *From Awareness to Funding*, OCLC, 2008

Who are the library's financial supporters?

The Detached are less inclined than others to see the importance of the role the library plays in the community

	Total Voting Respondents	Detached
Local support can make a big difference in the quality of the library	81%	70%
Having an excellent public library is a source of pride for a community	73%	55%
A top-notch public library is an important part of a good community	72%	55%
A reputable public library raises the status and image of a community	67%	49%
The public library stimulates growth and development in a community	63%	47%
I wish people in my community were more supportive of the library	48%	36%
Having a high-quality library helps raise property values in the community	45%	30%
You can measure the success of a community by the quality of the library	42%	28%

Percentage of voting respondents with an agreement rating of 8, 9 or 10
Source: *From Awareness to Funding*, OCLC, 2008

Barriers to Support—Detached

The Detached are less likely than other voting respondents to support tax increases that fund the library

	Total Voting Respondents	Detached
I feel like there's a lot of waste in local government spending	58%	67%
I can't afford to pay more taxes	50%	61%
I support tax increases that will improve my community	37%	26%
I would not be willing to pay higher taxes in order to fund the local library	23%	32%
I would be willing to pay more in taxes that would fund a new building or branch for the local library	23%	14%
I would be willing to pay more in taxes that would fund operating costs for the local library, like building maintenance and staff salaries	24%	11%
I would be willing to pay more in taxes if it meant better funding for the library	24%	10%

Percentage of voting respondents with an agreement rating of 8, 9 or 10
Source: *From Awareness to Funding*, OCLC, 2008

From Awareness to Funding: A study of library support in America

Who are the library's financial supporters?

Barriers to Support tier

The Web Wins segment

The Web Wins segment of the Barriers to Support tier represents 7.4% of total survey respondents and 6.6% of all respondents who said they would *definitely* vote favorably for a library referendum, ballot initiative or bond measure.

The Web Wins segment is characterized by a heavy reliance on the Internet as its information source and a belief that the library provides little added value over the Internet. Although it is nice for the community to have a good public library, this segment does not consider it an essential public service and is therefore less likely than average to vote for an increase in taxes to support library funding.

The Web Wins segment is demographically average across all survey respondents and shows no unique tendencies.

The Web Wins respondents are more likely than average to have an Internet connection at home and are more likely than other respondents to have high-speed Internet connections.

The Web Wins group believes that the information found on the Internet is as good as the information provided by the public library. They do not believe that research assistance from a librarian adds value. They visit the library six times annually, less than the average for all voting segments.

Trust in the power of the Internet and a lukewarm attitude toward the public library means that although they are more likely to support the public library financially than other segments on the Barriers to Support tier, The Web Wins respondents are still less likely than average to vote positively across all voters. In order to garner support from this segment, this segment would need to be convinced that the library is superior to the Web.

**Barriers to Support—
The Web Wins**

The Web Wins respondents are more likely than average to have an Internet connection at home and are the segment most likely to have high-speed Internet connections.

Who are the library's financial supporters?

1. Demographic profile

The Web Wins segment is demographically average. There are no demographic tendencies that differentiate this segment.

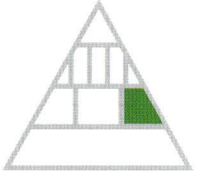

Demographic profile

The Web Wins segment

	Total Voting Respondents	The Web Wins
18–29	15%	11%
30–39	20%	22%
40–49	24%	23%
50–59	23%	25%
60–69	19%	19%
Female	50%	42%
Has at least one kid <18 years old	34%	35%
Less than $20,000	18%	21%
$20,000–$29,999	12%	6%
$30,000–$39,999	16%	10%
$40,000–$49,999	12%	9%
$50,000–$59,999	8%	12%
$60,000–$74,999	11%	11%
$75,000–$99,999	12%	18%
$100,000 or more	19%	23%

Source: *From Awareness to Funding*, OCLC, 2008

**Barriers to Support—
The Web Wins**

Who are the library's financial supporters?

2. Library usage

Annual Library Visits

The Web Wins
● 6.2

Total Voting Respondents
● 13.2

The Web Wins respondents are infrequent users of the public library. They report only 6.2 annual visits, representing only 4.2% of all annual visits for survey respondents.

Not surprisingly, they also report less than average usage of library services. Top services used are a mix of professional and recreational activities. Using the library for study, to do homework or to do research for work were the only services this group used more than other voting respondents.

The Web Wins respondents are infrequent users of the library and its services

The Web Wins segment

Below is a list of activities and services offered by public libraries. Please indicate how frequently you do each one at your local public library.

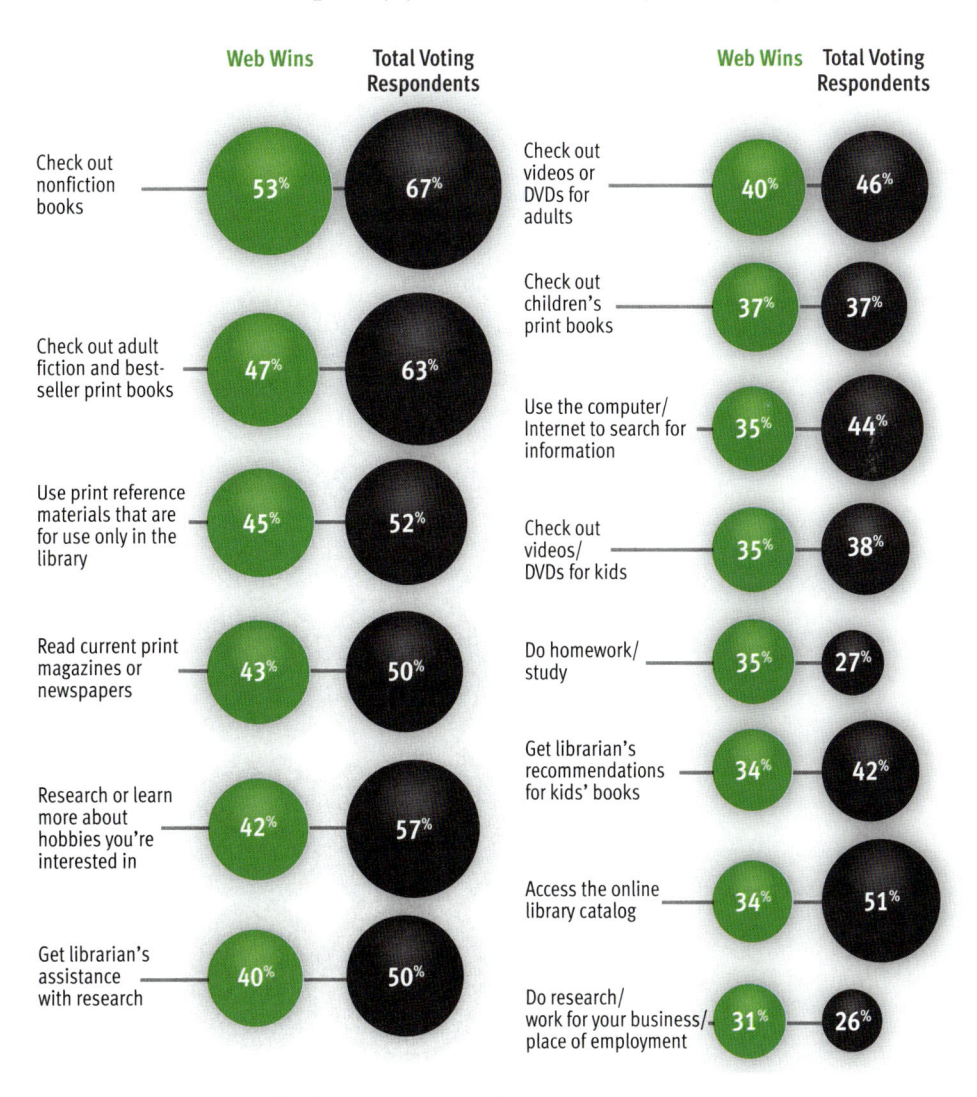

	Web Wins	Total Voting Respondents		Web Wins	Total Voting Respondents
Check out nonfiction books	53%	67%	Check out videos or DVDs for adults	40%	46%
Check out adult fiction and best-seller print books	47%	63%	Check out children's print books	37%	37%
Use print reference materials that are for use only in the library	45%	52%	Use the computer/Internet to search for information	35%	44%
Read current print magazines or newspapers	43%	50%	Check out videos/DVDs for kids	35%	38%
Research or learn more about hobbies you're interested in	42%	57%	Do homework/study	35%	27%
Get librarian's assistance with research	40%	50%	Get librarian's recommendations for kids' books	34%	42%
			Access the online library catalog	34%	51%
			Do research/work for your business/place of employment	31%	26%

The chart shows *once a month or more* responses only
Source: *From Awareness to Funding*, OCLC, 2008

From Awareness to Funding: A study of library support in America

Who are the library's financial supporters?

3. Public service support

Similar to the other segments on the Barriers to Support tier, The Web Wins segment is relatively unwilling to support an increase in taxes to fund the public library. The Web Wins segment is also reluctant to increase taxes for other local services. Less than half of its members are willing to raise taxes to support any of the seven local services surveyed.

The police department receives the most support from this group, with 47% of respondents showing a willingness to increase taxes for police services. Public schools rank second with 44% and the fire service ranks third at 43%. There is a large drop in support for the remaining services, all securing just 25% or less support for increased tax funding.

The public library ranked last across all services with 21% of The Web Wins respondents willing to increase their taxes for public libraries.

**Barriers to Support—
The Web Wins**

The library is the public service least likely to receive funding support from The Web Wins segment

The Web Wins segment

For each service, please rate how much you agree with the phrase "I'd be willing to pay more in local taxes to better fund this service." Please use a 10-point scale, where a 10 means you 'Completely Agree' and a 1 means you 'Completely Disagree.'

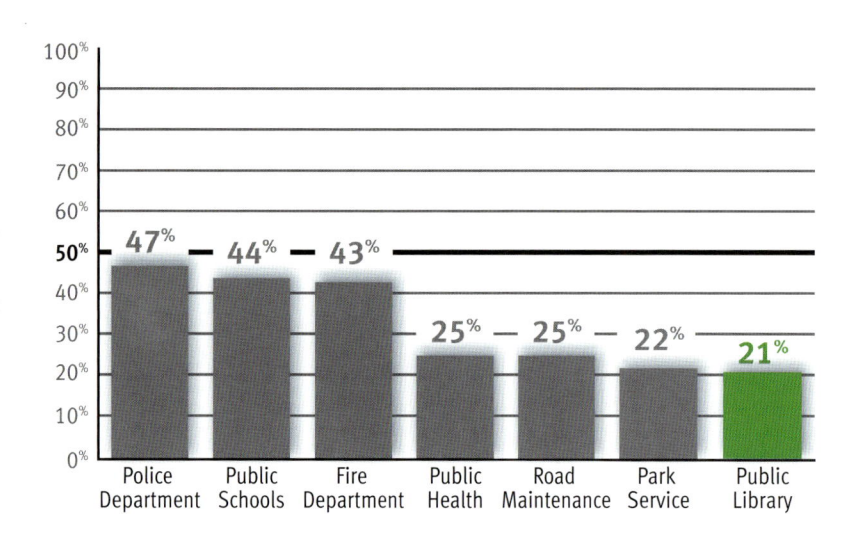

Service	Percentage
Police Department	47%
Public Schools	44%
Fire Department	43%
Public Health	25%
Road Maintenance	25%
Park Service	22%
Public Library	21%

Percentage of voting respondents with an agreement rating of 8, 9 or 10
Source: *From Awareness to Funding*, OCLC, 2008

Who are the library's financial supporters?

**Barriers to Support—
The Web Wins**

4. Library support compared to library usage

The Web Wins segment represents just 4.2% of all annual library visits.

Despite the infrequent use, this group is more likely to raise taxes for library funding than the other segments on the Barriers to Support tier. The percentage of respondents *definitely* willing to vote in support of a library referendum who are represented in The Web Wins segment is 6.6%. Definite support is still less than average, with a Library Support Index of 90.

The Web Wins respondents show below-average support for funding the library and are infrequent library users

The Web Wins segment

If there was a referendum, ballot initiative or bond measure for your local public library on the ballot, how do you think you would vote?

How many times have you visited your local public library in the past 12 months?

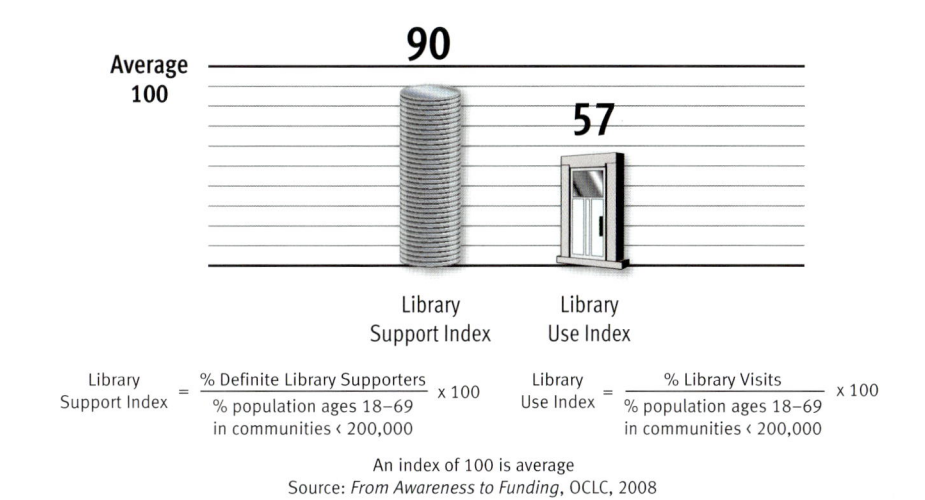

Average 100

90 — Library Support Index

57 — Library Use Index

$$\text{Library Support Index} = \frac{\text{\% Definite Library Supporters}}{\text{\% population ages 18–69 in communities < 200,000}} \times 100$$

$$\text{Library Use Index} = \frac{\text{\% Library Visits}}{\text{\% population ages 18–69 in communities < 200,000}} \times 100$$

An index of 100 is average
Source: *From Awareness to Funding*, OCLC, 2008

Who are the library's financial supporters?

5. Attitudes toward libraries and funding

The Web Wins segment is characterized by the juxtaposition of the respondents' attitudes to the public library and the Internet. Its members typically have Internet access at home and are the segment with the highest percentage of high-speed Internet connections.

The Web Wins respondents do not see value in the library for their own personal needs, as they believe the information on the Internet is sufficient. They believe it is easier to conduct research on the Internet than at the public library and do not think the librarian adds value to the research process.

The Web Wins respondents are not uninvolved with their communities but simply believe that the library is less relevant with the advent of the Internet and the ready availability of books online and at bookstores. They feel that television programming now provided for children has made the library less important to the current generation.

The Web Wins respondents are not opposed to the idea of the public library but do not consider it as an essential service for their communities. They are less willing than average for total voting respondents to raise taxes to fund the library.

Barriers to Support—The Web Wins

The Web Wins respondents do not see a value in the library for their own personal needs, as they believe the information on the Internet is sufficient.

Attitudes toward libraries and funding
The Web Wins segment

For each statement below, please rate your level of agreement on a scale from 1 to 10, where a 10 means 'Agree Strongly' and a 1 means 'Disagree Strongly.'

The Web Wins respondents have Internet access at home and the fastest connection

	Total Voting Respondents	The Web Wins
Have Internet access at home	69%	73%
Of those with home Internet access, % with cable modem access	38%	49%

Percentage of voting respondents with an agreement rating of 8, 9 or 10
Source: *From Awareness to Funding*, OCLC, 2008

The Web Wins segment believes the information on the Internet is as good as information available at the library

	Total Voting Respondents	The Web Wins
All the information in the library I could just as easily get on the Internet	26%	63%
The information you can find yourself using search engines like Google and Yahoo! is every bit as good as the information you can get by doing a library search	30%	61%
It's easier to do research on the Internet using search engines like Google and Yahoo! than in the local public library	37%	69%

Percentage of voting respondents with an agreement rating of 8, 9 or 10
Source: *From Awareness to Funding*, OCLC, 2008

Who are the library's financial supporters?

**Barriers to Support—
The Web Wins**

The Web Wins respondents do not believe that the librarian adds value over conducting independent research online

The public librarian:	Total Voting Respondents	The Web Wins
Can research topics better than you can do alone on the Internet	44%	24%
Recommends Web sites and other electronic information sources that you never would have thought of otherwise	39%	24%
Is able to access information through technology in ways that ordinary people can't	44%	31%

Percentage of voting respondents with an agreement rating of 8, 9 or 10
Source: *From Awareness to Funding*, OCLC, 2008

The Web Wins respondents do not believe that the librarian adds value over conducting independent research online.

The Web Wins segment considers the library a 'nice to have' for the community but not an essential public service

	Total Voting Respondents	The Web Wins
My community has much more important issues to worry about than funding the public library	13%	26%
Whether or not the local public library is good or bad has very little impact on the community	11%	24%
Since the advent of the Internet, the public library has become obsolete	11%	27%
A public library is nice to have in the community, but not necessary	11%	23%
People in my community don't use the library enough to justify spending additional money on it	14%	27%
It's just easier to buy books from a bookstore/online bookstore than to borrow them from the local public library	15%	30%
With all the great programming on public TV and the many activities children enjoy, libraries just aren't as important in kids' lives as they once were	24%	45%

Percentage of voting respondents with an agreement rating of 8, 9 or 10
Source: *From Awareness to Funding*, OCLC, 2008

Based on trust of the Internet and attitudes toward the library, The Web Wins segment is less willing than others to raise taxes for library support

	Total Voting Respondents	The Web Wins
I would be willing to pay more in taxes that would fund operating costs of the local public library, like building maintenance and staff salaries	24%	12%
I would be willing to pay more in taxes if it meant better funding for the local public library	24%	10%
I would be willing to pay more in taxes that would fund a new building or branch for the local public library	23%	5%
I support tax increases that will improve my community	37%	15%

Percentage of voting respondents with an agreement rating of 8, 9 or 10
Source: *From Awareness to Funding*, OCLC, 2008

Who are the library's financial supporters?

Probable Supporters tier

The Probable Supporters tier of the Library Supporter Segmentation Pyramid represents 32.3% of all survey respondents and approximately 44% of voting respondents. In local elections, Probable Supporters represent a slightly higher percentage (45%) of the voter turnout.

This tier represents a large number of voters and the largest percentage of *definite* library funding supporters. Fifty-six percent (55.7%) of all respondents who said they would *definitely* vote yes in support of a library referendum, ballot initiative or bond measure belong to the Probable Supporters tier.

Probable Supporters

Library Supporter Segmentation Pyramid
Probable Supporters

	Just for Fun	Kid Driven	Library as Office	Look to Librarians	Greater Good
	7.1%	6.6%	3.4%	6.5%	8.7%
	9.7%	11.5%	6.0%	12.2%	16.2%
	136	176	176	187	188

Super Supporters

Probable Supporters
32.3% | 55.6% | 172

Barriers to Support: Financially Strapped | Detached | The Web Wins

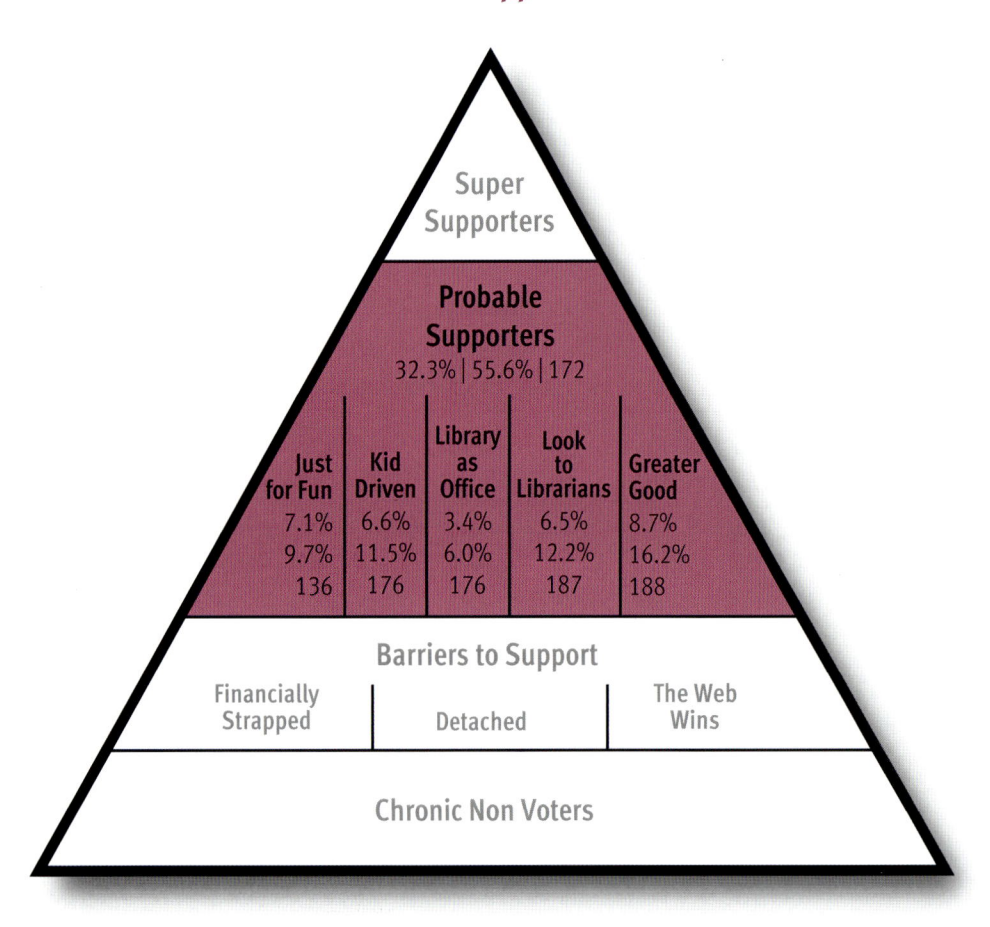

Chronic Non Voters

% Population ages 18–69 in communities < 200,000 | Definite Library Supporters | Library Support Index

$$\text{Library Support Index} = \frac{\text{\% Definite Library Supporters}}{\text{\% population ages 18–69 in communities < 200,000}} \times 100$$

Source: *From Awareness to Funding*, OCLC, 2008

Probable Supporters

Probable Supporters have a strong appreciation for the library. Probable Supporters appreciate the library's contribution to the 'greater good.'

The Probable Supporters' favorable perceptions of the library distinguish them from voters in the Barriers to Support tier. Voters in this tier see the library as an important asset to the community and are willing to increase taxes to fund it.

While a large number of Probable Supporters are open to the idea of increasing taxes in support of libraries, not all are firmly committed in their support. Understanding the attitudes and perceptions within this tier of voters is critical to increasing commitment for library funding initiatives. The segmentation analysis identified five distinct market segments within the Probable Supporter tier:

- **Just for Fun**
  The Just for Fun segment represents 7.1% of survey respondents and 9.7% of all *definite* library supporters.

- **Kid Driven**
  The Kid Driven segment represents 6.6% of respondents but almost double the percentage (11.5%) of respondents who would *definitely* vote in favor of a library referendum.

- **Library as Office**
  The Library as Office segment is the smallest segment at just 3.4% of respondents. Six percent (6.0%) of *definite* library supporters are in this segment.

- **Look to Librarians**
  The Look to Librarians segment represents 6.5% of survey respondents and 12.2% of all *definite* library supporters.

- **Greater Good**
  The largest segment of the Probable Supporters tier is the Greater Good, representing 8.7% of all survey respondents. It represents 16.2% of residents who would *definitely* vote in favor of increased library funding.

Before reviewing the segments of the Probable Supporters tier, it is helpful to review a number of characteristics that are common across respondents in all five segments. These overarching attitudes and beliefs about libraries are more likely to be held by Probable Supporters voters than by the general voting population surveyed. Supporting survey findings are presented and contrasted with the attitudes held by the total voting respondent base.

Probable Supporters' attitudes toward libraries and funding

Probable Supporters have a strong appreciation for the library. Probable Supporters appreciate the library's contribution to the 'greater good.' They believe that the library is a community resource for everyone, including members of the community not otherwise able to afford to purchase equivalent resources and services.

Who are the library's financial supporters?

Probable Supporters recognize that for many, the library is the only place where certain resources, like access to computers or the Internet, can be obtained.

Probable Supporters appreciate the library's contribution to the 'greater good'
Probable Supporters

Probable Supporters

For each statement below, please rate your level of agreement on a scale from 1 to 10, where a 10 means 'Agree Strongly' and a 1 means 'Disagree Strongly.'

	Total Voting Respondents	Probable Supporters
The local public library provides resources that some people couldn't otherwise afford	68%	79%
The local public library levels the playing field by providing access to books, technology and special classes for everyone	49%	60%
It's important in today's world that everyone has equal access to books and technology	83%	90%
For some people, the library is the only place to access computers or the Internet	79%	86%

Percentage of voting respondents with an agreement rating of 8, 9 or 10
Source: *From Awareness to Funding*, OCLC, 2008

Probable Supporters recognize that the research and information provided by the library is superior to the information available on the Web and that not everything is currently available on the Internet. The library provides more than search engines can provide.

Probable Supporters believe that the research and information the library provides are superior to the Web
Probable Supporters

For each statement below, please rate your level of agreement on a scale from 1 to 10, where a 10 means 'Agree Strongly' and a 1 means 'Disagree Strongly.'

	Total Voting Respondents	Probable Supporters
All the information in the library I could just as easily get on the Internet	26%	14%
It's easier to do research on the Internet using search engines like Google and Yahoo! than in the local public library	37%	23%
The information you can find yourself using search engines like Google and Yahoo! is every bit as good as the information you can get by doing a library search	30%	21%

Percentage of voting respondents with an agreement rating of 8, 9 or 10
Source: *From Awareness to Funding*, OCLC, 2008

Who are the library's financial supporters?

Probable Supporters

Probable Supporters believe the library plays an important role in children's education. They view the library as an excellent resource for children that helps prepare young children for school and they believe that children who regularly go to the public library do better in school than those who do not.

Probable Supporters see the library as an important asset to the community.

Probable Supporters believe the library is a key partner in a child's education

Probable Supporters

For each statement below, please rate your level of agreement on a scale from 1 to 10, where a 10 means 'Agree Strongly' and a 1 means 'Disagree Strongly.'

	Total Voting Respondents	Probable Supporters
Children who go regularly to the public library are better readers in the long run	71%	85%
The library is an excellent resource for kids to get help with their homework	71%	82%
Children who go regularly to the public library do better in school	65%	75%
The public library does an excellent job of helping prepare children for school	53%	65%

Percentage of voting respondents with an agreement rating of 8, 9 or 10
Source: *From Awareness to Funding*, OCLC, 2008

Probable Supporters see the library as an asset to the community. A significant number of Probable Supporters believe that a top-notch library is an important part of the community and believe that a reputable library raises the status and image of the community.

Probable Supporters feel the library is an important asset to the community

Probable Supporters

For each statement below, please rate your level of agreement on a scale from 1 to 10, where a 10 means 'Agree Strongly' and a 1 means 'Disagree Strongly.'

	Total Voting Respondents	Probable Supporters
A top-notch library is an important part of a good community	72%	87%
If the library in my community were to shut down, something essential and important would be lost, affecting the whole community	71%	87%
Having an excellent public library is a source of pride for a community	73%	85%
A reputable public library raises the status and image of a community	67%	81%

Percentage of voting respondents with an agreement rating of 8, 9 or 10
Source: *From Awareness to Funding*, OCLC, 2008

Who are the library's financial supporters?

Critically important, all segments of Probable Supporters are open to increasing taxes to fund public libraries. Just 12% of Probable Supporters are not willing to pay higher taxes to fund their local public libraries. An even smaller number, 5%, feel that raising taxes to fund the public library is a waste of the public funds. A majority of all Probable Supporters feel that libraries do not have sufficient operating funds.

Probable Supporters

Probable Supporters are not opposed to raising their taxes in order to fund the public library

Probable Supporters

For each statement below, please rate your level of agreement on a scale from 1 to 10, where a 10 means 'Agree Strongly' and a 1 means 'Disagree Strongly.'

	Total Voting Respondents	Probable Supporters
I would not be willing to pay higher taxes in order to fund the local public library	23%	12%
I think raising taxes to fund the public library would be a waste of the public's money	16%	5%
The public library should be able to operate on its current budget without an increase	23%	12%

Percentage of voting respondents with an agreement rating of 8, 9 or 10
Source: *From Awareness to Funding*, OCLC, 2008

The Probable Supporters represent a significant slice of the U.S. voting population. Their overall favorable view of libraries represents an important opportunity for increased library funding support. While this tier of respondents shares many common views, analysis of five distinct segments within this group provides important information that can be used to more effectively target and mobilize Probable Supporters.

Probable Supporters—Just for Fun

The Just for Fun respondents see the library as a place to relax, hang out and socialize.

They represent nearly a quarter of all library visits.

Probable Supporters tier
Just for Fun segment

The Just for Fun segment of the Probable Supporters tier represents 7.1% of all survey respondents and 9.7% of respondents who say they would *definitely* vote favorably for a library referendum, ballot initiative or bond measure.

The Just for Fun respondents are the heaviest users of the library, reporting an average of 36 visits per year. They have above-average usage of a large variety of library resources and services, but are particularly heavy users of recreational activities and services.

While the Just for Fun voters are the heaviest users of the library, they are the least likely of all Probable Supporters to vote in favor of an increase in library funding.

The Just for Fun segment shows several unique demographic tendencies. Respondents tend to be single, from low-income households and are less well-educated than the average for all voting respondents. They often do not have children and skew toward being blue-collar and nonwhite.

The Just for Fun respondents are responsible for 23.9% of all library visits reported by all respondents. They are avid readers who check out books and read magazines and newspapers. They also check out videos and DVDs and are heavy users of the computer and Internet at the library, because they are less likely than other segments to have access at home.

They see the library as a place to relax, hang out and socialize with others and recognize the library's role as a community gathering place. However, they are not as emotionally connected to the library as other segments on the Probable Supporters tier and are less likely to support it financially.

Who are the library's financial supporters?

1. Demographic profile

The Just for Fun segment shows several demographic tendencies. Just for Fun respondents tend to be single, from low-income households and are less well-educated than the average voting respondents. They are less likely to have children and skew toward blue-collar workers and nonwhite ethnicity.

Probable Supporters— Just for Fun

Demographic profile
Just for Fun segment

	Total Voting Respondents	Just For Fun
18–29	15%	15%
30–39	20%	23%
40–49	24%	9%
50–59	23%	27%
60–69	19%	26%
Female	50%	56%
Has at least one kid <18 years old	34%	7%
Less than $20,000	18%	36%
$20,000–$29,999	12%	16%
$30,000–$39,999	16%	13%
$40,000–$49,999	12%	5%
$50,000–$59,999	8%	7%
$60,000–$74,999	11%	8%
$75,000–$99,999	12%	7%
$100,000 or more	19%	16%
Demographic tendencies		
Less than $20,000	18%	36%
$20,000–$29,999	12%	16%
Single/never married	22%	36%
White-collar/professional	40%	28%
Blue-collar	46%	54%
Not currently employed, not retired	14%	18%
Completed some high school/high school graduate	27%	39%
Completed some college/college degree	60%	50%
Completed some postgraduate	4%	4%
Master/doctorate/professional degree	9%	8%
White/non-Hispanic	76%	65%
Black	7%	2%
Hispanic	6%	6%
Asian	5%	0%
Other	6%	26%

Source: *From Awareness to Funding*, OCLC, 2008

Who are the library's financial supporters?

Annual Library Visits

Just for Fun: 36.3

Total Voting Respondents: 13.2

2. Library usage

The Just for Fun respondents use the library more than any other segment, reporting an average of 36 visits a year. They use the library for a range of recreational activities, all with greater frequency than average.

Just for Fun respondents are avid readers of fiction and nonfiction, magazines and newspapers. They check out DVDs and videos and use the library to research and learn more about their hobbies. They are frequent users of the computer and Internet for e-mail and online research and like to relax in the library's comfortable seating areas.

Just for Fun respondents use the library more than any other segment

Just for Fun segment

Below is a list of activities and services offered by public libraries. Please indicate how frequently you do each one at your local public library.

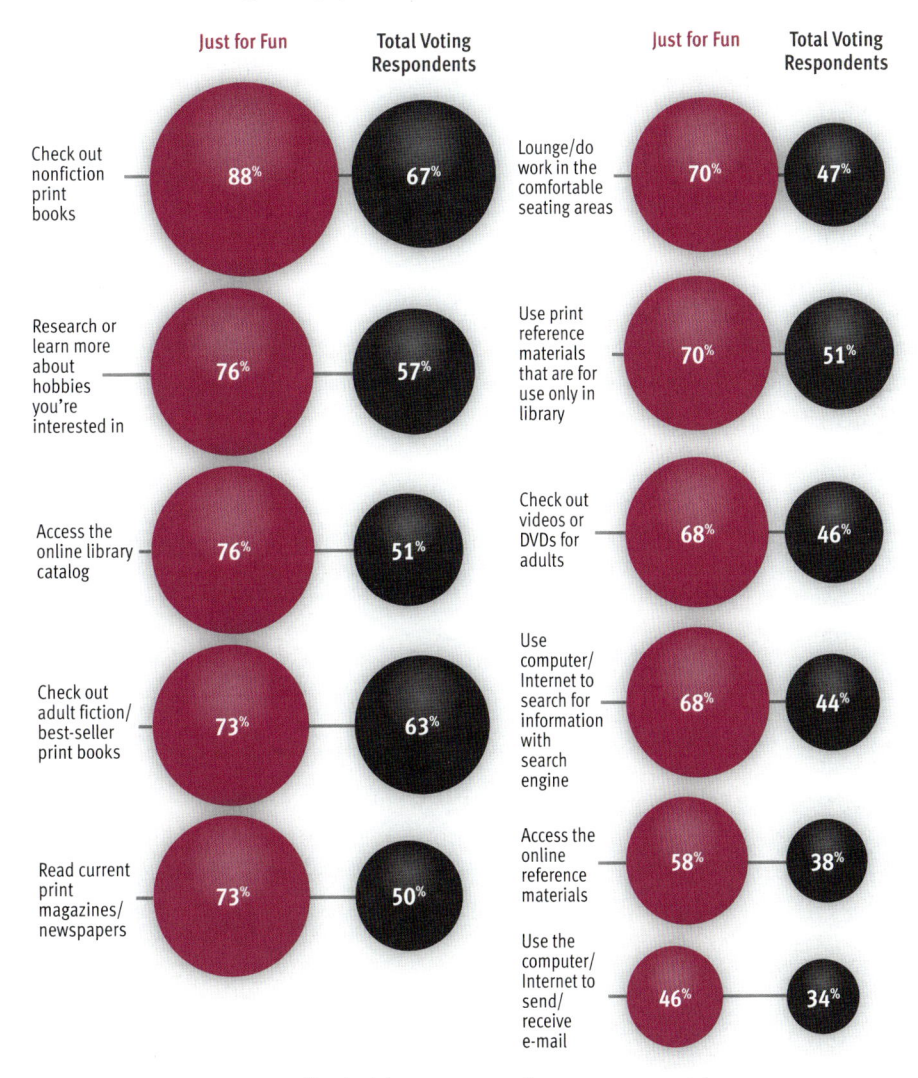

Activity	Just for Fun	Total Voting Respondents
Check out nonfiction print books	88%	67%
Research or learn more about hobbies you're interested in	76%	57%
Access the online library catalog	76%	51%
Check out adult fiction/best-seller print books	73%	63%
Read current print magazines/newspapers	73%	50%
Lounge/do work in the comfortable seating areas	70%	47%
Use print reference materials that are for use only in library	70%	51%
Check out videos or DVDs for adults	68%	46%
Use computer/Internet to search for information with search engine	68%	44%
Access the online reference materials	58%	38%
Use the computer/Internet to send/receive e-mail	46%	34%

The chart shows *once a month or more* responses only
Source: *From Awareness to Funding*, OCLC, 2008

From Awareness to Funding: A study of library support in America 2-45

Who are the library's financial supporters?

3. Public service support

The Just for Fun segment shows a greater willingness to increase taxes than segments on the Barriers to Support tier. Lower than average income does not keep its members from showing support across the seven public services surveyed.

Public services related to safety receive the greatest support from this segment with the police department (52%) and fire department (50%) ranked first and second respectively.

Although the level of support to fund the public library is below 50%, the public library ranks third, close to the level of support for police and fire department funding.

Probable Supporters—Just for Fun

The public library ranks in third place, after fire and police
Just for Fun segment

For each service, please rate how much you agree with the phrase "I'd be willing to pay more in local taxes to better fund this service." Please use a 10-point scale, where a 10 means you 'Completely Agree' and a 1 means you 'Completely Disagree.'

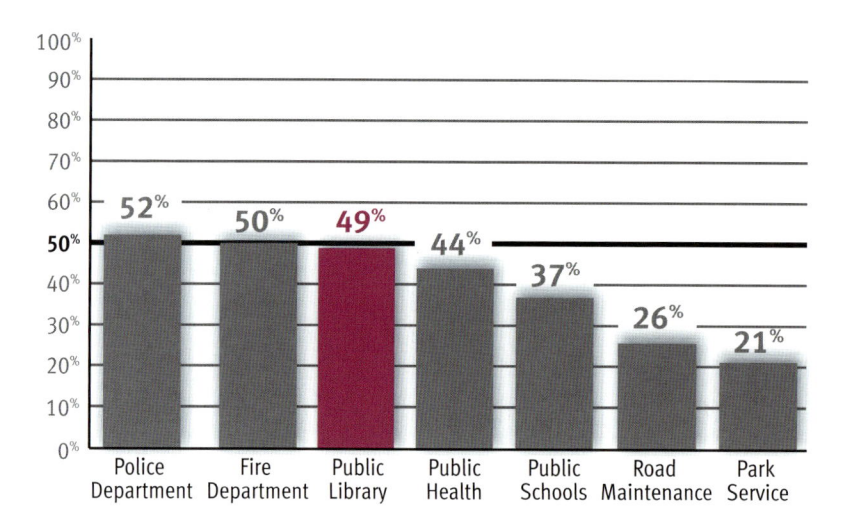

Service	Percentage
Police Department	52%
Fire Department	50%
Public Library	49%
Public Health	44%
Public Schools	37%
Road Maintenance	26%
Park Service	21%

Percentage of voting respondents with an agreement rating of 8, 9 or 10
Source: *From Awareness to Funding*, OCLC, 2008

2-46 From Awareness to Funding: A study of library support in America

Who are the library's financial supporters?

Probable Supporters—Just for Fun

4. Library support compared to library usage

The Just for Fun segment represents almost a quarter of all library visits (23.9%).

Their frequent use of the library does not directly translate into a high willingness to fund the library. Just for Fun respondents represent just 9.7% of respondents who say they would *definitely* vote in favor of a library funding measure. This puts them at a higher than average level of funding support (Library Support Index = 136) but with the lowest financial commitment to the library of any segment of the Probable Supporters tier.

Just for Fun respondents are the heaviest users but the least likely of the Probable Supporters to *definitely* vote to fund the library

Just for Fun segment

If there was a referendum, ballot initiative or bond measure for your local public library on the ballot, how do you think you would vote?

How many times have you visited your local public library in the past 12 months?

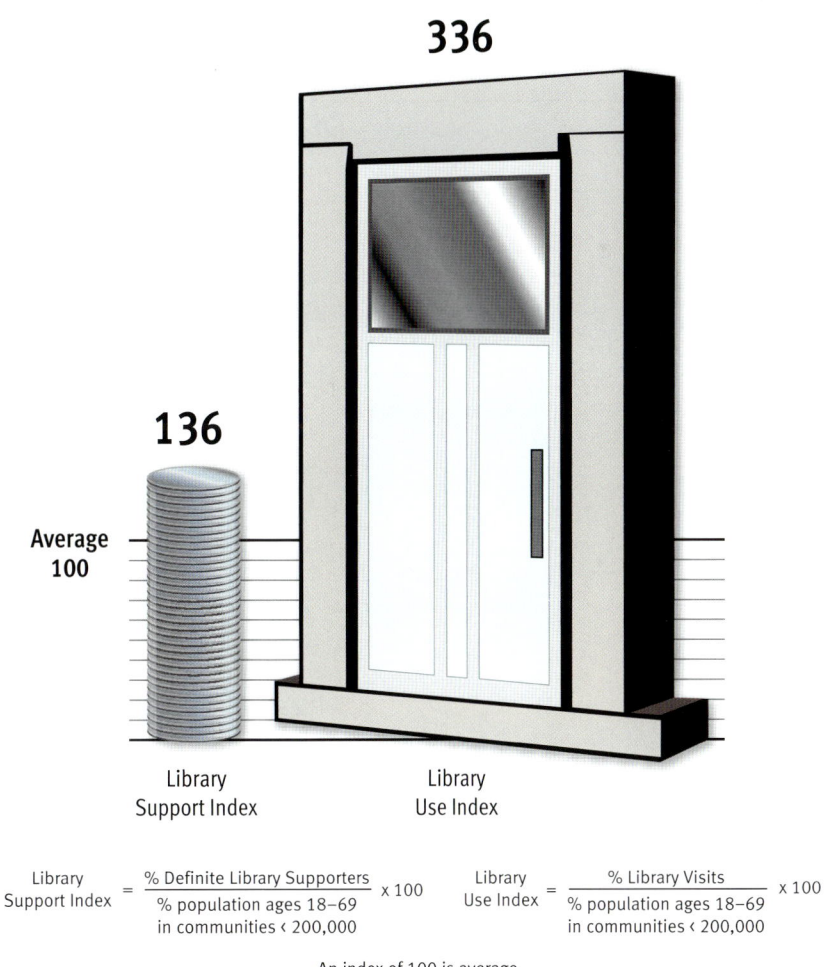

336 — Library Use Index

136 — Library Support Index

Average 100

$$\text{Library Support Index} = \frac{\text{\% Definite Library Supporters}}{\text{\% population ages 18–69 in communities < 200,000}} \times 100$$

$$\text{Library Use Index} = \frac{\text{\% Library Visits}}{\text{\% population ages 18–69 in communities < 200,000}} \times 100$$

An index of 100 is average
Source: *From Awareness to Funding*, OCLC, 2008

Who are the library's financial supporters?

5. Attitudes toward libraries and funding

The Just for Fun segment sees the library as a place for having fun and lots of it.

The Just for Fun segment has a greater awareness of what is available at the local public library than average for all voters. In particular, its members see the library's Internet access as a big draw and they love to read. They have the same positive associations with the library that are common across all Probable Supporters segments but have less of an emotional connection than other segments on this tier. Compared to other Probable Supporters, Just for Fun respondents are less likely to see the library as a place that helps them improve intellectually, creatively or personally.

The library is a place to hang out and socialize, and Just for Fun respondents value the library's role as a community gathering place and social hub.

Compared to other segments in the Probable Supporters tier, Just for Fun respondents are less likely to be committed to increased library funding, but are more likely than the voter average.

**Probable Supporters—
Just for Fun**

The Just for Fun segment sees the library as a place for having fun and lots of it.

Attitudes toward libraries and funding
Just for Fun segment

For each statement below, please rate your level of agreement on a scale from 1 to 10, where a 10 means 'Agree Strongly' and a 1 means 'Disagree Strongly.'

Just for Fun respondents frequently initiate visits to the library

	Total Voting Respondents	Just for Fun
I don't go to the library in my community very often	36%	4%
My public library is not top of mind—I just don't think to go there	24%	1%
How likely are you to initiate a trip to the library?	53%	79%
How likely is your spouse/significant other to initiate a trip to the library?	32%	42%
How likely is your child/children to initiate a trip to the library?	55%	72%

Percentage of voting respondents with an agreement rating of 8, 9 or 10
Source: *From Awareness to Funding*, OCLC, 2008

Who are the library's financial supporters?

Probable Supporters—Just for Fun

Just for Fun respondents know what resources the public library has to offer

	Total Voting Respondents	Just for Fun
Compared to most people, I know a lot about what my local public library has to offer	27%	50%
I spend a lot of time in the public library in my community	24%	51%
I don't pay much attention to what's going on at the library	24%	9%
It's been so long since I've been to the library that I'm not even sure what it has to offer anymore	19%	1%
Know that library has:		
Print magazines/newspapers	87%	98%
Music CDs to check out	65%	88%
Community meeting rooms	59%	88%
Online library catalog	70%	89%
Library Web site	68%	84%
Special events such as author readings	49%	71%
Computer/Internet/technology training programs	36%	57%
Ability to play games on the computer/Internet	38%	56%
Wi-Fi Internet access	27%	50%
Literacy training programs	33%	46%
Coffee/snack shop	16%	34%

Percentage of voting respondents with an agreement rating of 8, 9 or 10
Source: *From Awareness to Funding*, OCLC, 2008

The Just for Fun segment has a greater awareness of what is available at the local public library than average for all voters. In particular, they see the library's Internet access as a big draw and love to read.

The library's Internet access is a big draw for Just for Fun respondents, who are less likely to have access elsewhere

	Total Voting Respondents	Just for Fun
Have Internet access at home or work	69%	58%
Have Internet access at school	9%	7%
Have Internet access at library	43%	66%
Accesses Internet to read Web sites/blogs once every 2–3 weeks or more	69%	81%

Percentage of voting respondents with an agreement rating of 8, 9 or 10
Source: *From Awareness to Funding*, OCLC, 2008

Just for Fun respondents are avid readers

	Total Voting Respondents	Just for Fun
I consider myself an avid reader	52%	66%
People would consider me kind of a bookworm	34%	49%
Average number of books read per month	4.6	7.2

Percentage of voting respondents with an agreement rating of 8, 9 or 10
Source: *From Awareness to Funding*, OCLC, 2008

Who are the library's financial supporters?

Just for Fun respondents value the library as a place to hang out and socialize

	Total Voting Respondents	Just for Fun
The public library should be a place for communities to gather together	45%	63%
The public library is a social hub in my community where people frequently get together	18%	29%
The public library is a welcoming place to hang out and spend time	43%	57%
The public library is a place for people in the community to gather and socialize	35%	52%

Percentage of voting respondents with an agreement rating of 8, 9 or 10
Source: *From Awareness to Funding*, OCLC, 2008

Probable Supporters—Just for Fun

The library is seen as a place to participate in fun activities, relax, use the Wi-Fi or visit the café

The public library:	Total Voting Respondents	Just for Fun
Offers a wide variety of activities and entertainment	37%	54%
Offers activities and entertainment you can't find anywhere else in the community	34%	43%
Offers comfortable seating areas for lounging and reading books	57%	72%
Offers the most popular books and best-sellers	56%	71%
Provides Wi-Fi Internet access	36%	52%
Has a café inside the library	13%	31%

Percentage of voting respondents with an agreement rating of 8, 9 or 10
Source: *From Awareness to Funding*, OCLC, 2008

While the library is enjoyable, Just for Fun respondents don't feel as strong a personal connection as other Probable Supporters

The public library:	Total Voting Respond.	Probable Supporters	Just for Fun
Connects with people in a real human way	53%	63%	45%
Makes you feel like part of a social group	35%	39%	22%

Percentage of voting respondents with an agreement rating of 8, 9 or 10
Source: *From Awareness to Funding*, OCLC, 2008

While the library is enjoyable, Just for Fun respondents don't feel as strong a personal connection as other Probable Supporters.

From Awareness to Funding: A study of library support in America

Who are the library's financial supporters?

Probable Supporters—Just for Fun

The library is seen less by Just for Fun respondents as a place to better themselves intellectually, creatively or personally

The public library:	Total Voting Respond.	Probable Supporters	Just for Fun
Enables you to become a more creative person	58%	67%	55%
Helps you become a better person	54%	65%	49%
Makes you feel like you're part of a group of people who are well-educated	51%	59%	48%
Encourages you to develop your own point of view	52%	61%	48%

Percentage of voting respondents with an agreement rating of 8, 9 or 10
Source: *From Awareness to Funding*, OCLC, 2008

Just for Fun respondents are the least likely Probable Supporters to definitely vote yes for a library referendum.

Just for Fun respondents have a tendency to be uninvolved in the community

	Total Voting Respondents	Just for Fun
I have a lot of friends in my community	36%	20%
I am very involved with the public schools in my community	18%	4%
People would consider me somewhat influential in the town where I live	16%	1%
I am involved in learning about and discussing issues or decisions that affect my city/town	20%	8%

Percentage of voting respondents with an agreement rating of 8, 9 or 10
Source: *From Awareness to Funding*, OCLC, 2008

Just for Fun respondents make a point of voting in local elections and their voting habits tend to be liberal

	Total Voting Respondents	Just for Fun
Almost certain to vote in elections that involve local issues	48%	59%
Voted for Kerry/Edwards in 2004 U.S. presidential election	43%	53%
Describe themselves as Democrat	36%	47%
Consider themselves liberal	28%	40%

Percentage of voting respondents with an agreement rating of 8, 9 or 10
Source: *From Awareness to Funding*, OCLC, 2008

However, Just for Fun respondents are the least likely Probable Supporters to *definitely* vote yes for a library referendum

	Total Voting Respondents	Just for Fun
Would *definitely* vote in favor of library referendum if it were on the ballot	37%	37%

Percentage of voting respondents with an agreement rating of 8, 9 or 10
Source: *From Awareness to Funding*, OCLC, 2008

Who are the library's financial supporters?

Probable Supporters tier
Kid Driven segment

The Kid Driven segment represents 6.6% of all survey respondents. Although it is a relatively small segment, its members account for 11.5% of all *definite* voting support for the library.

As the name indicates, this group is most likely to have at least one child in the household. Kid Driven respondents visit the library more than average with 19 visits reported annually. They are typically accompanied by at least one child. They regularly check out materials for children and participate in the children's programming. Kid Driven respondents are willing to support the library financially because of the role it plays in educating and inspiring their children to be the best that they can be.

The majority of the people in the Kid Driven segment have at least one child under 18 and are more likely to be women.

Kid Driven voters visit the library more than average and their children often initiate the trips. Child-oriented activities are what draw this group to the library, including checking out books and videos for children, attending story time and other children's programs. The parents are not leaving empty-handed, however, as they also check out books and videos for themselves.

The Kid Driven segment sees the library as a valuable resource for children of all ages and also values the role of the librarian. Kid Driven respondents think librarians are proactive and helpful and really understand how to engage children with books and technology. They are emotionally connected to the library and believe that it offers an exciting and stimulating experience that can inspire them and their children.

The Kid Driven voters' emotional connection to the library and their recognition of its importance to their children and the community is the underlying driver for their willingness to support the library financially. Forty-eight percent (48%) claim that they would *definitely* vote yes in a library referendum, ballot initiative or bond measure. Kid Driven voters are average supporters within the segments of the Probable Supporters tier.

Probable Supporters— Kid Driven

Kid Driven voters visit the library more than average and children often initiate the trips. Child-oriented activities are what draw this group to the library, including checking out books and videos for children.

1. Demographic profile

The majority of the Kid Driven segment have at least one child under 18 and are more likely to be women. Members of this group are also more likely to be white, non-Hispanic and in their thirties.

Probable Supporters—Kid Driven

Demographic profile
Kid Driven segment

	Total Voting Respondents	Kid Driven
18–29	15%	8%
30–39	20%	34%
40–49	24%	29%
50–59	23%	13%
60–69	19%	15%
Female	50%	64%
Has at least one kid <18 years old	34%	73%
Less than $20,000	18%	12%
$20,000–$29,999	12%	14%
$30,000–$39,999	16%	13%
$40,000–$49,999	12%	15%
$50,000–$59,999	8%	12%
$60,000–$74,999	11%	16%
$75,000–$99,999	12%	11%
$100,000 or more	19%	14%
Demographic tendencies		
Female	50%	64%
Has at least one kid <18 years old	34%	73%
30–39	20%	34%
% White/non-Hispanic	76%	87%

Source: *From Awareness to Funding*, OCLC, 2008

Who are the library's financial supporters?

2. Library usage

Kid Driven voters visit the library more often than average, reporting 19 visits annually. This segment has the highest usage of programs for children, such as story time, and checks out children's print books, videos and DVDs more than other segments. The Kid Driven parents do not leave the library empty-handed. They frequently check out books and movies for themselves.

Annual Library Visits

Kid Driven: 19.0

Total Voting Respondents: 13.2

Kid Driven respondents are the most likely segment to check things out for children and use materials for adults as well

Kid Driven segment

Below is a list of activities and services offered by public libraries. Please indicate how frequently you do each one at your local public library.

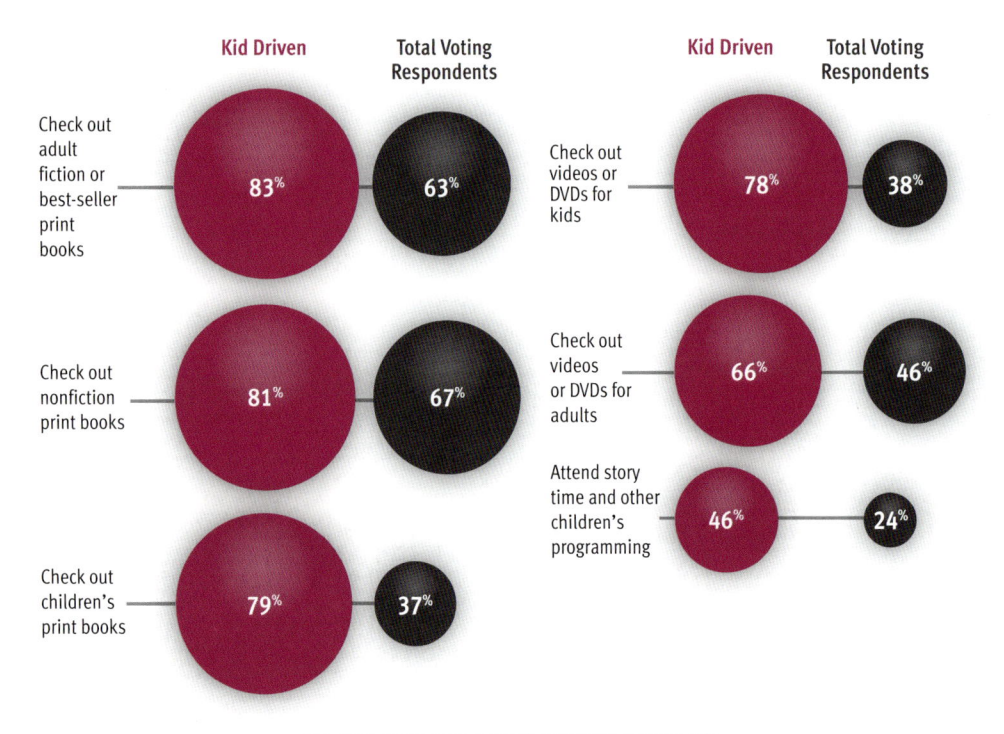

Activity	Kid Driven	Total Voting Respondents
Check out adult fiction or best-seller print books	83%	63%
Check out nonfiction print books	81%	67%
Check out children's print books	79%	37%
Check out videos or DVDs for kids	78%	38%
Check out videos or DVDs for adults	66%	46%
Attend story time and other children's programming	46%	24%

The chart shows *once a month or more* responses only
Source: *From Awareness to Funding*, OCLC, 2008

Who are the library's financial supporters?

Probable Supporters— Kid Driven

3. Public service support

The Kid Driven segment shows a strong level of support for a number of public services. More than half the voters in this segment are willing to increase their taxes for four of the seven services: public schools, fire department, police department and the public library.

Given the role that children play in the lives of this segment, it is not surprising that public schools receive the highest level of support with 65% of voters agreeing they would be willing to increase their taxes. Safety is also important to this group, with fire and police receiving support from 62% and 61% of voters respectively.

The Kid Driven segment places the library fourth with 51% of respondents willing to increase their taxes for libraries.

The public library falls in the middle of the public services Kid Driven voters are willing to support

Kid Driven segment

For each service, please rate how much you agree with the phrase "I'd be willing to pay more in local taxes to better fund this service." Please use a 10-point scale, where a 10 means you 'Completely Agree' and a 1 means you 'Completely Disagree.'

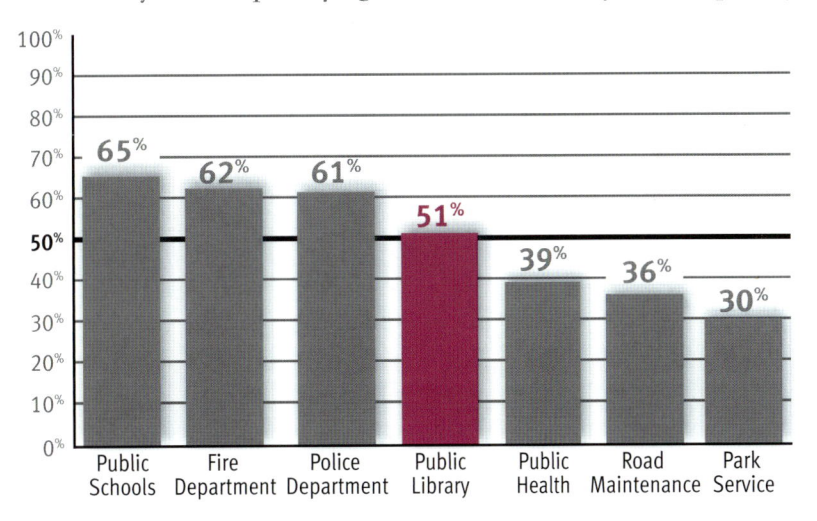

Service	%
Public Schools	65%
Fire Department	62%
Police Department	61%
Public Library	51%
Public Health	39%
Road Maintenance	36%
Park Service	30%

Percentage of voting respondents with an agreement rating of 8, 9 or 10
Source: *From Awareness to Funding*, OCLC, 2008

Who are the library's financial supporters?

4. Library support compared to library usage

The Kid Driven segment is the only segment of the pyramid where usage and funding support are parallel. Kid Driven respondents are responsible for 11.6% of all library visits. And the Kid Driven segment represents 11.5% of respondents who said they would *definitely* vote in favor of a library funding measure.

Kid Driven support for library funding is on par for the Probable Supporters tier.

**Probable Supporters—
Kid Driven**

For the Probable Supporters tier, the Kid Driven respondents are on par as users and supporters of the library

Kid Driven segment

If there was a referendum, ballot initiative or bond measure for your local public library on the ballot, how do you think you would vote?

How many times have you visited your local public library in the past 12 months?

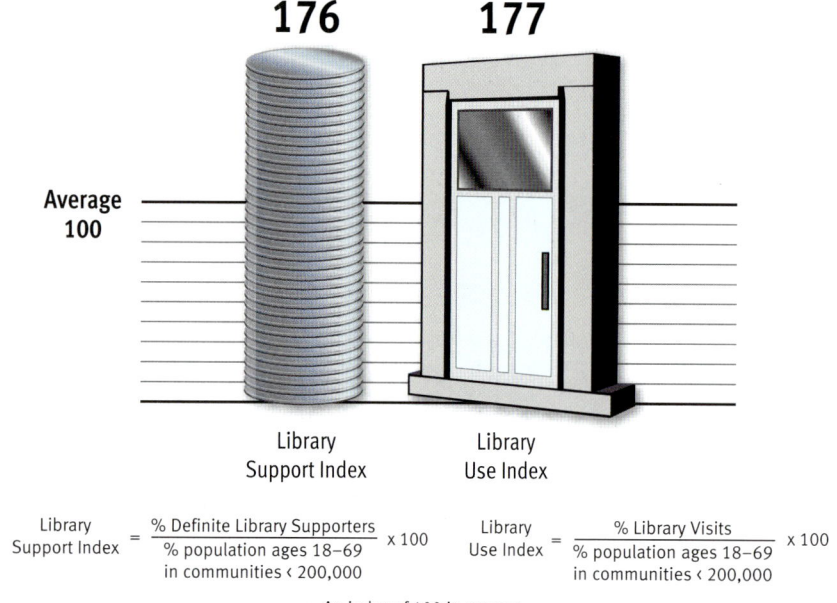

176   **177**

Average 100

Library Support Index   Library Use Index

$$\text{Library Support Index} = \frac{\text{\% Definite Library Supporters}}{\text{\% population ages 18–69 in communities < 200,000}} \times 100$$

$$\text{Library Use Index} = \frac{\text{\% Library Visits}}{\text{\% population ages 18–69 in communities < 200,000}} \times 100$$

An index of 100 is average
Source: *From Awareness to Funding*, OCLC, 2008

Who are the library's financial supporters?

Probable Supporters—Kid Driven

5. Attitudes toward libraries and funding

The attitudes of the Kid Driven segment toward their libraries and their communities are influenced by the important role that children play in their lives.

The Kid Driven segment believes that the library is a great resource for children of all ages. Its members value the role the library plays in inspiring a love of learning in young children, preparing children for school and providing a great resource for homework help.

The Kid Driven voters place a lot of value on the role of the librarian. They believe that librarians understand the needs of children and are proactive and helpful in supporting library patrons.

The Kid Driven voters also see the public library as a community social center. They value the library both for its traditional offerings and the access to technology it provides for the community as a whole. They believe the library is organized and up-to-date.

The Kid Driven voters are emotionally connected to the library, seeing it as offering an exciting and diverse experience that inspires them and helped shape their identity. They hope the library will do the same for their children.

The Kid Driven voters place a lot of value on the role of the librarian. They believe that librarians understand the needs of children and are proactive and helpful in supporting library patrons.

Attitudes toward libraries and funding
Kid Driven segment

For each statement below, please rate your level of agreement on a scale from 1 to 10, where a 10 means 'Agree Strongly' and a 1 means 'Disagree Strongly.'

The Kid Driven voters who visit the library are usually accompanied by at least one child who often initiates the trip

	Total Voting Respondents	Kid Driven
Library visits accompanied by at least one child	28%	73%
How likely are you to initiate a trip to the library	53%	76%
How likely is your child/children to initiate a trip to the library	55%	69%

Percentage of voting respondents with an agreement rating of 8, 9 or 10
Source: *From Awareness to Funding*, OCLC, 2008

Who are the library's financial supporters?

Kid Driven respondents believe the library is a great resource for children of all ages

The public library:	Total Voting Respondents	Kid Driven
Inspires a love of learning in young children	59%	76%
Offers excellent classes and special events for children	47%	60%
Is a place for moms and dads to bond with their kids	46%	62%
Prepares young children for school	50%	61%
Is a great resource for teens	56%	66%
Offers an excellent resource for students to get help with homework	60%	70%
Is committed to lifelong learning	63%	74%

Percentage of voting respondents with an agreement rating of 8, 9 or 10
Source: *From Awareness to Funding*, OCLC, 2008

Probable Supporters—Kid Driven

Kid Driven respondents believe the library is a great resource for children of all ages.

Kid Driven respondents strongly believe librarians understand the needs of children

The public librarian:	Total Voting Respondents	Kid Driven
Really understands how to engage kids with computers and technology	42%	51%
Knows better than anyone else what music and movies kids would love	33%	42%
Knows better than anyone else what books children would love	47%	62%

Percentage of voting respondents with an agreement rating of 8, 9 or 10
Source: *From Awareness to Funding*, OCLC, 2008

Kid Driven respondents are more likely to believe librarians are proactive and helpful

The public librarian:	Total Voting Respondents	Kid Driven
Is proactive in helping patrons	56%	70%
Takes the time to coach people in how to use the public library	52%	67%
Is always available to answer questions	59%	79%
Always helps you find the information and materials you need	59%	68%
Is friendly and approachable	67%	76%

Percentage of voting respondents with an agreement rating of 8, 9 or 10
Source: *From Awareness to Funding*, OCLC, 2008

The public library is seen as a community social center

The public library:	Total Voting Respondents	Kid Driven
Is a place for people in the community to gather and socialize	35%	44%
Offers a wide variety of activities and entertainment	37%	50%
Offers activities you can't find anywhere else in the community	34%	47%
Is a welcoming place to hang out and spend time	43%	57%

Percentage of voting respondents with an agreement rating of 8, 9 or 10
Source: *From Awareness to Funding*, OCLC, 2008

Who are the library's financial supporters?

Probable Supporters—Kid Driven

Kid Driven respondents value the library's traditional offerings and the access to technology it provides

The public library:	Total Voting Respondents	Kid Driven
Is able to draw the community together around knowledge	43%	56%
Is a place of serious thought and education	56%	69%
Offers a comfortable seating area for lounging around and reading books	57%	72%
Provides access to a wide variety of music and movies	36%	53%
Provides access to the latest releases of music and movies	33%	42%
Offers free access to computers and the Internet for everyone	68%	82%
Provides all the resources needed to do work, like a copier, fax machine, Internet access	62%	74%
Has enough computers and online services for all those who want to use them	44%	56%
Offers access to computer programs	51%	62%

Percentage of voting respondents with an agreement rating of 8, 9 or 10
Source: *From Awareness to Funding*, OCLC, 2008

Kid Driven respondents consider the library as organized and up-to-date

Kid Driven respondents value the library's traditional offerings and the access to technology it provides.

The public library:	Total Voting Respondents	Kid Driven
Is organized in a way where you can find exactly what you're looking for	62%	73%
Provides the most up-to-date and recent information available	55%	67%
Has the right staff to meet the needs of the community	57%	66%
Provides access to books you can't find anywhere else	53%	67%

Percentage of voting respondents with an agreement rating of 8, 9 or 10
Source: *From Awareness to Funding*, OCLC, 2008

The library offers a unique, exciting and diverse experience that inspires them and helped shape their identity

The public library:	Total Voting Respond.	Probable Supporters	Kid Driven
Is dramatic and exciting	26%	29%	39%
Allows you to immerse yourself in a different culture	55%	60%	69%
Is creative and innovative	45%	53%	61%
Helps create who you are	40%	46%	56%
Is inspirational	41%	50%	59%

Percentage of voting respondents with an agreement rating of 8, 9 or 10
Source: *From Awareness to Funding*, OCLC, 2008

Who are the library's financial supporters?

Probable Supporters tier
Library as Office segment

Library as Office is the smallest segment on the Library Supporter Segmentation Pyramid and represents just 3.4% of all survey respondents. This group represents 6.0% of all *definite* voting support for the library.

As the name implies, the library is an extension of the workplace for this segment. Its members are more likely than any other segment to be business owners and they take advantage of the library's technology and other resources to conduct work. The library fulfills a practical function and is more about knowledge than a personal connection for the Library as Office segment.

Library as Office respondents are more likely than other segments to be male, age 40 to 49 and have children. They are the segment most likely to be employed, either full-time or part-time, or own their own business.

Because their local libraries provide them all the things they need to do work, like computer, Internet access, photocopier, fax machine and a relaxing atmosphere, the Library as Office voters spend their time at the library conducting business and business research. They see the librarian as a key resource when conducting research but they are computer-savvy and able to do their own Internet research. In fact, Library as Office respondents are more likely than other segments to use the Internet at the library. For this group, the library is not about an emotional connection or a life-changing experience, but about practical knowledge and access to resources.

Library as Office respondents tend to operate, or work for, companies based in the towns where they live. They are involved in and informed about local matters. They recognize that a good library is a reflection on the community and are willing to raise taxes to support it. Half would *definitely* vote positively for a library referendum.

Probable Supporters—
Library as Office

The library fulfills a practical function and is more about knowledge than a personal connection for the Library as Office segment.

Who are the library's financial supporters?

**Probable Supporters—
Library as Office**

1. Demographic profile

Library as Office respondents have demographic tendencies. They tend toward being male, age 40–49 and have children. They are more likely than other segments to be employed and are the segment most likely to own their own business.

Library as Office respondents are more likely than other segments to operate businesses or work in the same towns where they live. They have a tendency to live in smaller, rural towns across the Midwest.

Demographic profile
Library as Office segment

	Total Voting Respondents	Library as Office
18–29	15%	9%
30–39	20%	14%
40–49	24%	39%
50–59	23%	27%
60–69	19%	11%
Female	50%	40%
Has at least one kid <18 years old	34%	47%
Less than $20,000	18%	24%
$20,000–$29,999	12%	4%
$30,000–$39,999	16%	18%
$40,000–$49,999	12%	6%
$50,000–$59,999	8%	7%
$60,000–$74,999	11%	8%
$75,000–$99,999	12%	17%
$100,000 or more	19%	17%
Demographic tendencies		
40–49	24%	39%
Male	50%	60%
Employed full-time or part-time	63%	88%
Business owner	8%	34%
Business or workplace located in the same town or city you live in	54%	78%
% Live in city/town with fewer than 10,000 people	22%	36%
% From the Midwest/North Central Region	31%	48%
% Describe city/town as rural	32%	41%

Source: *From Awareness to Funding*, OCLC, 2008

Library as Office respondents are more likely than other segments to operate businesses or work in the same towns where they live.

Who are the library's financial supporters?

2. Library usage

The Library as Office segment visits the library less than the Just for Fun or Kid Driven segments but still visits more than average with 18 visits annually.

The library is a place of work for this group and the Library as Office segment primarily uses the business-related resources and services. This segment is most likely to use the computer and Internet at the library for e-mail and online research. Library as Office voters do a large amount of business research, in addition to research for personal investing and they appreciate the research assistance the library provides. The library also provides this group with resources for outside of work. They check out videos and DVDs for children and adults and ask the librarian for recommendations for books for their children.

Annual Library Visits

Library as Office: 18.0

Total Voting Respondents: 13.2

Library as Office respondents use the library to access the Internet and conduct research for their places of business

Library as Office segment

Below is a list of activities and services offered by public libraries. Please indicate how frequently you do each one at your local public library.

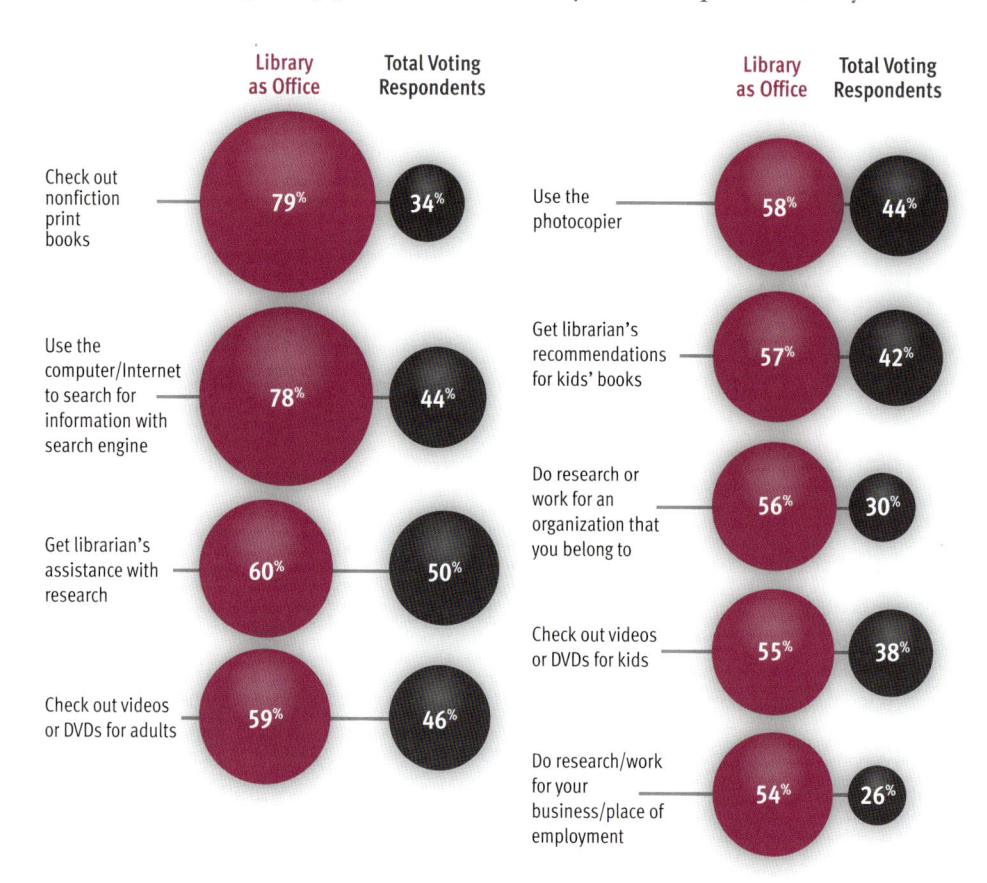

Activity	Library as Office	Total Voting Respondents
Check out nonfiction print books	79%	34%
Use the computer/Internet to search for information with search engine	78%	44%
Get librarian's assistance with research	60%	50%
Check out videos or DVDs for adults	59%	46%
Use the photocopier	58%	44%
Get librarian's recommendations for kids' books	57%	42%
Do research or work for an organization that you belong to	56%	30%
Check out videos or DVDs for kids	55%	38%
Do research/work for your business/place of employment	54%	26%

The chart shows *once a month or more* responses only
Source: *From Awareness to Funding*, OCLC, 2008

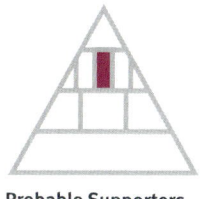

Probable Supporters— Library as Office

3. Public service support

The Library as Office segment is less willing to agree with an increase in taxes for the support of local services than other Probable Supporter segments. Not one of the seven services surveyed receives support from more than half of this segment.

The fire department (48%) receives the most support from Library as Office voters and the police department is a close second (47%).

Although the library plays a practical and important role as an extension of the work environment for the Library as Office segment, the library ranks fifth with only 31% of the segment willing to increase taxes for the library.

Library as Office respondents prioritized other public services higher than the library

Library as Office segment

For each service, please rate how much you agree with the phrase "I'd be willing to pay more in local taxes to better fund this service." Please use a 10-point scale, where a 10 means you 'Completely Agree' and a 1 means you 'Completely Disagree.'

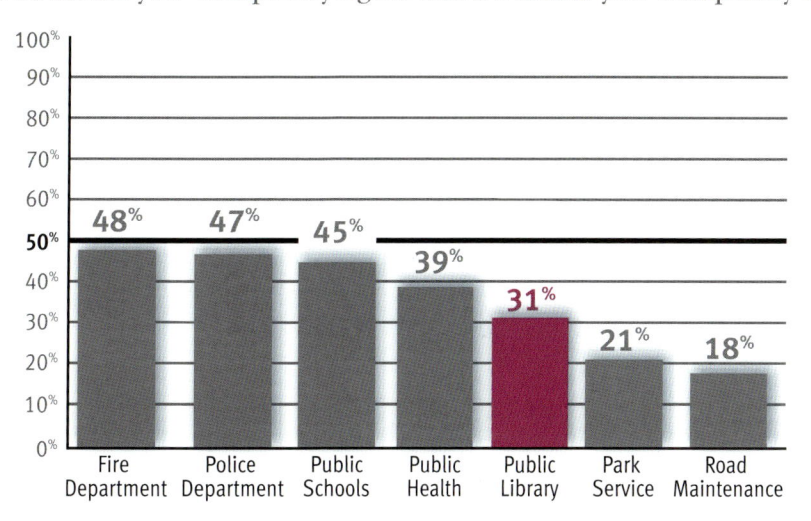

Service	Percentage
Fire Department	48%
Police Department	47%
Public Schools	45%
Public Health	39%
Public Library	31%
Park Service	21%
Road Maintenance	18%

Percentage of voting respondents with an agreement rating of 8, 9 or 10
Source: *From Awareness to Funding*, OCLC, 2008

Who are the library's financial supporters?

4. Library support compared to library usage

The Library as Office voters are responsible for 5.7% of all library visits for a Library Use Index of 167, slightly lower than other segments on the Probable Supporters tier, but above average overall.

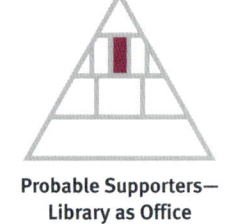

The Library as Office segment represents 6.0% of all respondents who say they will *definitely* vote favorably in a library referendum (Library Support Index = 176).

Probable Supporters—Library as Office

Library as Office respondents visit the library less frequently but are above average for support within the Probable Supporters tier

Library as Office segment

If there was a referendum, ballot initiative or bond measure for your local public library on the ballot, how do you think you would vote?

How many times have you visited your local public library in the past 12 months?

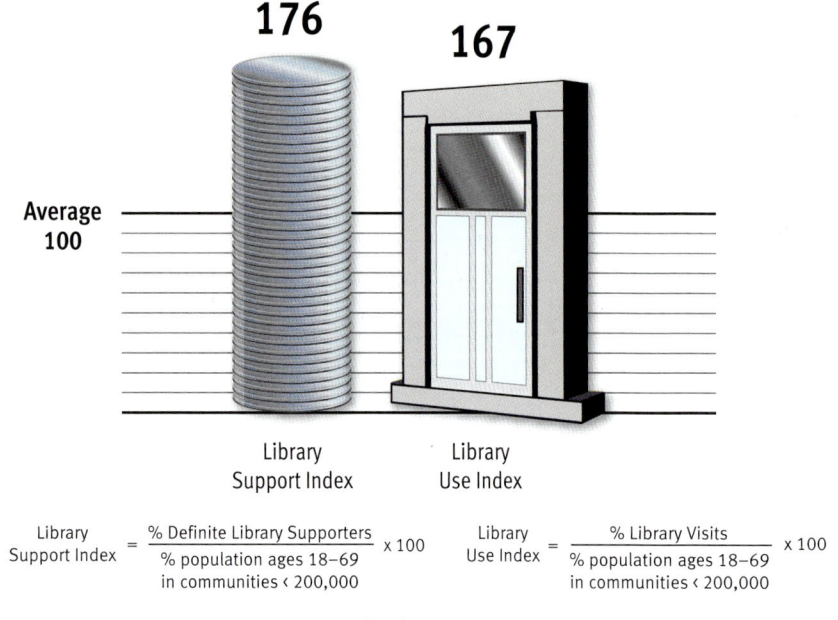

176 — Library Support Index

167 — Library Use Index

Average 100

$$\text{Library Support Index} = \frac{\text{\% Definite Library Supporters}}{\text{\% population ages 18–69 in communities < 200,000}} \times 100$$

$$\text{Library Use Index} = \frac{\text{\% Library Visits}}{\text{\% population ages 18–69 in communities < 200,000}} \times 100$$

An index of 100 is average
Source: *From Awareness to Funding*, OCLC, 2008

Who are the library's financial supporters?

Probable Supporters—Library as Office

5. Attitudes toward libraries and funding

The Library as Office voters visit the library more than average and they believe they know a lot about what the library has to offer. They believe that the library provides them with everything they need to work and they appreciate the business research resources in particular.

Library as Office voters are computer-savvy and self-sufficient Internet searchers. They are the segment most likely to use the computer and Internet access available at the library, partly because they are less likely to have access at home or at work and partly because they like the library atmosphere. The Library as Office voters feel that they always leave the library having learned something new. Their connection to the library is practical rather than emotional and their ideal library would offer services tailored to the business user.

The Library as Office respondents are more involved in local civic matters than other segments and are willing to actively make their views known within the community. About half of the Library as Office segment would *definitely* support a library referendum.

The Library as Office respondents are more involved in local civic matters than other segments and are willing to actively make their views known within the community.

Attitudes toward libraries and funding
Library as Office segment

For each statement below, please rate your level of agreement on a scale from 1 to 10, where a 10 means 'Agree Strongly' and a 1 means 'Disagree Strongly.'

This segment visits the library more than average and believes it knows more than others what the library has to offer

	Total Voting Respondents	Library as Office
I go to the library in my community very often	34%	62%
I spend a lot of time in the public library in my community	24%	40%
Compared to most people, I know a lot about what my local public library has to offer	29%	46%
The librarians at my local public library know me by name	24%	35%

Percentage of voting respondents with an agreement rating of 8, 9 or 10
Source: *From Awareness to Funding*, OCLC, 2008

From Awareness to Funding: A study of library support in America

Who are the library's financial supporters?

Library as Office respondents believe the library provides them with all the resources they need to conduct work

The public library:	Total Voting Respondents	Library as Office
Offers free access to computers and the Internet for everyone	68%	82%
Provides all the resources needed to do work, like a copier, fax machine, Internet access, etc.	62%	72%
Provides an expert in technology	37%	47%
Has enough computers and online services for all those who want to use them	44%	53%

Percentage of voting respondents with an agreement rating of 8, 9 or 10
Source: *From Awareness to Funding*, OCLC, 2008

Probable Supporters— Library as Office

Library as Office respondents are computer-savvy and self-sufficient Internet searchers

	Total Voting Respondents	Library as Office
I consider myself very computer-savvy	42%	51%
I know how to find exactly what I'm looking for on the Internet	52%	64%
I access the Internet to do research on topics of interest at least once a week	66%	89%

Percentage of voting respondents with an agreement rating of 8, 9 or 10
Source: *From Awareness to Funding*, OCLC, 2008

Library as Office respondents believe the library provides them with all the resources they need to conduct work.

Library as Office respondents use the Internet at the library because they are less likely to have access at home and because they enjoy the atmosphere and learning new things

	Total Voting Respondents	Library as Office
Have Internet access at the library	43%	79%
Have Internet access at home or work	69%	60%
The library makes you feel safe and secure	49%	71%
The library really allows you to relax	53%	64%
The library provides an escape from your own world	58%	70%
You come away feeling like you really learned something	61%	80%
The library helps you be the first to know new things	42%	59%
The library is a source you trust	71%	91%

Percentage of voting respondents with an agreement rating of 8, 9 or 10
Source: *From Awareness to Funding*, OCLC, 2008

Who are the library's financial supporters?

Probable Supporters—Library as Office

For the Library as Office segment, the library is more about information and less about a personal connection

	Total Voting Respond.	Probable Supporters	Library as Office
Connects with people in a real human way	53%	63%	55%
Creates fond memories	55%	69%	59%

Percentage of voting respondents with an agreement rating of 8, 9 or 10
Source: *From Awareness to Funding*, OCLC, 2008

The ideal library for Library as Office respondents would be tailored to businesses

The ideal library:	Total Voting Respondents	Library as Office
A resource for small businesses: Provides all of the resources a small business would need, including free temporary office space, computers with Internet access, phone, copier, scanner and fax machine. It would also provide access to online databases like ABI/Inform as well as other business-related resources like books about finances, marketing, etc.	39%	50%
Resource for tax preparation: Provides tax forms, access to tax preparation resources and step-by-step guidance during tax season	49%	58%
Workforce training center: Provides instructor-led classes on entrepreneurship, presentation skills, computer skills, sales generation, financial planning, marketing and other business-related topics in order to improve the workplace skills and marketability of community members	44%	53%

Percentage of voting respondents with an agreement rating of 8, 9 or 10
Source: *From Awareness to Funding*, OCLC, 2008

The ideal library for Library as Office respondents would be tailored to businesses.

Library as Office are very informed about local civic matters, and are more likely than other respondents to be Friends of the Library

	Total Voting Respondents	Library as Office
Involvement in learning about and discussing issues or decisions that affect your city or town	20%	39%
Very or somewhat closely follow news about local politics in town	78%	91%
Very interested in public policy and economic decisions that take place in your community	32%	46%
Member of the Friends of the Library	9%	19%

Percentage of voting respondents with an agreement rating of 8, 9 or 10
Source: *From Awareness to Funding*, OCLC, 2008

From Awareness to Funding: A study of library support in America

Who are the library's financial supporters?

Library as Office respondents are vocal about their opinions and more likely than other segments to actively make their views heard

	Total Voting Respondents	Library as Office
Attended a public meeting on local affairs or a local political event in recent years	41%	66%
Contacted a local public official to express your views on an issue or problem	44%	64%
Wrote an article or letter to the editor for the local newspaper in recent years	20%	34%

Percentage of voting respondents with an agreement rating of 8, 9 or 10
Source: *From Awareness to Funding*, OCLC, 2008

Probable Supporters— Library as Office

About half would *definitely* support a library referendum

	Total Voting Respondents	Library as Office
Will *definitely* support a library referendum	37%	49%

Percentage of voting respondents with an agreement rating of 8, 9 or 10
Source: *From Awareness to Funding*, OCLC, 2008

Probable Supporters tier

Look to Librarians segment

The Look to Librarians segment represents 6.5% of respondents and 12.2% of respondents who said they would *definitely* vote favorably in a library referendum, ballot initiative or bond measure.

The Look to Librarians segment has a deep appreciation of the value of the librarian in providing services and research expertise. Its members also believe that the librarian is a passionate advocate for the library within the community. Look to Librarians voters give librarians the most favorable rating of any segment.

Look to Librarians respondents are more likely than other segments to be female (65%), Hispanic (20%) and have children (45%). They also show a tendency to be in the lower middle-income bracket and to be part-time college students.

Look to Librarians voters are avid readers who use the library almost twice the average for all voting respondents, with just under 25 visits a year. They have very positive associations with the library, recognizing the important role the library plays as a partner in children's education and in providing equal access to knowledge for residents of their communities.

Look to Librarians voters have the foundation of a strong emotional relationship with the library and they see the library as a place where they can better themselves intellectually and feel like they belong. They also see the library as a place to escape from everyday life.

The Look to Librarians group is responsible for more than its fair share of library visitation and voter support. In fact, this is the only segment to rank public libraries as the number-one priority for an increase in taxes across all seven public services surveyed, outranking the police and fire departments and public schools. The Look to Librarians voters are open to increasing taxes for the library because they value it highly and use it frequently; 50% would *definitely* vote in favor of a library referendum.

Look to Librarians voters have the foundation of a strong emotional relationship with the library and they see the library as a place where they can better themselves intellectually and feel like they belong.

Who are the library's financial supporters?

1. Demographic profile

The Look to Librarians segment trends toward female and Hispanic and having at least one child under the age of 18. The segment also tends to be in the lower middle-income bracket and more likely to include part-time students.

**Probable Supporters—
Look to Librarians**

Demographic profile

Look to Librarians segment

	Total Voting Respondents	Look to Librarians
18–29	15%	20%
30–39	20%	19%
40–49	24%	26%
50–59	23%	21%
60–69	19%	15%
Female	50%	65%
Has at least one kid <18 years old	34%	45%
Less than $20,000	18%	6%
$20,000–$29,999	12%	23%
$30,000–$39,999	16%	20%
$40,000–$49,999	12%	7%
$50,000–$59,999	8%	10%
$60,000–$74,999	11%	14%
$75,000–$99,999	12%	9%
$100,000 or more	19%	22%
Demographic tendencies		
Female	50%	65%
Has at least one kid <18 years old	34%	45%
$20,000–$29,999	12%	23%
$30,000–$39,999	16%	20%
Hispanic	6%	20%
Part-time student	5%	17%
Not a student	87%	79%

Source: *From Awareness to Funding*, OCLC, 2008

Who are the library's financial supporters?

Annual Library Visits

Look to Librarians

24.5

Total Voting Respondents

13.2

2. Library usage

The Look to Librarians segment visits the library almost twice as much as the average for all voting respondents, reporting an average of 24.5 annual visits. Only the Just for Fun segment uses the library more than this group.

Look to Librarians voters use the library to check out books, both fiction and nonfiction. They are more likely than other segments to take advantage of the assistance of the librarian for research and for recommendations. They use the library as a resource for home schooling.

Look to Librarians respondents check out books and take advantage of the assistance provided by the librarian

Look to Librarians segment

Below is a list of activities and services offered by public libraries. Please indicate how frequently you do each one at your local public library.

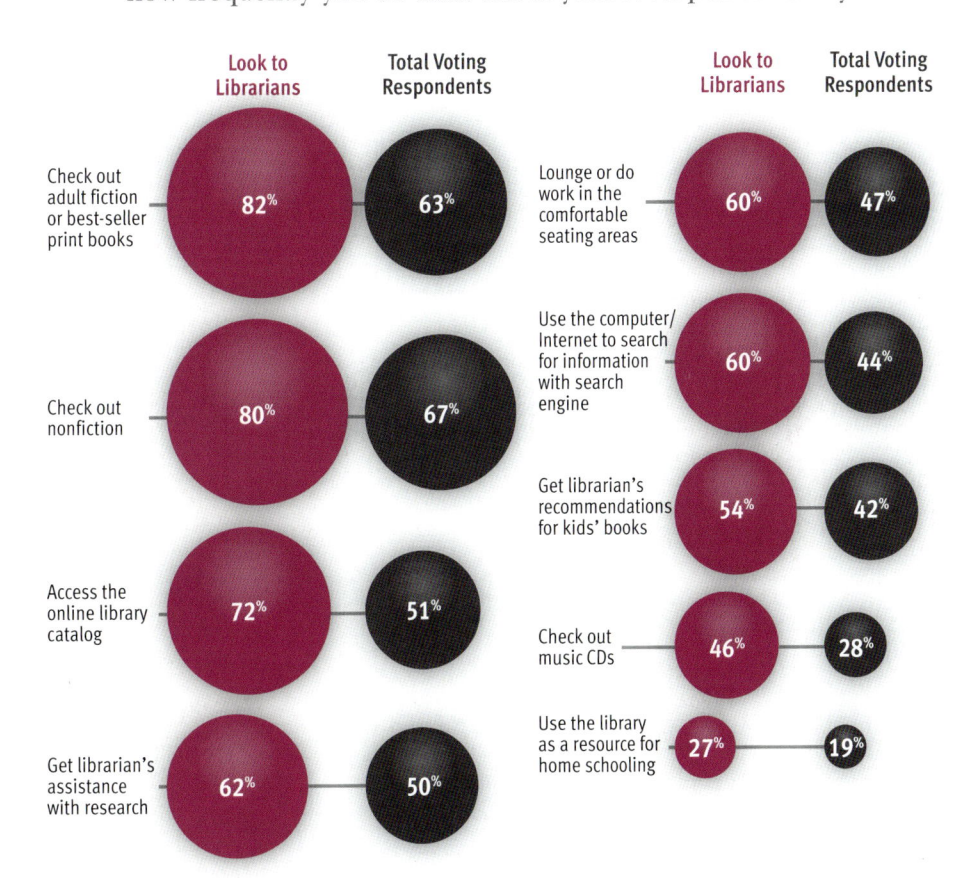

Activity	Look to Librarians	Total Voting Respondents
Check out adult fiction or best-seller print books	82%	63%
Check out nonfiction	80%	67%
Access the online library catalog	72%	51%
Get librarian's assistance with research	62%	50%
Lounge or do work in the comfortable seating areas	60%	47%
Use the computer/Internet to search for information with search engine	60%	44%
Get librarian's recommendations for kids' books	54%	42%
Check out music CDs	46%	28%
Use the library as a resource for home schooling	27%	19%

The chart shows *once a month or more* responses only
Source: *From Awareness to Funding*, OCLC, 2008

From Awareness to Funding: A study of library support in America

Who are the library's financial supporters?

3. Public service support

Look to Librarians voters are 'equal opportunity' supporters of tax increases and hold similar attitudes about increasing taxes for six of the seven public services surveyed. The Look to Librarians segment was the only segment to rank the library first for an increase in taxes. Fifty-five percent (55%) of Look to Librarians voters agreed with the statement "I'd be willing to pay more in local taxes to better fund this service."

All other public services except road maintenance have about the same level of support for increased taxes with 46% for the fire department and police departments and 45% for public schools, public health and parks.

**Probable Supporters—
Look to Librarians**

Look to Librarians respondents are the only segment to rank libraries first in comparison to other public services

Look to Librarians segment

For each service, please rate how much you agree with the phrase "I'd be willing to pay more in local taxes to better fund this service." Please use a 10-point scale, where a 10 means you 'Completely Agree' and a 1 means you 'Completely Disagree.'

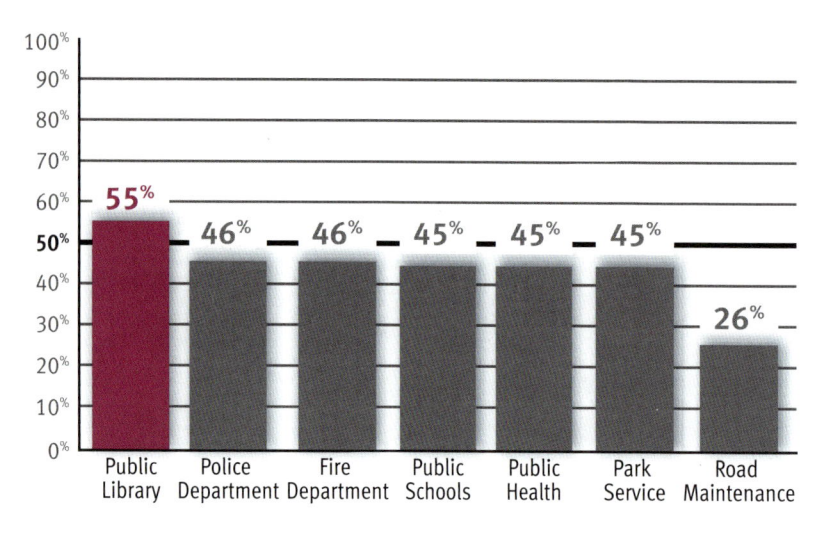

Service	Percentage
Public Library	55%
Police Department	46%
Fire Department	46%
Public Schools	45%
Public Health	45%
Park Service	45%
Road Maintenance	26%

Percentage of voting respondents with an agreement rating of 8, 9 or 10
Source: *From Awareness to Funding*, OCLC, 2008

Who are the library's financial supporters?

Probable Supporters—Look to Librarians

4. Library support compared to library usage

The Look to Librarians respondents are frequent users of the library and represent 14.8% of all library visits, resulting in a Library Use Index of 227, which is almost twice the average.

The Look to Librarians segment has a high level of commitment to library funding support. More than 12% of people who said they would *definitely* vote in favor of a library referendum, ballot initiative or bond measure are Look to Librarians voters (Library Support Index = 187).

This segment prioritizes public library tax funding ahead of all other public services surveyed. Its members place significant value in the library and the librarian for their lives and for their communities.

Look to Librarians respondents were more than willing to support the library they use and value

Look to Librarians segment

If there was a referendum, ballot initiative or bond measure for your local public library on the ballot, how do you think you would vote?

How many times have you visited your local public library in the past 12 months?

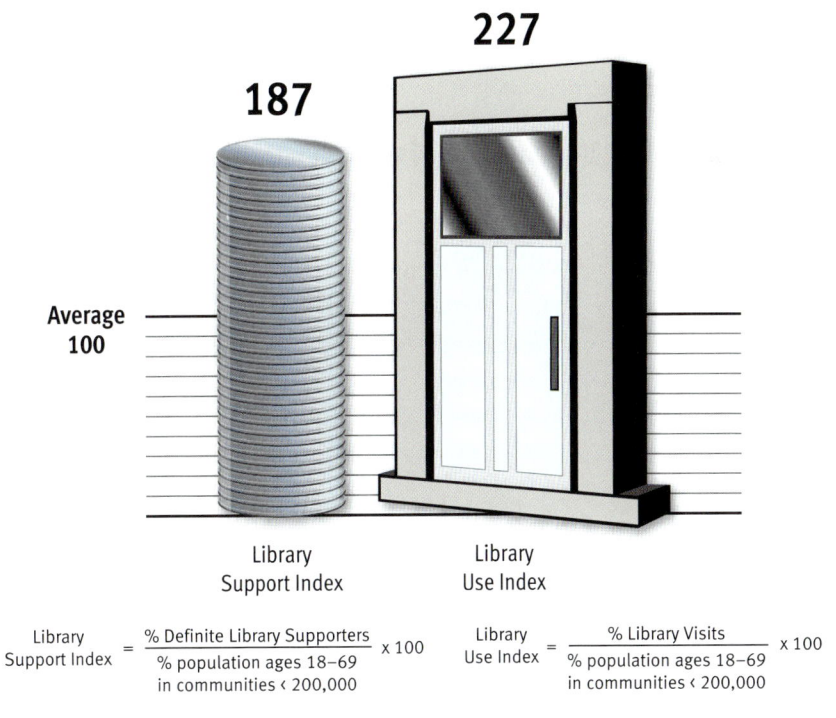

227

187

Average 100

Library Support Index

Library Use Index

$$\text{Library Support Index} = \frac{\text{\% Definite Library Supporters}}{\text{\% population ages 18-69 in communities < 200,000}} \times 100$$

$$\text{Library Use Index} = \frac{\text{\% Library Visits}}{\text{\% population ages 18-69 in communities < 200,000}} \times 100$$

An index of 100 is average
Source: *From Awareness to Funding*, OCLC, 2008

From Awareness to Funding: A study of library support in America

Who are the library's financial supporters?

5. Attitudes toward libraries and funding

The Look to Librarians voters are heavy users of the library and know what it has to offer. They are particularly appreciative of librarians and the role they play in providing knowledge, research expertise and support for the library in the community.

Look to Librarians voters believe that the library has kept up with technological advancements. They feel the library offers the latest in music and movies and remains relevant in people's lives today. They believe that the library is well-organized and full of quality information but it is the librarian they appreciate most of all. They respect librarians for their knowledge and expertise and for their passionate advocacy on behalf of the library. The Look to Librarians voters have the most positive overall impression of the librarians at their local public library. Respondents believe that the librarian understands the needs of the community.

Look to Librarians voters volunteer in their community and at the library and are active participants in local organizations. They have a long-standing and ongoing relationship with the library. This relationship has led to a strong emotional connection and a sense of belonging. Look to Librarians voters are solid supporters of increased funding for libraries; half would *definitely* vote in favor of a library referendum.

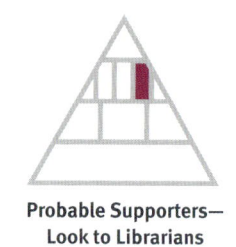

Probable Supporters—Look to Librarians

Look to Librarians voters believe that the library has kept up with technological advancements. They feel the library offers the latest in music and movies and remains relevant in people's lives today.

Attitudes toward libraries and funding
Look to Librarians segment

For each statement below, please rate your level of agreement on a scale from 1 to 10, where a 10 means 'Agree Strongly' and a 1 means 'Disagree Strongly.'

Look to Librarians respondents visit the library frequently and live close by

	Total Voting Respondents	Look to Librarians
I don't go to the library in my community very often	36%	7%
I have a library card	77%	90%
I live 1–2 miles from public library	29%	41%
How likely are you to initiate a trip to the library?	53%	79%

Percentage of voting respondents with an agreement rating of 8, 9 or 10
Source: *From Awareness to Funding*, OCLC, 2008

Who are the library's financial supporters?

Probable Supporters—Look to Librarians

Look to Librarians respondents know what the library has to offer.

Look to Librarians respondents know what the library has to offer

	Total Voting Respondents	Look to Librarians
It's been so long since I've been to the library that I'm not even sure what it has to offer anymore	19%	4%
Know that library has:		
Print magazines/newspapers	87%	97%
Audiobooks/books on tape	80%	90%
Videos/DVDs to check out	83%	97%
Story time and other children's programming	80%	97%
Library Web site	68%	86%
Online library catalog	66%	86%
Tax/government documents	70%	85%
Music CDs to check out	65%	84%
Books/materials in languages other than English	62%	82%
High-speed Internet access	64%	75%
Special programs for teens	42%	68%
Book discussion groups	47%	66%
Fax machine	57%	65%
Electronic magazines and books	45%	58%
Ability to play games on the computer/Internet	38%	56%
Online databases like ABI/Inform	28%	44%
ESL Classes	17%	26%

Percentage of voting respondents with an agreement rating of 8, 9 or 10
Source: *From Awareness to Funding*, OCLC, 2008

Look to Librarians respondents believe the library is current with technological advancements and offers the latest in music and movies

The public library:	Total Voting Respondents	Look to Librarians
Is one of the first places I would go if I wanted to engage my children with computers and technology	30%	39%
In my town is one of the best places to go to learn computer skills	26%	36%
Is on the forefront of technology	39%	49%
Is an expert in technology	37%	45%
Uses technology to meet the changing needs of the community	48%	62%
Provides access to a wide variety of music and movies	36%	48%
Provides access to the latest releases in music and movies	33%	41%

Percentage of voting respondents with an agreement rating of 8, 9 or 10
Source: *From Awareness to Funding*, OCLC, 2008

From Awareness to Funding: A study of library support in America

Who are the library's financial supporters?

Look to Librarians respondents believe the library is relevant to people's lives

	Total Voting Respondents	Look to Librarians
The public library has done a good job of keeping up with changing technology	60%	75%
The library is no longer necessary in the Internet age	13%	2%

Percentage of voting respondents with an agreement rating of 8, 9 or 10
Source: *From Awareness to Funding*, OCLC, 2008

Probable Supporters— Look to Librarians

The library is seen as well-organized and full of quality information

The public library:	Total Voting Respondents	Look to Librarians
Is organized in a way where you can find exactly what you're looking for	62%	78%
Provides the most up-to-date information available	55%	68%
Provides access to books you can't find anywhere else	53%	66%
Provides more trustworthy information than what you can find on the Internet	50%	68%
Offers access to databases not available on the Internet	39%	52%

Percentage of voting respondents with an agreement rating of 8, 9 or 10
Source: *From Awareness to Funding*, OCLC, 2008

The librarians are what Look to Librarians respondents appreciate most: their vast knowledge, research expertise and material recommendations

The public librarian:	Total Voting Respondents	Look to Librarians
Is knowledgeable about every aspect of the public library	63%	79%
Is well-educated	61%	77%
Has excellent computer skills	50%	69%
Is someone you'd go to with a question before going to the Internet	41%	56%
Utilizes all the public library resources to perform the most thorough research possible	54%	70%
Is a trained expert in finding the right information, wherever it is	51%	69%
Is able to access information through technology in ways that ordinary people can't	44%	65%
Can research topics better than you can do alone on the Internet	44%	63%
Recommends Web sites and other electronic information sources that you never would have thought of otherwise	39%	53%
Provides more trustworthy information than search engines like Google and Yahoo!	40%	53%

Percentage of voting respondents with an agreement rating of 8, 9 or 10
Source: *From Awareness to Funding*, OCLC, 2008

The librarians are what Look to Librarians respondents appreciate most: their vast knowledge, research expertise and material recommendations.

Who are the library's financial supporters?

**Probable Supporters—
Look to Librarians**

Look to Librarians respondents see librarians as passionate advocates for the library and believe the librarian understands their community and their patrons' needs.

Look to Librarians respondents have the highest impression of librarians of any segment

	Total Voting Respondents	Look to Librarians
[Positive] overall impression of the librarians at the local public library	60%	83%

Percentage of voting respondents with an agreement rating of 8, 9 or 10
Source: *From Awareness to Funding*, OCLC, 2008

Look to Librarians respondents see librarians as passionate advocates for the library and believe the librarian understands their community and their patrons' needs

The public librarian:	Total Voting Respondents	Look to Librarians
Is a true advocate for lifelong learning	56%	67%
Is passionate about making the public library relevant again	53%	64%
Recommends books that you never would have thought to read otherwise	45%	60%
Understands the community's needs and how to address them through the public library	48%	56%
Really understands how to engage kids with computers and technology	42%	51%

Percentage of voting respondents with an agreement rating of 8, 9 or 10
Source: *From Awareness to Funding*, OCLC, 2008

Look to Librarians respondents are active volunteers— at the library and in their community

	Total Voting Respondents	Look to Librarians
I do a lot of volunteer work in my community	19%	30%
Donated books and other goods to the library	31%	45%
Donated time to the library	8%	22%

Percentage of voting respondents with an agreement rating of 8, 9 or 10
Source: *From Awareness to Funding*, OCLC, 2008

Look to Librarians respondents are active participants in local organizations

Member of:	Total Voting Respondents	Look to Librarians
Church or other religious organization	41%	56%
Local nonprofit organization	17%	28%
Humane society or other animal charity	13%	26%
Chamber of commerce	4%	14%
Currently an active member of a local community organization, social volunteer group, trade or professional association	31%	45%

Percentage of voting respondents with an agreement rating of 8, 9 or 10
Source: *From Awareness to Funding*, OCLC, 2008

Who are the library's financial supporters?

Look to Librarians respondents have a long-standing relationship with the library

	Total Voting Respondents	Look to Librarians
The public library was an important part of my life growing up	49%	61%
I go to the library a lot more than one year ago	10%	23%

Percentage of voting respondents with an agreement rating of 8, 9 or 10
Source: *From Awareness to Funding*, OCLC, 2008

Probable Supporters— Look to Librarians

Look to Librarians respondents have an emotional connection to the library that gives them a sense of belonging and helps them become a better person

The public library:	Total Voting Respond.	Probable Supporters	Look to Librarians
Makes you feel like a part of a group of people who are well-educated	51%	59%	67%
Makes you feel like part of a social group	35%	39%	49%
Helps you gain a broader perspective on life	59%	68%	80%
Empowers you	55%	67%	75%
Helps you be self-reliant	54%	65%	75%
Helps you become a better person	54%	65%	74%
Encourages you to develop a point of view	52%	61%	69%

Percentage of voting respondents with an agreement rating of 8, 9 or 10
Source: *From Awareness to Funding*, OCLC, 2008

2-78 From Awareness to Funding: A study of library support in America

Probable Supporters—
Greater Good

The Greater Good respondents believe that the library plays an important role in contributing to the 'greater good' by bringing the community together and providing access to the technology and resources that residents need.

Probable Supporters tier

Greater Good segment

The Greater Good segment represents 8.7% of the population and 16.2% of *definite* voting support for a library referendum.

As the name suggests, this final segment of the Probable Supporters tier values the library's contribution to 'the greater good.' Although this group uses the library infrequently with only 4.5 visits a year, its members believe that the library plays an important role in serving the needs of the community and can be a great source of pride.

The Greater Good respondents are more likely than other segments to trend toward female and white/non-Hispanic. They are more likely to describe themselves as liberal.

The Greater Good segment uses the library significantly less than average and is more likely to check out books than take advantage of the other services and resources the library makes available. The only activity this group participates in more than average is to attend meetings in the community meeting rooms.

The Greater Good respondents are involved in their communities, participate in local organizations and charities and follow the news about local events and politics. They believe that the library plays an important role in contributing to the 'greater good' by bringing the community together and providing access to the technology and resources that residents need.

The Greater Good respondents are the least opposed to tax increases of any Probable Supporters segment. This segment is willing to support a tax increase to fund the library; 50% of voters would *definitely* vote yes in a library referendum.

Who are the library's financial supporters?

1. Demographic profile

The Greater Good respondents are more likely than other segments to be female and white/non-Hispanic. They are one of the few segments that exhibits a political tendency, being more likely to describe themselves as liberal.

Probable Supporters—Greater Good

Demographic profile
Greater Good segment

	Total Voting Respondents	Greater Good
18–29	15%	18%
30–39	20%	12%
40–49	24%	25%
50–59	23%	25%
60–69	19%	21%
Female	50%	61%
Has at least one kid <18 years old	34%	28%
Less than $20,000	18%	20%
$20,000–$29,999	12%	11%
$30,000–$39,999	16%	13%
$40,000–$49,999	12%	18%
$50,000–$59,999	8%	10%
$60,000–$74,999	11%	8%
$75,000–$99,999	12%	12%
$100,000 or more	19%	17%
Demographic tendencies		
Female	50%	61%
White/non-Hispanic	76%	87%
Slightly liberal/liberal/extremely liberal	28%	45%

Source: *From Awareness to Funding*, OCLC, 2008

Who are the library's financial supporters?

Annual Library Visits

Greater Good
● 4.5

Total Voting Respondents
● 13.2

2. Library usage

The Greater Good voters are infrequent users of the library, reporting only 4.5 visits a year. The only segment that uses the library less than this group is the Detached segment in the Barriers to Support tier.

The Greater Good voters use very few of the services and resources provided by the library. They primarily check out books, but at a rate less than average for all voting respondents. The only library service that the Greater Good segment uses more than average is attending meetings in community meeting rooms.

Greater Good respondents mainly use the library to check out books; the only thing they do more than average is attend meetings

Greater Good segment

Below is a list of activities and services offered by public libraries. Please indicate how frequently you do each one at your local public library.

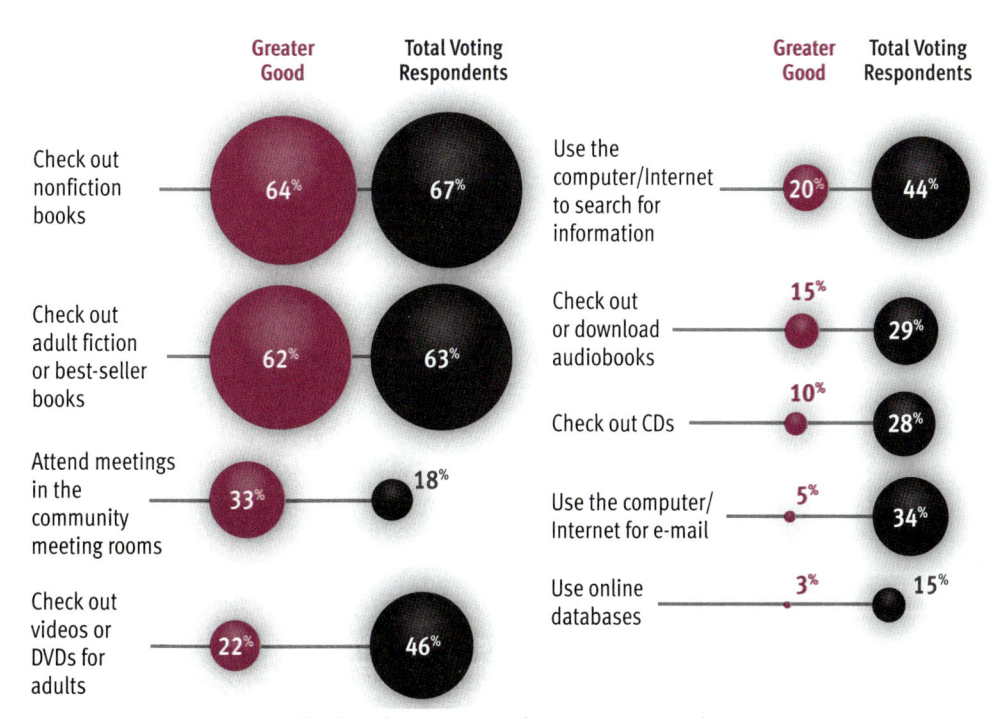

	Greater Good	Total Voting Respondents		Greater Good	Total Voting Respondents
Check out nonfiction books	64%	67%	Use the computer/Internet to search for information	20%	44%
Check out adult fiction or best-seller books	62%	63%	Check out or download audiobooks	15%	29%
Attend meetings in the community meeting rooms	33%	18%	Check out CDs	10%	28%
Check out videos or DVDs for adults	22%	46%	Use the computer/Internet for e-mail	5%	34%
			Use online databases	3%	15%

The chart shows *once a month or more* responses only
Source: *From Awareness to Funding*, OCLC, 2008

Who are the library's financial supporters?

3. Public service support

The Greater Good voters are generally willing to increase taxes for the services they believe provide value to their communities.

The fire department is the public service with the greatest support for a tax increase among Greater Good voters. Sixty-three percent (63%) agree that they would be willing to increase their taxes to support the fire service. Public schools follow at 57% and the police department is third with 52%. While the Greater Good voters place high value on the library, it ranks fourth with 42% of the segment willing to increase taxes for the library.

Probable Supporters—Greater Good

The library places fourth on the list for the Greater Good segment, after safety and education

Greater Good segment

For each service, please rate how much you agree with the phrase "I'd be willing to pay more in local taxes to better fund this service." Please use a 10-point scale, where a 10 means you 'Completely Agree' and a 1 means you 'Completely Disagree.'

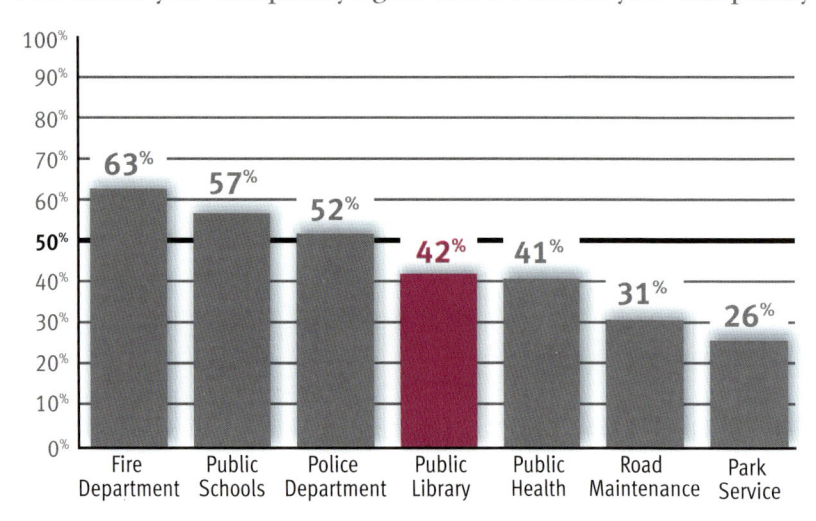

Service	Percentage
Fire Department	63%
Public Schools	57%
Police Department	52%
Public Library	42%
Public Health	41%
Road Maintenance	31%
Park Service	26%

Percentage of voting respondents with an agreement rating of 8, 9 or 10
Source: *From Awareness to Funding*, OCLC, 2008

Who are the library's financial supporters?

Probable Supporters—Greater Good

4. Library support compared to library usage

The Greater Good segment uses the library well below average representing only 3.6% of all library visits (Library Use Index = 42). Only the Detached segment indexes lower for library usage.

However, the Greater Good voters represent proportionately the greatest level of commitment to library funding support of any segment on the Probable Supporters tier. Sixteen percent (16.2%) of people who said they would *definitely* vote in favor of a library referendum, ballot initiative or bond measure are members of the Greater Good segment (Library Support Index = 188). This percentage of *definite* voting support is surpassed only by the Super Supporters segment.

Greater Good respondents had the lowest library visitation for this tier but were the most likely to be *definite* library supporters

Greater Good segment

If there was a referendum, ballot initiative or bond measure for your local public library on the ballot, how do you think you would vote?

How many times have you visited your local public library in the past 12 months?

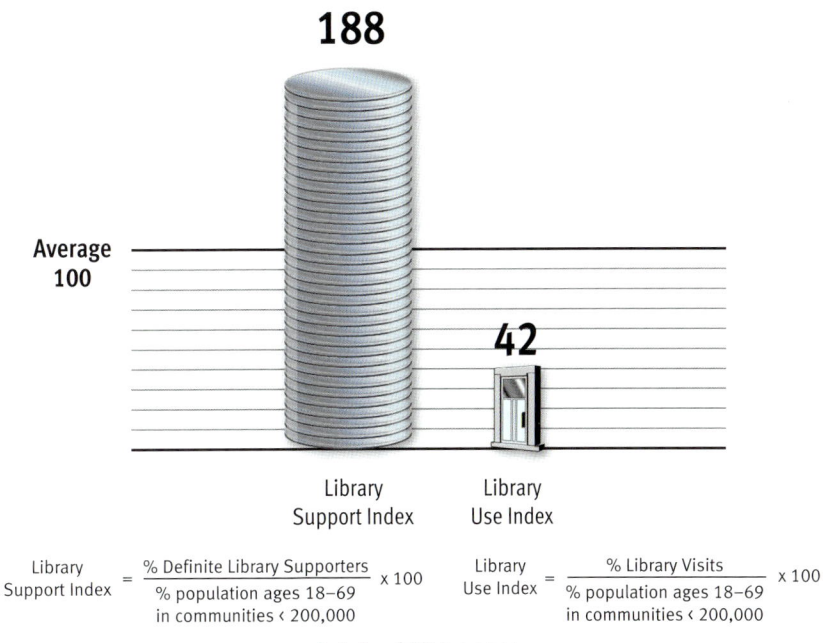

188

Average 100

42

Library Support Index   Library Use Index

$$\text{Library Support Index} = \frac{\text{\% Definite Library Supporters}}{\text{\% population ages 18–69 in communities < 200,000}} \times 100$$

$$\text{Library Use Index} = \frac{\text{\% Library Visits}}{\text{\% population ages 18–69 in communities < 200,000}} \times 100$$

An index of 100 is average
Source: *From Awareness to Funding*, OCLC, 2008

From Awareness to Funding: A study of library support in America

Who are the library's financial supporters?

5. Attitudes toward libraries and funding

The Greater Good voters are more concerned with the library needs of their local communities than with their own library usage.

The Greater Good voters are less familiar than other respondents with what the library has to offer. They use the library less than anyone else in the Probable Supporters tier, but value the library's contribution to the 'greater good' more highly than any segment outside of the Super Supporters.

The Greater Good respondents see the library as a noble and necessary institution, a source of pride in a community and a place that brings people together. They believe that the library turns people into thinkers and achievers instead of passive participants in life.

The Greater Good respondents are the Probable Supporters least opposed to tax increases.

Probable Supporters—Greater Good

Attitudes toward libraries and funding
Greater Good segment

For each statement below, please rate your level of agreement on a scale from 1 to 10, where a 10 means 'Agree Strongly' and a 1 means 'Disagree Strongly.'

The Greater Good segment knows less than others about what the library has to offer

Don't know that library has:	Total Voting Respondents	Greater Good
Wi-Fi Internet access	58%	72%
English as second language (ESL) classes	60%	72%
Ability to play games on computer/Internet	48%	61%
Computer/technology training programs	49%	60%
Electronic magazines or books	46%	58%
Movie showings	43%	55%

Percentage of voting respondents with an agreement rating of 8, 9 or 10
Source: *From Awareness to Funding*, OCLC, 2008

From Awareness to Funding: A study of library support in America

Who are the library's financial supporters?

Probable Supporters—Greater Good

The Greater Good segment values the library's contribution to the 'greater good' more than any segment outside of Super Supporters

	Total Voting Respondents	Greater Good
It's important in today's world that everyone has equal access to books and technology	83%	97%
The primary purpose of the library is to ensure free and equal access to books and information for everyone	81%	90%
For some people, the library is the only place to access computers or the Internet	79%	87%

Percentage of voting respondents with an agreement rating of 8, 9 or 10
Source: *From Awareness to Funding*, OCLC, 2008

The Greater Good respondents are more involved in their communities than average for the voting population

The Greater Good respondents are very involved in their communities.

	Total Voting Respondents	Greater Good
Member of church or other religious organization	41%	49%
Member of local nonprofit organization	17%	25%
Member of humane society or other animal charity	13%	28%
Very interested in following news about local politics in your city	31%	40%
Watch local news on TV every day	57%	67%
Access community information online on a regular basis	42%	52%
Made a financial contribution to a local community organization or to a local political campaign in recent years	44%	58%

Percentage of voting respondents with an agreement rating of 8, 9 or 10
Source: *From Awareness to Funding*, OCLC, 2008

The Greater Good respondents believe the library can be a source of pride, given the proper funding

	Total Voting Respondents	Greater Good
Having an excellent public library is a source of pride for a community	73%	91%
Local support can make a big difference in the quality of a library	81%	97%

Percentage of voting respondents with an agreement rating of 8, 9 or 10
Source: *From Awareness to Funding*, OCLC, 2008

From Awareness to Funding: A study of library support in America

Who are the library's financial supporters?

The Greater Good respondents believe that the library should be a place that brings communities together

	Total Voting Respondents	Greater Good
The public library should be a place for communities to gather together	45%	58%
It is important that the library provides a place for people in the community to gather and socialize	36%	47%

Percentage of voting respondents with an agreement rating of 8, 9 or 10
Source: *From Awareness to Funding*, OCLC, 2008

Probable Supporters— Greater Good

The Greater Good respondents do not see the library as a place of indulgence and fun as much as other Probable Supporters

The public library:	Total Voting Respond.	Probable Supporters	Greater Good
Lets you indulge and enjoy yourself	53%	64%	54%
Surrounds you with a feeling of magic and fantasy	40%	46%	33%
Is the kind of thing you can really immerse yourself in and savor	51%	65%	56%

Percentage of voting respondents with an agreement rating of 8, 9 or 10
Source: *From Awareness to Funding*, OCLC, 2008

The Greater Good respondents are the least opposed to tax increases of all Probable Supporters.

The Greater Good respondents are the least opposed to tax increases of all Probable Supporters

	Total Voting Respondents	Greater Good
I oppose tax increases across the board	35%	20%
I feel like I pay too much in property taxes	41%	21%
People in my community can't afford to have their taxes raised	45%	33%
Local politicians are too quick to raise taxes instead of finding ways to cut spending	55%	41%
Would *definitely* vote in favor of a library referendum	37%	50%

Percentage of voting respondents with an agreement rating of 8, 9 or 10
Source: *From Awareness to Funding*, OCLC, 2008

Who are the library's financial supporters?

Super Supporters tier

The Super Supporters tier of the Library Support Segmentation Pyramid represents 7.1% of the U.S. population ages 18–69 in communities of less than 200,000 and 9.7% of voting respondents. In local elections, Super Supporters represent an even greater 12% of the voter turnout. While this tier represents just 7.1% of the population, it provides the largest proportion of *definite* library funding support of any segment on the Library Supporter Segmentation Pyramid. Twenty-one percent (21.0%) of all respondents who report that they will *definitely* vote yes for a library referendum, ballot initiative or bond measure are Super Supporters.

Research did not identify any segments within the Super Supporters tier. The attitudes and actions that drive Super Supporters are consistent across respondents.

Library Supporter Segmentation Pyramid
Super Supporters

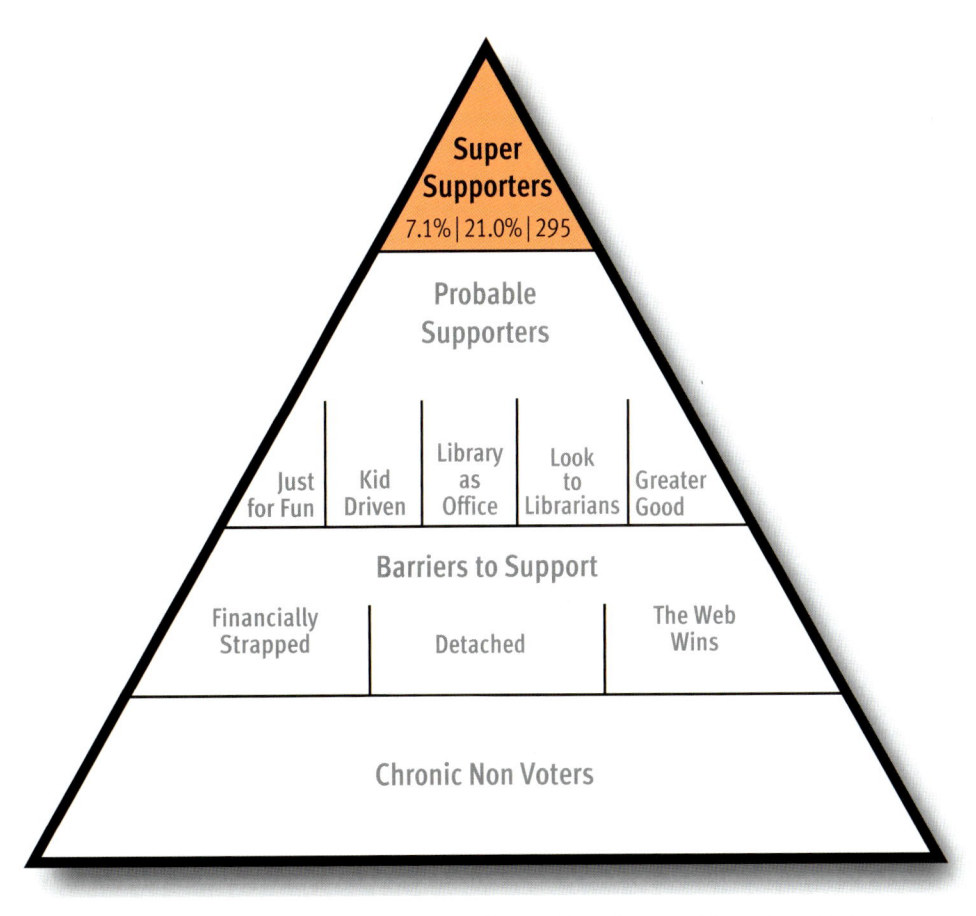

Super Supporters 7.1% | 21.0% | 295

Probable Supporters
- Just for Fun
- Kid Driven
- Library as Office
- Look to Librarians
- Greater Good

Barriers to Support
- Financially Strapped
- Detached
- The Web Wins

Chronic Non Voters

% Population ages 18–69 in communities < 200,000 | Definite Library Supporters | Library Support Index

$$\text{Library Support Index} = \frac{\text{\% Definite Library Supporters}}{\text{\% population ages 18–69 in communities < 200,000}} \times 100$$

Source: *From Awareness to Funding*, OCLC, 2008

Who are the library's financial supporters?

Super Supporters segment

The Super Supporters segment is the pinnacle of the Library Supporter Segmentation Pyramid and represents the public library's core supporter group.

Super Supporters are not defined by any particular demographic. They are demographically average, but share a common mindset, attitudes and beliefs about the library, their community and library funding.

Super Supporters are avid readers with a long-standing relationship with the library. Although they use the library only a little more than average, their relationship with the library is strong because their emotional connection to the library transcends the library's practical functions.

More than any other segment, Super Supporters see the library as a place where they can better themselves and become the person they always wanted to be. They hold the librarian in high regard and recognize the value that librarians bring to the research process. They are the segment that most appreciates the librarian as a passionate advocate for the library.

Super Supporters recognize the library's contribution to a successful community and, more than anyone else, see the library as a place that can help bring a community together.

Super Supporters are very informed about community matters and are the most likely segment to be involved in local organizations and charities. They are well-known, influential members of their communities who are not afraid to openly voice their opinions.

Super Supporters are the segment most likely to vote in both general and local elections. Their voting habits trend toward liberal. Their favorable vote for library support is virtually assured with 80% reporting they would *definitely* vote in favor of a library referendum.

Super Supporters

More than any other segment, Super Supporters see the library as a place where they can better themselves and become the people they always wanted to be. They hold the librarian in high regard and recognize the value that librarians bring to the research process.

Who are the library's financial supporters?

1. Demographic profile

Super Supporters are not defined by any particular demographic. They are demographically average, but have a common mindset, attitudes and beliefs about the library, their community and library funding.

Super Supporters

Super Supporters are not defined by any particular demographic. They are demographically average but have a common mindset, attitudes and beliefs about the library, their community and library funding.

Demographic profile
Super Supporters segment

	Total Voting Respondents	Super Supporters
18–29	15%	7%
30–39	20%	18%
40–49	24%	28%
50–59	23%	28%
60–69	19%	19%
Female	50%	49%
Has at least one kid <18 years old	34%	42%
Less than $20,000	18%	8%
$20,000–$29,999	12%	16%
$30,000–$39,999	16%	24%
$40,000–$49,999	12%	13%
$50,000–$59,999	8%	9%
$60,000–$74,999	11%	15%
$75,000–$99,999	12%	8%
$100,000 or more	19%	15%

Source: *From Awareness to Funding*, OCLC, 2008

Who are the library's financial supporters?

2. Library usage

Super Supporters report an average of 15.9 annual visits to their local public library, only slightly greater than average for all voting respondents.

Super Supporters use traditional library offerings. They check out books for adults and children and they depend on the librarian for recommendations. They read magazines and newspapers and make use of online reference materials.

Annual Library Visits

Super Supporters
15.9

Total Voting Respondents
13.2

Super Supporters use the library to feed their voracious reading habits and to recommend children's books

Super Supporters segment

Below is a list of activities and services offered by public libraries. Please indicate how frequently you do each one at your local public library.

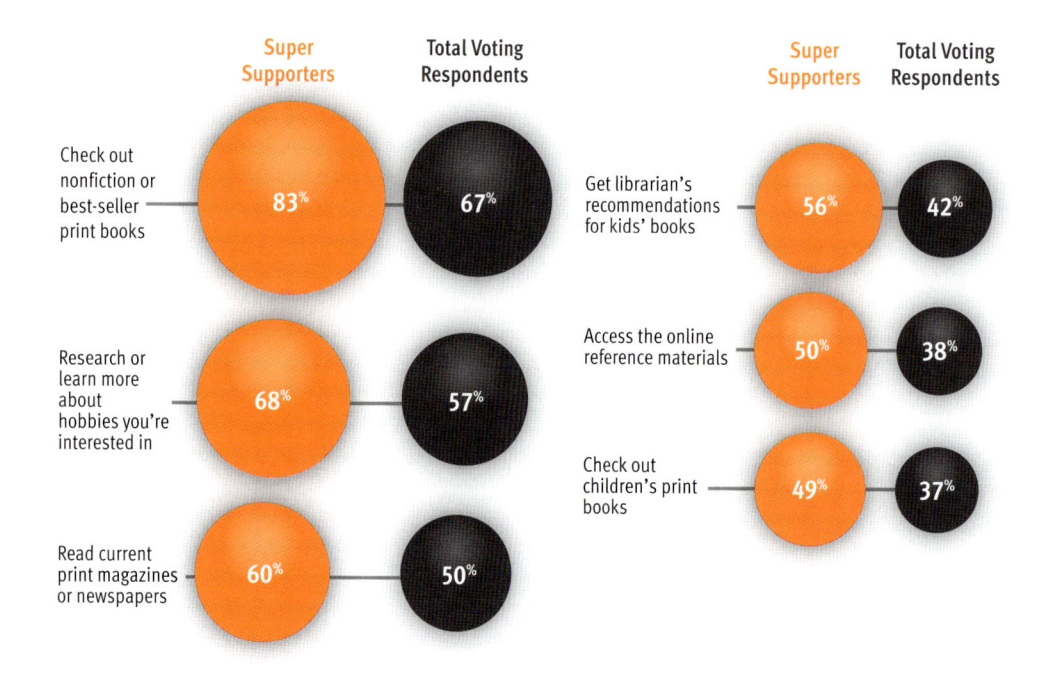

Activity	Super Supporters	Total Voting Respondents
Check out nonfiction or best-seller print books	83%	67%
Research or learn more about hobbies you're interested in	68%	57%
Read current print magazines or newspapers	60%	50%
Get librarian's recommendations for kids' books	56%	42%
Access the online reference materials	50%	38%
Check out children's print books	49%	37%

The chart shows *once a month or more* responses only
Source: *From Awareness to Funding*, OCLC, 2008

2-90 From Awareness to Funding: A study of library support in America

Who are the library's financial supporters?

3. Public service support

When compared to all other segments, the Super Supporters' willingness to increase taxes to fund all seven of the public services included in the survey is high. Essentially, Super Supporters for the public library are Super Supporters for all public services. Even the public service that ranked last, the park service, gained support from over half (58%) of Super Supporters.

Super Supporters

The library is in second place on the Super Supporters' list of public services to support through increased taxes

Super Supporters segment

For each service, please rate how much you agree with the phrase "I'd be willing to pay more in local taxes to better fund this service." Please use a 10-point scale, where a 10 means you 'Completely Agree' and a 1 means you 'Completely Disagree.'

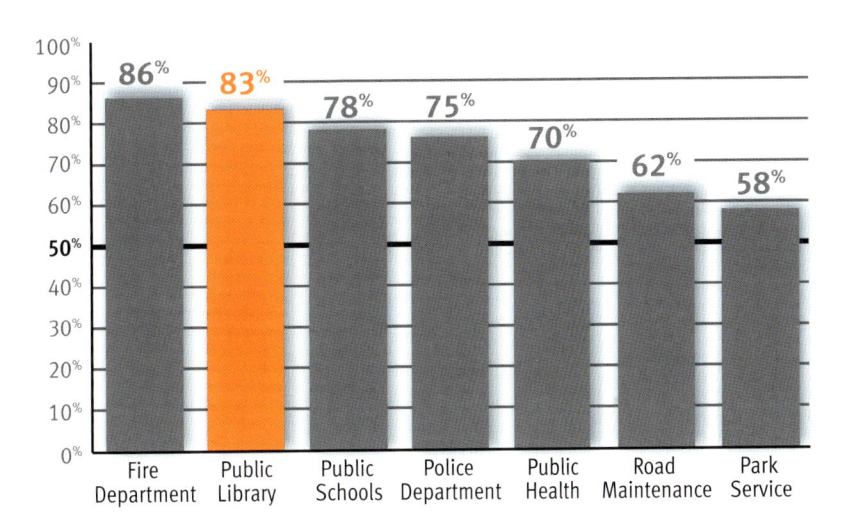

Service	Percentage
Fire Department	86%
Public Library	83%
Public Schools	78%
Police Department	75%
Public Health	70%
Road Maintenance	62%
Park Service	58%

Percentage of voting respondents with an agreement rating of 8, 9 or 10
Source: *From Awareness to Funding*, OCLC, 2008

Who are the library's financial supporters?

4. Library support compared to library usage

The Super Supporters are responsible for 9.4% of library visits reported by all respondents, which places them at just above average (Library Use Index = 132).

In contrast, the Super Supporters are very committed supporters of the library and represent almost three times the average amount of *definite* voting support for the library across all segments. Twenty-one percent (21%) of all respondents who say they would *definitely* vote in favor of a library referendum, ballot initiative or bond measure are Super Supporters (Library Support Index = 295).

The favorable vote of the Super Supporters for an increase in library funding is virtually guaranteed.

Super Supporters

Super Supporters account for, by far, the most financial support for libraries despite only somewhat higher usage

Super Supporters segment

If there was a referendum, ballot initiative or bond measure for your local public library on the ballot, how do you think you would vote?

How many times have you visited your local public library in the past 12 months?

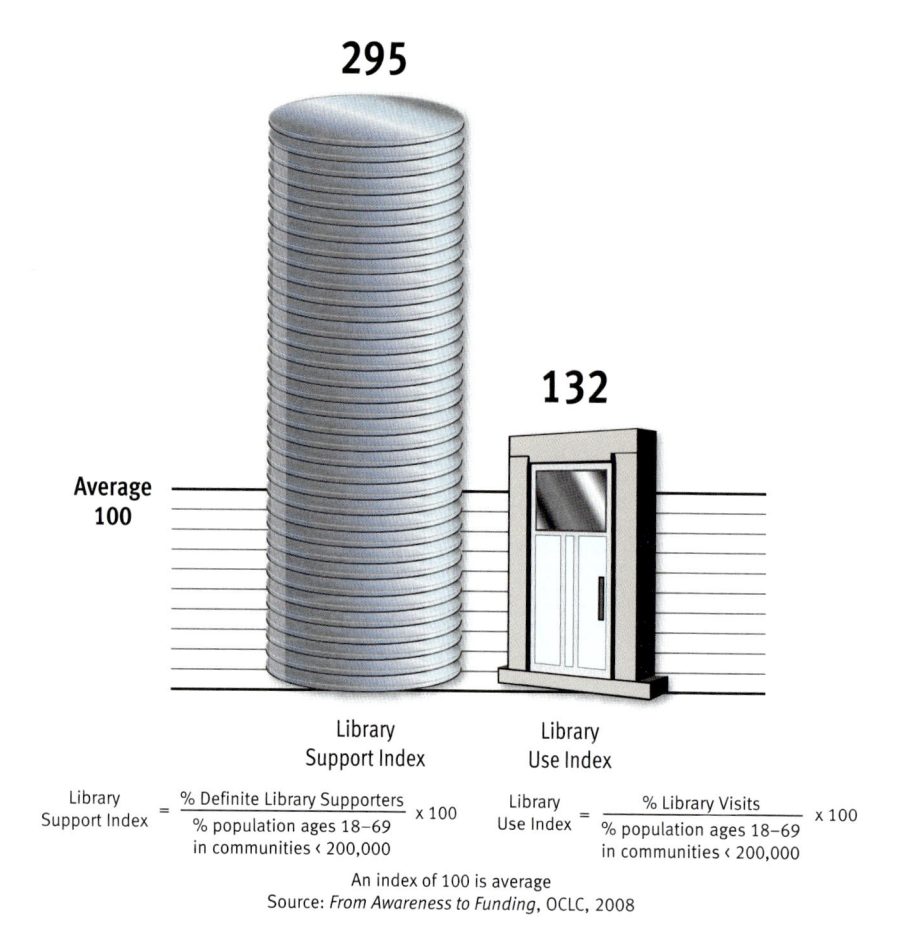

295 — Library Support Index

132 — Library Use Index

Average 100

$$\text{Library Support Index} = \frac{\% \text{ Definite Library Supporters}}{\% \text{ population ages 18–69 in communities } < 200{,}000} \times 100$$

$$\text{Library Use Index} = \frac{\% \text{ Library Visits}}{\% \text{ population ages 18–69 in communities } < 200{,}000} \times 100$$

An index of 100 is average
Source: *From Awareness to Funding*, OCLC, 2008

5. Attitudes toward libraries and funding

Super Supporters are characterized by a high level of involvement and commitment in everything they do. They are not the most frequent users of the library, but are passionate about the vital role that it plays in the lives of individuals and the community as a whole. They are heavily involved in a variety of aspects of the community and are strong advocates for all local services.

The Super Supporters are involved in their local communities. They are the most informed segment about local civic matters and are willing to take action on local issues by voicing their opinions at public meetings and to officials. They make it a point to always vote. The Super Supporters are the segment most involved in local organizations and charities and, not surprisingly, are influential and well-known in their communities.

The Super Supporters are voracious readers and have a long history with the library that continues to flourish. More than those in other segments, Super Supporters recognize the library's contribution to a successful community and see the library as an important partner in a child's education. They believe in the importance of equal access to the resources and information provided by the public library, and see the library as a place that brings the community together, maintaining its relevance to people through all stages of life.

Super Supporters recognize that the library is superior to the Internet, partially due to the role played by the librarian. They appreciate the librarian's superior research capabilities and the librarian's passion for the library and its role in lifelong learning. They see librarians as outspoken advocates for the library.

Super Supporters have a deep emotional connection to the library that goes far beyond the practical functions the library provides to a deeper level of learning that helped transform them into the people they always wanted to be.

Super Supporters have a deep emotional connection to the library that goes far beyond the practical functions the library provides to a deeper level of learning that helped transform them into the people they always wanted to be.

Attitudes toward libraries and funding

Super Supporters segment

For each statement below, please rate your level of agreement on a scale from 1 to 10, where a 10 means 'Agree Strongly' and a 1 means 'Disagree Strongly.'

Super Supporters are the most informed segment about local civic matters

	Total Voting Respondents	Super Supporters
Involved in learning about and discussing issues or decisions that affect your city or town	20%	30%
Very closely follow news about local politics in town	31%	51%
Very interested in public policy and economic decisions that take place in your community	32%	51%
Watch the local news on TV every day	57%	73%

Percentage of voting respondents with an agreement rating of 8, 9 or 10
Source: *From Awareness to Funding*, OCLC, 2008

Who are the library's financial supporters?

Super Supporters are the most involved segment in local organizations and charities

	Total Voting Respondents	Super Supporters
Member of church or other religious organization	41%	49%
Member of local nonprofit organization	17%	26%
Member of Friends of the Library	9%	22%
Member of humane society or other animal charity	13%	19%
Member of local PTA	8%	13%
Currently are an active member of a local community organization, social volunteer group, trade or professional association	31%	47%
I'm very involved with the public schools in my community	18%	30%

Percentage of voting respondents with an agreement rating of 8, 9 or 10
Source: *From Awareness to Funding*, OCLC, 2008

Super Supporters are the most involved segment in local organizations and charities.

Super Supporters are influential and well-known in the community

	Total Voting Respondents	Super Supporters
I have a lot of friends in my community	36%	57%
People in my community often come to me for advice	15%	27%

Percentage of voting respondents with an agreement rating of 8, 9 or 10
Source: *From Awareness to Funding*, OCLC, 2008

Super Supporters are willing to take action when it comes to local issues by voicing their opinions

	Total Voting Respondents	Super Supporters
Contacted a local public official to express your views on an issue or problem	44%	60%
Attended a public meeting on local affairs or a local political event in recent years	41%	56%
Made a financial contribution to a local community organization or local political organization in recent years	44%	55%

Percentage of voting respondents with an agreement rating of 8, 9 or 10
Source: *From Awareness to Funding*, OCLC, 2008

Super Supporters are influential and well-known in the community.

Super Supporters also voice their opinions by making a point to always vote

Very likely to vote in...	Total Voting Respondents	Super Supporters
Presidential elections	73%	84%
Primary/special elections	47%	66%
Elections that involve local issues	48%	66%

Percentage of voting respondents with an agreement rating of 8, 9 or 10
Source: *From Awareness to Funding*, OCLC, 2008

Who are the library's financial supporters?

Super Supporters

The voting habits of Super Supporters tend to be more liberal than average

	Total Voting Respondents	Super Supporters
Voted for Kerry/Edwards in 2004 U.S. presidential election	43%	56%
Identify themselves as liberal-leaning	28%	44%

Percentage of voting respondents with an agreement rating of 8, 9 or 10
Source: *From Awareness to Funding*, OCLC, 2008

Super Supporters are voracious readers with a long history with the library

	Total Voting Respondents	Super Supporters
Average number of books read in typical 2-month period	4.6	6.7
Average number of magazines read in typical 2-month period	6.0	8.6
I consider myself an avid reader	52%	83%
People would consider me kind of a bookworm	34%	56%
The public library was an important part of my life growing up	49%	83%
I visit the library a little/a lot more than a year ago	23%	33%

Percentage of voting respondents with an agreement rating of 8, 9 or 10
Source: *From Awareness to Funding*, OCLC, 2008

More than other segments, Super Supporters recognize the library's contribution to a successful community.

More than other segments, Super Supporters recognize the library's contribution to a successful community

	Total Voting Respondents	Super Supporters
Having an excellent public library is a source of pride for a community	73%	96%
A top-notch library is an important part of a good community	72%	95%
The public library stimulates growth and development in a community	71%	85%
You can measure the success of a community by the quality of the public library	42%	68%

Percentage of voting respondents with an agreement rating of 8, 9 or 10
Source: *From Awareness to Funding*, OCLC, 2008

Super Supporters see the library as an important partner in a child's education

	Total Voting Respondents	Super Supporters
Children who go regularly to the public library are better readers in the long run	70%	88%
Children who go regularly to the public library do better in school	65%	87%
The public library does an excellent job of helping prepare children for school	53%	79%

Percentage of voting respondents with an agreement rating of 8, 9 or 10
Source: *From Awareness to Funding*, OCLC, 2008

Who are the library's financial supporters?

Super Supporters believe in the importance of equal access to resources, uniquely available at the public library

	Total Voting Respondents	Super Supporters
It's important in today's world that everyone has equal access to books and technology	83%	96%
For some people, the library is the only place to access computers or the Internet	79%	95%
The primary purpose of the library is to ensure free and equal access to books and information for everyone	81%	94%
The public library provides essential resources that some people may not be able to otherwise afford	68%	92%

Percentage of voting respondents with an agreement rating of 8, 9 or 10
Source: *From Awareness to Funding*, OCLC, 2008

Super Supporters

Super Supporters believe the library helps bring a community together

	Total Voting Respondents	Super Supporters
It is important that the library is able to draw the community together around knowledge	58%	79%
The public library should be a place for communities to gather together	45%	68%
The public library is a social hub in my community where people frequently get together	18%	34%

Percentage of voting respondents with an agreement rating of 8, 9 or 10
Source: *From Awareness to Funding*, OCLC, 2008

Super Supporters believe that the library maintains its relevance to people through all stages of life.

Super Supporters believe that the library maintains its relevance to people through all stages of life

The public library:	Total Voting Respondents	Super Supporters
Is committed to lifelong learning	63%	82%
Is an excellent resource for students to get help with homework	60%	81%

Percentage of voting respondents with an agreement rating of 8, 9 or 10
Source: *From Awareness to Funding*, OCLC, 2008

Super Supporters recognize the library's superiority to the Internet

The public library:	Total Voting Respondents	Super Supporters
Provides more trustworthy information than you can find on the Internet	50%	70%
Offers access to databases not available on the Internet	39%	57%

Percentage of voting respondents with an agreement rating of 8, 9 or 10
Source: *From Awareness to Funding*, OCLC, 2008

Who are the library's financial supporters?

Super Supporters

Super Supporters believe librarians are more than researchers— they are passionate advocates for the library.

Super Supporters recognize the librarian's superior researching capabilities

The public librarian:	Total Voting Respondents	Super Supporters
Utilizes all public library resources to perform the most thorough searches possible	54%	76%
Is a trained expert in finding the right information wherever it is	51%	68%
Is someone you'd go to with a question before going to the Internet	41%	57%

Percentage of voting respondents with an agreement rating of 8, 9 or 10
Source: *From Awareness to Funding*, OCLC, 2008

Super Supporters believe librarians are more than researchers— they are passionate advocates for the library

Public librarians:	Total Voting Respondents	Super Supporters
Are true advocates for lifelong learning	56%	85%
Are passionate about making the public library relevant again	53%	80%
Are knowledgeable about every aspect of the public library	63%	86%
Are knowledgeable about my community	54%	79%
Are outspoken advocates for the library	51%	68%
Are committed to rekindling the importance of the public library in the world of technology	50%	64%
Work closely with local politicians and community leaders to get public funding and support	41%	61%

Percentage of voting respondents with an agreement rating of 8, 9 or 10
Source: *From Awareness to Funding*, OCLC, 2008

Super Supporters have a deep emotional connection to the library that extends beyond its practical function to a deeper level of learning

The public library:	Total Voting Respondents	Super Supporters
Provides you with basic information and answers to your questions	73%	90%
Provides tools for very practical purposes	68%	89%
Puts information and answers right at your fingertips	71%	88%
Provides instant access to information	67%	87%
Is something of great importance	66%	93%
Helps you seek truth	62%	86%
Serves a serious purpose	74%	98%
Allows you to get really in-depth on a subject	71%	85%

Percentage of voting respondents with an agreement rating of 8, 9 or 10
Source: *From Awareness to Funding*, OCLC, 2008

Who are the library's financial supporters?

Super Supporters believe the library transforms lives, including their own

The public library:	Total Voting Respondents	Super Supporters
Helps you come away feeling like you really learned something	61%	86%
Allows you to pursue your passions and interests	59%	83%
Helps you gain a broader perspective on life	59%	80%
Makes you feel smart	56%	77%
Encourages you to develop your own point of view	52%	73%
Makes you feel good about yourself	48%	75%
Allows you to appreciate the beauty in life	46%	71%
Helps create who you are	40%	64%
Fills you with hope and optimism	40%	62%

Percentage of voting respondents with an agreement rating of 8, 9 or 10
Source: *From Awareness to Funding*, OCLC, 2008

Super Supporters

Super Supporters believe the library transforms lives, including their own.

For Super Supporters, the closing of the library would be felt deeply

	Total Voting Respondents	Super Supporters
If the library were to close, it would be a great loss	73%	93%
If the library in my community were to shut down, something essential and important would be lost, affecting the whole community	71%	89%

Percentage of voting respondents with an agreement rating of 8, 9 or 10
Source: *From Awareness to Funding*, OCLC, 2008

Super Supporters' favorable library vote is virtually guaranteed

	Total Voting Respondents	Super Supporters
Would definitely vote in favor of a library referendum	37%	80%
Voted in favor of the most recent library referendum in the community (among those who had such a referendum)	89%	100%

Percentage of voting respondents with an agreement rating of 8, 9 or 10
Source: *From Awareness to Funding*, OCLC, 2008

Who are the library's financial supporters?

Segmentation in review

A primary goal of the quantitative research was to create a market segmentation and targeting framework of U.S. residents to understand the following:

- Which segments of the public are most interested in financially supporting their local libraries and what motivations drive their support
- Which segments are least likely to support libraries and what are their barriers to support
- Whether it is viable to use marketing and advocacy techniques to target interested segments and positively impact library funding.

The research informed the creation of a Library Supporter Segmentation Pyramid that profiled 10 distinct segments based on the likelihood for financial support of public libraries. Assessment of the characteristics and attitudes of the population represented in each segment provides new understanding of what drives library funding support.

Which segments of the public are most likely to financially support their local libraries and what motivations drive their support?

The Super Supporters and the Probable Supporters tiers of the Library Supporter Segmentation Pyramid are the most likely to increase financial support for their local libraries.

Super Supporters

The Super Supporters segment is the segment most committed to increasing funding for libraries. They represent almost three times the average number of *definite* voting supporters. Super Supporters are not only committed supporters of the library, but of a broad range of local public services. Super Supporters are almost guaranteed (80%) to *definitely* vote in favor of a library referendum, ballot initiative or bond measure.

Super Supporters represent just 7.1% of residents in U.S. cities, towns and suburbs under 200,000 population but comprise a larger proportion of voters due to the higher likelihood of voting, especially in local elections. Super Supporters represent 9.7% of people who vote on library funding measures and 12% of voters in local elections.

Super Supporters are the core of library funding support as their favorable vote for library funding is almost guaranteed. They play a critical role in influencing other members of their community to commit their financial support because of their high involvement in the community, and their willingness to voice their opinions.

Any library funding advocacy or marketing campaign must leverage the commitment of the Super Supporters. Super Supporters must feel like a part of the library support

Who are the library's financial supporters?

campaign, sharing their opinions and using their influence to impact the favorable vote of others in the community. In particular, the Super Supporters can play a vital role in increasing the commitment to library funding among Probable Supporters.

Probable Supporters

The five segments in the Probable Supporters tier are the pool of U.S. residents offering the most potential to increase library funding. Probable Supporters represent a third (32.3%) of U.S. residents ages 18–69 in cities, towns and suburbs under 200,000 population. They have strong positive associations with the library and the role it plays in their lives, their families' lives and their local communities.

Probable Supporters offer the most potential to increase library funding.

Probable Supporters are predisposed to supporting an increase in taxes to fund the local library, and together represent 55.6% of all respondents who said they would *definitely* vote favorably in a library referendum. However, their favorable vote is not guaranteed.

The key to increasing the percentage of Probable Supporters who would be *definite* 'yes' voters is to leverage the attitudes, beliefs and behaviors they already share with the Super Supporters and to increase the intensity of those beliefs. A library funding advocacy or marketing campaign must develop messaging and tactics that would ignite those attitudes and behaviors.

Which segments are least likely to support libraries and what are their barriers to support?

The bottom two tiers of the Library Supporter Segmentation Pyramid are unlikely to provide financial support for libraries at the ballot box.

Chronic Non Voters

The Chronic Non Voters segment of the Library Supporter Segmentation Pyramid represents 26.6% of the U.S. population ages 18–69 in communities with populations of less than 200,000. Chronic Non Voters are the group least likely to improve funding support for libraries. Chronic Non Voters are not registered to vote, or they are registered to vote but report a track record of not voting in primary elections, presidential elections or local elections. Chronic Non Voters are unlikely to be motivated to vote in the future. This segment represents 0% of respondents who said they would *definitely* vote yes in a library referendum.

To gain library voting support from this segment, Chronic Non Voters would first need to be persuaded to register to vote and subsequently motivated to exercise that vote. Increasing voter registration and turnout is an important activity but not a realistic goal for a library support campaign.

Barriers to Support

The three segments in the Barriers to Support tier—the Financially Strapped, the Detached and The Web Wins—have significant barriers to funding their public libraries. This large segment of the population represents a third of all residents ages 18–69 in U.S. communities with populations of less than 200,000. These residents vote, use public library services and are at least modestly involved in their communities. While about half are willing to increase taxes for the fire or police departments, in general they are not supportive of tax increases for other public services, including the public library.

This tier does include a number of people who say they would either *probably* or *definitely* vote yes, but in general their support is unlikely. Any advocacy or marketing campaign for library funding support should recognize the needs of this group, but not target these market segments.

Is it viable to target interested Super Supporters and Probable Supporters to positively impact library funding?

There are sufficient numbers of voters in the Super Supporters and Probable Supporters tiers of the U.S. population—57% of voters in local elections—to potentially increase the success rate of library funding referenda, ballot initiatives and bond measures via a targeted campaign aimed at these groups. This analysis is discussed further in "Chapter 6: Mobilizing Probable and Super Supporters—what makes the difference."

Who are the library's financial supporters?

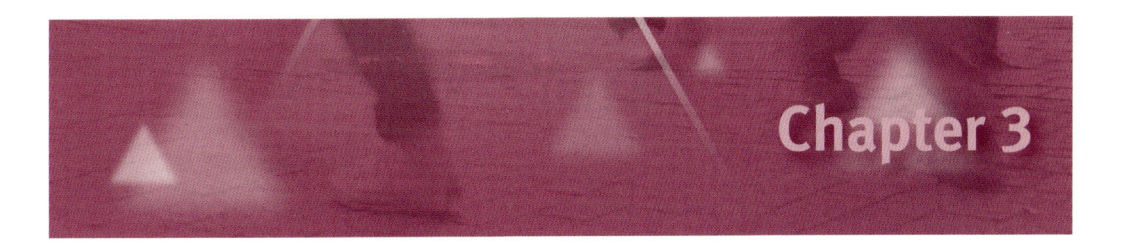

Elected officials and library funding

Understanding the motivations and voting intent of the U.S. population is a critical foundation for developing any initiative aimed at impacting library funding. But an understanding of voter attitudes is only part of the funding environment.

Elected and appointed local government officials play a critical role in determining library funding and their attitudes and behaviors must also be understood. Before residents can vote on a library referendum, elected officials must agree to put the issue on the ballot. And local funding for public libraries is not always decided at the ballot box. In many communities, the public library is allocated a share of the general fund and that allocation is often decided by the locally elected and appointed officials.

Local funding for libraries is not always decided at the ballot box. In many communities public library funds are allocated from general operating funds.

To understand the motivations and behaviors of this important group, elected and appointed officials were also surveyed. Unlike the general population, there are no national survey panels for local officials. A questionnaire for elected officials was administered online and survey participation was solicited via an e-mail sent to subscribers of *Governing* magazine, a monthly magazine whose primary audience is state and local government officials. All qualifying elected officials had some responsibility for making decisions about the local library. The survey was an abbreviated version of the voter questionnaire. Due to the process by which respondents were recruited, they represent a convenience sample that is quantitative but not statistically representative of all local elected officials in the United States.

While the smaller survey data set did not allow for segmentation of elected officials, it did allow for quantified comparisons between elected officials and the public they serve. Eighty-four elected and appointed officials completed the survey.

In addition to the quantitative survey, a number of phone interviews were also conducted with elected officials and political consultants to understand the role the elected official plays in library funding, the attitudes they hold about the library and their perspective on increasing library funding.

The elected and appointed officials surveyed tended to be city managers, city council members or library board members. Most of those who completed the survey were still in office. Half had held their positions for less than five years and expected to remain in their positions for a few more years.

Elected officials surveyed tend to be well-educated males who are employed full-time in addition to their appointed or elected positions. They are long-time residents of their communities and are very involved as members or volunteers in local civic organizations. The officials surveyed are fans of their local libraries and report a higher number of annual library visits than average for the total voting respondents. They see the library as a place where anyone, regardless of race, religion or income, can go to get access to information and technology.

Elected officials have views about the library similar to those of the Probable Supporters. They appreciate the added value librarians offer and see librarians as important figures in rallying community support. Elected officials are knowledgeable about libraries and their value, but they often do not see the library as a necessity for the community. The library is seen as a community 'amenity' rather than a 'must have.'

The research indicates that when weighing budget decisions, elected officials are not fully committed to increasing funding for the library, even though they may feel personally connected to the library. The elected officials surveyed all had some responsibility for making decisions about the public library, but when asked about supporting a local library referendum, only 60% indicate that they would *definitely* support putting a funding measure on the ballot.

This chapter provides an overview of the findings from the quantitative survey and the phone interviews, and presents a slightly different set of profile dimensions than the voter segmentation:

1. Demographic profile
2. Professional situation
3. Library visits
4. Public service support
5. Attitudes toward public libraries
6. Attitudes toward public library funding.

The chapter concludes with advice from elected officials on the required components of a successful library funding campaign.

1. Demographic profile

Elected officials surveyed tend to be well-educated males who are employed full-time in addition to their appointed or elected positions.

Demographic profile
Elected officials

	Total Voting Respondents	Elected Officials
18–29	15%	17%
30–39	20%	12%
40–49	24%	18%
50–59	23%	30%
60–69	19%	20%
Female	50%	33%
Less than $20,000	18%	25%
$20,000–$29,999	12%	9%
$30,000–$39,999	16%	13%
$40,000–$49,999	12%	6%
$50,000–$59,999	10%	6%
$60,000–$74,999	11%	13%
$75,000–$99,999	12%	19%
$100,000 or more	10%	9%
Demographic tendencies		
Completed some high school/high school graduate	27%	21%
Completed some college/college degree	60%	44%
Completed some post-grad/masters/doctorate/professional degree	13%	35%

Source: *From Awareness to Funding*, OCLC, 2008

Elected officials and library funding

2. Professional situation

The elected officials surveyed tend to be city managers, on the city council or on the library board. In most of the communities surveyed, the public library is overseen by a library board.

Most of those who completed the survey are still in office. Half have held their positions for less than five years and most expect to remain in their positions for only a few more years.

Elected officials surveyed tend to be city managers, on the city council or on the library board—most are currently in office

	Elected Officials
Currently holding appointed/elected position	89%
Member of:	
City/town council	24%
Local library board	21%
City manager	17%
School board	7%
Other	31%

Source: *From Awareness to Funding*, OCLC, 2008

Half of the elected officials surveyed have held their positions for less than five years and expect to serve only a few years longer

	Elected Officials
How many years have you HELD this appointed/elected position?	
Less than 3 years	26%
3–4 years	27%
5–9 years	31%
10 years or more	15%
How many more years do you EXPECT to hold an appointed/elected position?	
Less than 3 years	27%
3–4 years	31%
5–9 years	14%
10 years or more	27%

Source: *From Awareness to Funding*, OCLC, 2008

In most of the communities surveyed, a library board oversees the public library

	Elected Officials
Have library board that is responsible for overseeing the public library	88%
Library board is responsible for making:	
Financial and budgetary decisions	65%
Policy and programming decisions	84%

Source: *From Awareness to Funding*, OCLC, 2008

3. Library visits

Elected officials report visiting the library more frequently than average for the voting population. They report 19 visits a year, a similar frequency to the average across Probable Supporters (19.9).

Elected officials report visiting the library more frequently than average for the voting population.

Annual library visits

Probable Supporters: 19.9
Elected Officials: 19.0
Super Supporters: 15.9
Barriers to Support: 6.4
Total Voting Respondents: 13.2

Source: *From Awareness to Funding*, OCLC, 2008

Elected officials and library funding

4. Public service support

The majority of elected officials are reluctant to support a tax increase for local services, including the public library. The elected officials' willingness to increase taxes to fund the seven public services surveyed was low; no services reached 50% support.

The police department receives the highest level of support with 49% of elected officials agreeing that they would be willing to increase taxes.

The public library ranked fifth on the list, with just 40% of elected officials willing to increase taxes to support their public library.

The library ranks in the lower half of a list of public services that elected officials are willing to support with a tax increase

Elected officials

For each service, please rate how much you agree with the phrase "I'd be willing to pay more in local taxes to better fund this service." Please use a 10-point scale, where a 10 means you 'Completely Agree' and a 1 means you 'Completely Disagree.'

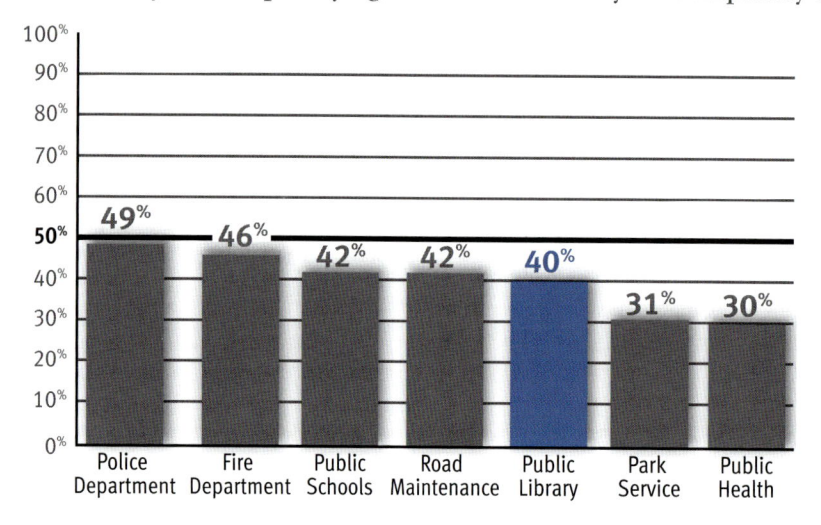

Service	%
Police Department	49%
Fire Department	46%
Public Schools	42%
Road Maintenance	42%
Public Library	40%
Park Service	31%
Public Health	30%

Percentage of elected officials respondents with an agreement rating of 8, 9 or 10
Source: *From Awareness to Funding*, OCLC, 2008

The majority of elected officials are reluctant to support a tax increase for local services, including the public library.

5. Attitudes toward public libraries

Elected officials who participated in the survey are very involved in their local communities. They are also long-term residents of their communities. Local elected officials (68%) are more likely than voters (59%) to have lived in their community for more than 10 years. Elected officials are more likely to be members of a variety of local organizations, including Friends of the Library groups. Forty percent (40%) of elected officials surveyed were members of Friends of the Library, compared to 9% of voters and 11% of Probable Supporters.

Elected officials have a positive opinion of the library, similar to the views held by Probable Supporters. They believe the library plays an important role in the community by providing equal access to information and technology. Elected officials also recognize the positive influence the library has on the community by providing a community gathering place.

Elected officials appreciate the added value the librarians provide to library patrons, and the role librarians play in rallying community support for the library. Seventy-one percent (71%) have a positive impression of the leadership at their local library, yet just half (53%) believe that their local librarian works closely with local politicians and community leaders to find ways to better the community.

Attitudes toward public libraries
Elected officials

For each statement below, please rate your level of agreement on a scale from 1 to 10, where a 10 means 'Agree Strongly' and a 1 means 'Disagree Strongly.'

Elected officials are very involved in their communities

	Total Voting Respond.	Probable Supporters	Elected Officials
Have lived in their city/town for 10 or more years	59%	62%	68%
Member of:			
Local nonprofit organization	17%	23%	45%
Friends of the Library	9%	11%	40%
Chamber of Commerce	4%	6%	38%
Local city board	2%	1%	36%
Neighborhood planning association	6%	6%	21%
Local PTA	8%	8%	17%
Rotary club	3%	1%	15%
League of Women Voters	2%	1%	11%
Local park district board	1%	1%	11%

Percentage of elected officials and voting respondents with an agreement rating of 8, 9 or 10
Source: *From Awareness to Funding*, OCLC, 2008

Elected officials and library funding

Local elected officials have a positive opinion of the public library

	Total Voting Respond.	Probable Supporters	Elected Officials
[Positive] overall impression of the local public library	61%	73%	73%
[Positive] overall impression of the librarians at the local public library	60%	72%	64%
[Positive] overall impression of the leadership at the local public library	—	—	71%

Percentage of elected officials and voting respondents with an agreement rating of 8, 9 or 10
Source: *From Awareness to Funding*, OCLC, 2008

Local elected officials have a positive opinion of the public library.

Elected officials see the library as a key player in providing equal access to information and technology

	Total Voting Respond.	Probable Supporters	Elected Officials
The local public library provides essential resources that some people couldn't otherwise afford	68%	79%	77%
The local public library levels the playing field by providing access to books, technology and special classes for everyone	49%	60%	65%
A lot of people who use the public library in my community don't have Internet access at home	44%	52%	58%
My local public library offers special events and programs that are not offered anywhere else in the community	34%	38%	61%

Percentage of elected officials and voting respondents with an agreement rating of 8, 9 or 10
Source: *From Awareness to Funding*, OCLC, 2008

Local elected officials see the library as a great resource for information technology and activities

The public library:	Total Voting Respond.	Probable Supporters	Elected Officials
Offers access to computer programs/software people don't have at home	51%	59%	61%
Offers access to databases not available on the Internet	39%	40%	53%
Offers activities and entertainment you can't find anywhere else in the community	34%	42%	46%

Percentage of elected officials and voting respondents with an agreement rating of 8, 9 or 10
Source: *From Awareness to Funding*, OCLC, 2008

Elected officials and library funding

Elected officials recognize the library has a positive influence on the community by providing a community gathering place

	Total Voting Respond.	Probable Supporters	Elected Officials
Public libraries can be a preventative measure against crime by providing kids an alternative to the streets	56%	63%	70%
Having a high-quality public library helps raise property values in the community	45%	56%	57%
The public library is a social hub in my community where people frequently get together	18%	19%	37%

Percentage of elected officials and voting respondents with an agreement rating of 8, 9 or 10
Source: *From Awareness to Funding*, OCLC, 2008

Elected officials appreciate the added value librarians offer patrons

The public librarian:	Total Voting Respond.	Probable Supporters	Elected Officials
Really understands how to engage kids with computers and technology	42%	46%	57%
Recommends books that you never would have thought to read otherwise	45%	49%	57%
Develops interesting classes and programs that you can't find anywhere else	34%	39%	49%

Percentage of elected officials and voting respondents with an agreement rating of 8, 9 or 10
Source: *From Awareness to Funding*, OCLC, 2008

Elected officials recognize the library has a positive influence on the community by providing a community gathering place.

Elected officials see librarians as important figures in rallying community support for the library

The public librarian:	Total Voting Respond.	Probable Supporters	Elected Officials
Is passionate about making the public library relevant again	53%	61%	64%
Is committed to rekindling the importance of the public library in the world of technology	50%	58%	59%

Percentage of elected officials and voting respondents with an agreement rating of 8, 9 or 10
Source: *From Awareness to Funding*, OCLC, 2008

Elected officials and library funding

6. Attitudes toward public library funding

Elected officials surveyed report positive opinions and attitudes toward their public libraries and librarians. These positive opinions did not directly translate into increased financial support for the library.

All elected officials who participated in the survey had some responsibility for making decisions about the local library. When asked about supporting a local library referendum, 60% indicate they would *definitely* support putting a library funding measure on the ballot.

While elected officials are more likely than the voting public to recognize the financial struggles the library faces, the majority (73%) think the library has enough money for day-to-day operations.

While many of the elected officials report that their local libraries have Friends of the Library chapters (to which many elected officials surveyed belong) they do not feel these groups are effective in raising funds.

Attitudes toward public library funding
Elected officials

For each statement below, please rate your level of agreement on a scale from 1 to 10, where a 10 means 'Agree Strongly' and a 1 means 'Disagree Strongly.'

Elected officials are more likely than voters to recognize library financial needs; yet 73% believe the library has sufficient operating funds

	Total Voting Respond.	Probable Supporters	Elected Officials
My local library doesn't have enough money for day-to-day operations	14%	10%	27%

Percentage of elected officials and voting respondents with an agreement rating of 8, 9 or 10
Source: *From Awareness to Funding*, OCLC, 2008

73% of local elected officials believe the library has sufficient operating funds.

Elected officials tend to think their communities could afford a tax increase

	Total Voting Respond.	Probable Supporters	Elected Officials
The local government in my community tends to make responsible financial decisions	24%	22%	56%
I support tax increases that will improve my community	37%	38%	61%
I feel like I/my community pays too much in property taxes	41%	31%	33%
People in my community can't afford to have their taxes raised	45%	40%	33%
I feel like there's a lot of waste in local government spending	58%	54%	30%

Percentage of elected officials and voting respondents with an agreement rating of 8, 9 or 10
Source: *From Awareness to Funding*, OCLC, 2008

Elected officials and library funding

Half the elected officials surveyed believe that librarians work closely with community leaders

	Total Voting Respond.	Probable Supporters	Elected Officials
The public librarian works closely with other community leaders to find ways to better the community	38%	42%	53%
The public librarian works closely with local politicians and community leaders to get public library funding and support	41%	45%	53%
Elected officials in my community strongly support the local public library	30%	31%	43%

Percentage of elected officials and voting respondents with an agreement rating of 8, 9 or 10
Source: *From Awareness to Funding*, OCLC, 2008

Over half of elected officials surveyed state that they would *definitely* support putting a local library funding measure on the ballot

	Total Voting Respond.	Probable Supporters	Elected Officials
Would definitely support putting a library referendum, ballot initiative or bond measure on the ballot	37%*	47%*	60%

*Would *definitely* vote yes
Percentage of elected officials and voting respondents with an agreement rating of 8, 9 or 10
Source: *From Awareness to Funding*, OCLC, 2008

Elected officials do not view voluntary fund-raising for libraries as effective

	Total Voting Respond.	Probable Supporters	Elected Officials
Public library has a voluntary fund-raising group such as Friends of the Library	49%	57%	81%
Please rate how effective the fund-raising group for your local library is at gaining community and financial support for the public library	—	—	46%

Percentage of elected officials and voting respondents with an agreement rating of 8, 9 or 10
Source: *From Awareness to Funding*, OCLC, 2008

Advice from elected officials

Elected officials involved in library funding initiatives offered important advice and suggestions for increasing library funding in their communities.

Stress the library's return on investment (ROI) to the community

The elected officials acknowledge and appreciate the public library's value to their community, often referring to this as the return on investment, or ROI, of the library. Officials noted that the library's ROI is often unique to a community and can change over time. This value ranges from keeping children off the street (Salinas, California) to education of residents leading to wealth creation for the community (Boise, Idaho). Officials also speak frequently of the universal and important role libraries play in providing access to technology for the broader community.

Build strategic partnerships

Elected officials interviewed believe that the libraries have a funding challenge, but admit that the library often falls lower in the pecking order for financing than other public services, particularly public safety. Finding opportunities to partner or create joint ventures with other public services and programs increases the level of elected official support.

Be proactive

Although elected officials recognize the need for increased library funding, they are rarely, if ever, the first to push for increased funding support for libraries. The new library projects they mentioned were typically initiated by a passionate and committed library director, a small group of voters or by private groups including Friends of the Library organizations.

Engage voters in the campaign

Elected officials said that they and their colleagues are most likely to be influenced to support an increase in library funding in response to pressure from their constituents. There is an opportunity to influence the elected officials (in the same way as Probable Supporters) by leveraging their recognition of the library's value to the community.

Stress the broad appeal of the library

Elected officials can take on the cause of the library without substantially alienating or competing with another core group of funders or political party supporters. The public library represents a safe, neutral topic on which an elected official could campaign or speak with broad appeal to nonpartisan audiences.

Elected officials on library funding campaigns

Elected officials cited a number of important components required of a successful library funding campaign:

- Messaging that focuses on the broader value of the library to the community, specifically a community gathering place, access to technology and programs for teenagers and other groups

- A passionate, committed and active champion(s) who can rally support among the elected officials and community influencers

- Civic engagement, including a commitment to speak with every relevant group in the community to encourage grassroots support

- A willingness to partner with other public services in a joint effort where strategically advantageous

- The ability to ask for the right support at the right time:
    - Voter turnout is greater for general elections than local elections
    - It is often easier to campaign for a new building than for operating funds.

Chapter 4

Library funding support is an attitude, not a demographic

Library funding behavior is driven by attitudes and beliefs, not by demographics. Voters' perceptions of the role the library plays in their lives and in their communities are more important determinants of their willingness to increase funding than their age, gender, race, political affiliation, life stage or income level. The more that can be learned about library perceptions, the better the chances of constructing a successful library support campaign to improve library funding.

The Library Supporter Segmentation discussed in Chapter 2 identified important constructs that drive a voter's willingness to support an increase in library funding. The quantitative research uncovered many additional and related insights into voters' attitudes toward libraries.

This chapter will explore eight key insights:

1. **Most people claim they would support the library at the ballot box—fewer are firmly committed to it.**
2. **There is a lot that people don't know about their public libraries.**
3. **Library support is only marginally related to visitation. Advocating for library support to library users focuses effort and energy on the wrong target group.**
4. **Perceptions of the librarian are highly related to support. 'Passionate librarians' who are involved in the community make a difference.**
5. **The library occupies a very clear position in people's minds as a provider of practical answers and information. This is a very crowded space, and to remain relevant in today's information landscape, repositioning will be required.**
6. **Belief that the library is a transformational force in people's lives is directly related to their level of funding support.**
7. **Increasing support for libraries may not necessarily mean a trade-off with financial support for other public services.**
8. **Elected officials are supportive of the library—but not fully committed to increasing funding. Engaging Super Supporters and Probable Supporters to help elevate library funding needs is required.**

Library funding support is an attitude, not a demographic

1. Most people claim they would support the library at the ballot box—fewer are firmly committed to it.

"Think ahead to the next election and assume that you were at the ballot box, ready to cast your vote. If there was a referendum, ballot initiative or bond measure for your local public library on the ballot, how do you think you would vote?"

A. I would definitely vote in favor of it

B. I would probably vote in favor of it

C. I may vote either way

D. I would probably vote against it

E. I would definitely vote against it

Just 3% of the voting respondents indicate that they would *probably* or *definitely* vote against a library levy when they were asked this question in the survey. A strong 74% had a favorable response, stating that they would *probably* or *definitely* vote yes and 23% may vote either way. But of those who indicated that they would probably or definitely vote in favor, the strength of commitment was evenly split. Thirty-seven percent (37%) of residents said they would *probably* vote yes. An equal 37% indicated they would *definitely* vote yes—a strong showing, but not enough to carry an election.

Only 37% of voters say that they will *definitely* support the library at the ballot box

Total Voting Respondents

If there was a referendum, ballot initiative or bond measure for your local public library on the ballot, how do you think you would vote?

- Definitely vote yes
- Probably vote yes
- Definitely vote no, probably vote no, or may vote either way

Definitely vote yes: 37%
Probably vote yes: 37%
Definitely vote no, probably vote no, or may vote either way: 26%

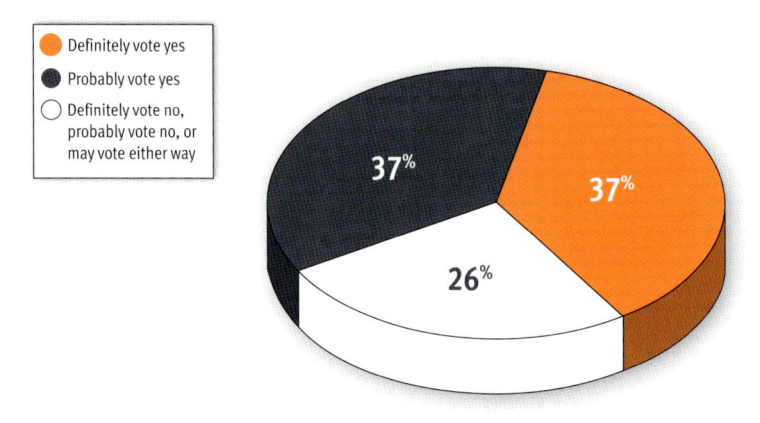

Source: *From Awareness to Funding*, OCLC, 2008

Relying on the *probably* favorable support of voters for funding libraries is not sufficient to drive the needed outcome at the polls. As discussed in Chapter 2, understanding and identifying which voters have barriers to supporting library funding, which voters are *probable* supporters and which voters are *definite* funding supporters is critical to mounting a successful library support campaign.

The segmentation analysis revealed that *definite* support varies across segments of the voting population and this formed the basis of the stratification of the Library Supporter Segmentation Pyramid. There is a measurable increase in the percentage of voters who are *definitely* likely to vote yes in a library referendum in upper tiers of the segmentation pyramid. The proportion of voters who will *definitely* vote yes for a library referendum is greatest in the top two tiers. Forty-seven percent (47%) of Probable Supporters indicate that they would *definitely* vote yes on a library levy; 80% of Super Supporters are *definite* library supporters.

'*Definitely* vote yes' is a critical measure of which voters are truly committed to providing financial support to the library

Total Voting Respondents

If there was a referendum, ballot initiative or bond measure for your local public library on the ballot, how do you think you would vote?

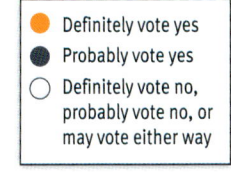

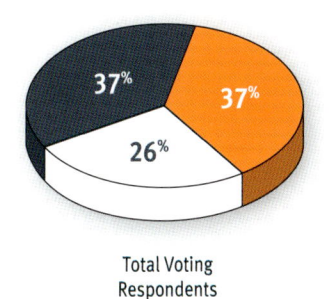

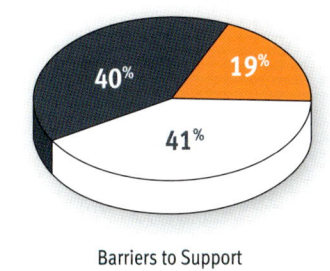

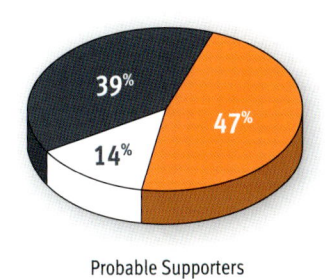

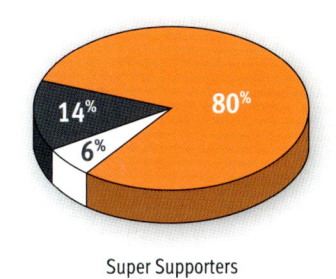

- Definitely vote yes
- Probably vote yes
- Definitely vote no, probably vote no, or may vote either way

	Total Voting Respondents	Barriers to Support	Probable Supporters	Super Supporters
Definitely vote yes	37%	19%	47%	80%
Probably vote yes	37%	40%	39%	14%
Definitely/probably no or either way	26%	41%	14%	6%

Source: *From Awareness to Funding*, OCLC, 2008

A library support campaign targeted at voters in the top two segmentation tiers has a much higher likelihood of success in increasing the percentage of 'yes' votes than a campaign that attempts to reach the broader population.

Library funding support is an attitude, not a demographic

2. There is a lot that people don't know about their public libraries.

People are generally unaware of many of the services provided by their local libraries. Respondents indicate awareness of traditional offerings: books, newspapers and magazines, photocopiers, videos/DVDs, etc. And the majority of respondents are aware of services providing public access computing and Internet access. However, respondents have much lower awareness of many of the value-added community-focused programs, such as programming for seniors and teens, literacy training and book discussion groups. Awareness of the availability of online databases, electronic books and electronic journals/magazines is also low, despite the growing proportion of the public library's collections budget spent on electronic content.

Awareness of services provided by the local public library
Total Respondents

Below are some services or types of information that public libraries may or may not offer. For each one, please indicate whether or not your local public library offers this.

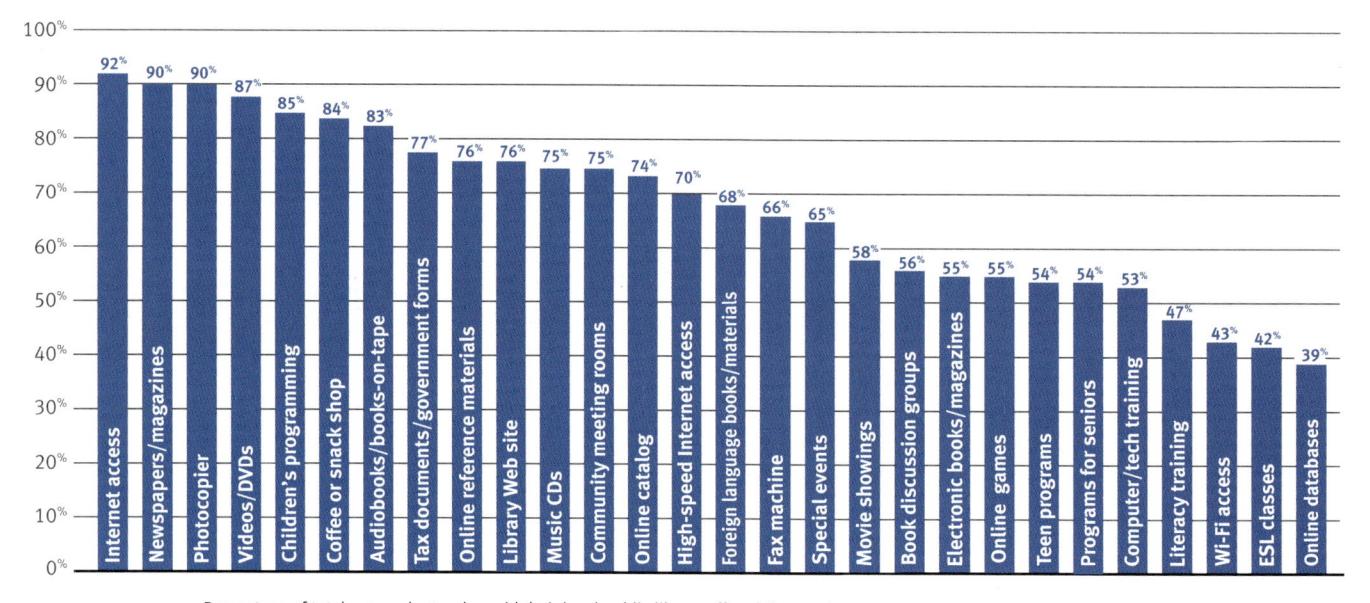

Service	%
Internet access	92%
Newspapers/magazines	90%
Photocopier	90%
Videos/DVDs	87%
Children's programming	85%
Coffee or snack shop	84%
Audiobooks/books-on-tape	83%
Tax documents/government forms	77%
Online reference materials	76%
Library Web site	76%
Music CDs	75%
Community meeting rooms	75%
Online catalog	74%
High-speed Internet access	70%
Foreign language books/materials	68%
Fax machine	66%
Special events	65%
Movie showings	58%
Book discussion groups	56%
Electronic books/magazines	55%
Online games	55%
Teen programs	54%
Programs for seniors	54%
Computer/tech training	53%
Literacy training	47%
Wi-Fi access	43%
ESL classes	42%
Online databases	39%

Percentage of total respondents who said their local public library offered the service
Source: *From Awareness to Funding*, OCLC, 2008

An important insight uncovered by the research is that this lack of awareness may not be a deterrent for funding support. Unfamiliarity with the full range of library services does not dampen the positive attitudes about library funding held by Probable Supporters and Super Supporters. Even when unaware of the range of programs offered by their libraries, Probable Supporters and Super Supporters view the library as an important asset to the community. Familiarity with the full range of library services was not a determinant of library funding support for the library's top funding supporters.

Library funding support is an attitude, not a demographic

3. Library support is only marginally related to visitation. Advocating for library support to library users focuses effort and energy on the wrong target group.

Frequency of library visitation is not a determinant of funding support.

Respondents were asked how often they visited their local public library in the past 12 months. On average, the voting respondents visited their library 13.2 times annually. While overall visitation rates indicate that voters are users of the library, analysis indicates that the frequency of library visits has almost no relationship to a respondent's willingness to support the library at the ballot box. In fact, the correlation between frequency of visitation and library funding support was only 0.06. (A correlation of 0 would indicate no relationship.)

There is no correlation between frequency of library visits and library funding support.

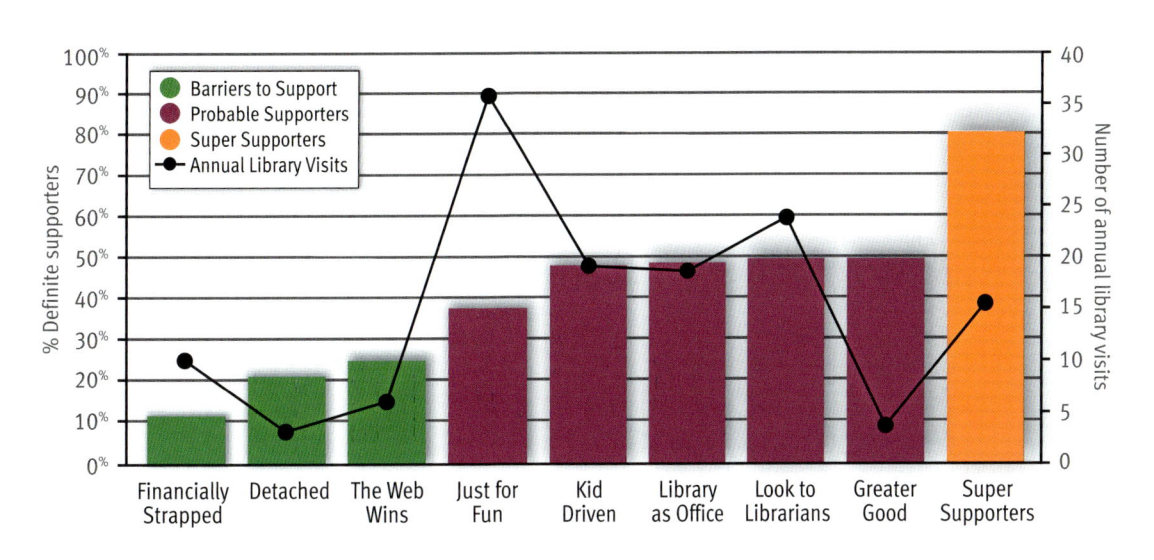

Library visitation and *definite* library support by segment
Total Voting Respondents

How many times have you visited your local public library in the past 12 months?

If there was a referendum, ballot initiative or bond measure for your local public library on the ballot, how do you think you would vote?

Percentage of voting respondents who would *definitely* vote 'yes' for a library referendum
Source: *From Awareness to Funding*, OCLC, 2008

From Awareness to Funding: A study of library support in America

Library funding support is an attitude, not a demographic

To illustrate the important finding that library support is not driven, or limited, by frequency of library visits, consider the usage and support profiles for two of the segments, Super Supporters and Just for Fun.

The most committed library funding supporters, the Super Supporters, do not visit the library any more frequently than other segments. Super Supporters show the greatest commitment to library funding support—almost three times the average—yet their frequency of library visits is only slightly above average.

Super Supporters account for, by far, the most financial support for libraries despite only somewhat higher usage

Super Supporters segment

If there was a referendum, ballot initiative or bond measure for your local public library on the ballot, how do you think you would vote?

How many times have you visited your local public library in the past 12 months?

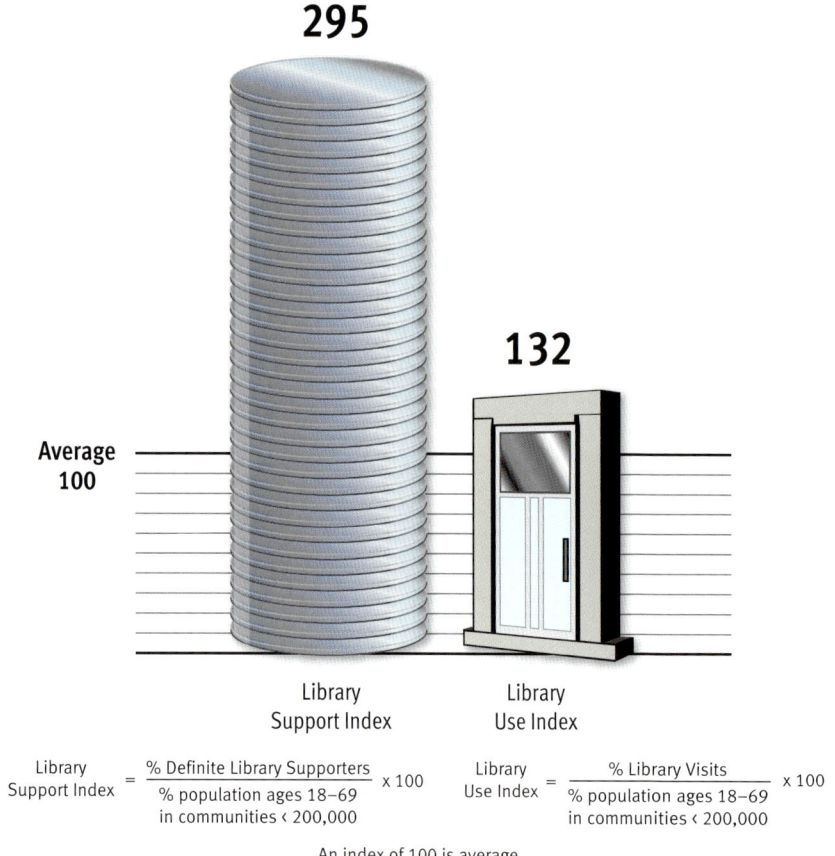

295

132

Average 100

Library Support Index

Library Use Index

$$\text{Library Support Index} = \frac{\%\ \text{Definite Library Supporters}}{\%\ \text{population ages 18-69 in communities} < 200{,}000} \times 100$$

$$\text{Library Use Index} = \frac{\%\ \text{Library Visits}}{\%\ \text{population ages 18-69 in communities} < 200{,}000} \times 100$$

An index of 100 is average
Source: *From Awareness to Funding*, OCLC, 2008

Conversely, the Just for Fun segment of Probable Supporters reports by far the most frequent use of the library with more than three times the average. However, this segment is only somewhat more likely than average to *definitely* vote in favor of a library funding measure.

The most frequent library visitors are not the right target market for a library funding campaign. Library support is driven by voter attitudes and beliefs, not by awareness of library services or the frequency of library usage.

Just for Fun respondents are the heaviest users but the least likely of the Probable Supporters to *definitely* vote to fund the library

Just for Fun segment

If there was a referendum, ballot initiative or bond measure for your local public library on the ballot, how do you think you would vote?

How many times have you visited your local public library in the past 12 months?

The most frequent library visitors are not the right target market for a library funding campaign.

336

136

Average 100

Library Support Index

Library Use Index

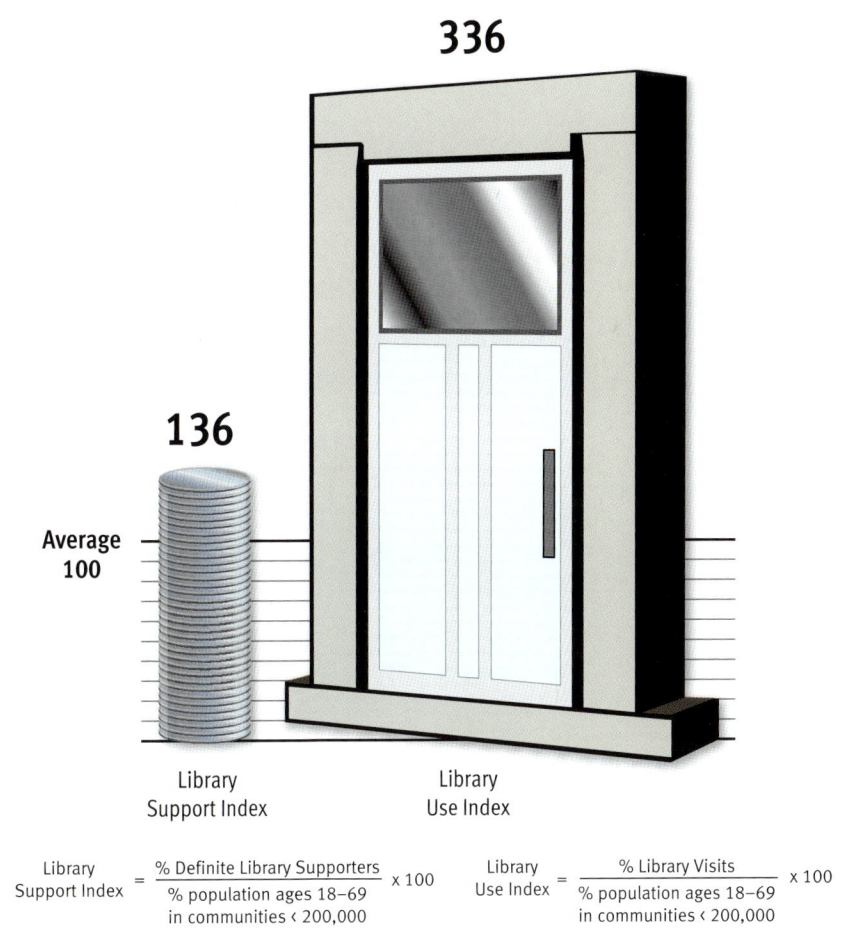

$$\text{Library Support Index} = \frac{\text{\% Definite Library Supporters}}{\text{\% population ages 18–69 in communities < 200,000}} \times 100$$

$$\text{Library Use Index} = \frac{\text{\% Library Visits}}{\text{\% population ages 18–69 in communities < 200,000}} \times 100$$

An index of 100 is average
Source: *From Awareness to Funding*, OCLC, 2008

Library funding support is an attitude, not a demographic

4. Perceptions of the librarian are highly related to support. 'Passionate librarians' who are involved in the community make a difference.

While frequency of library visitation and awareness of the full range of library services are not key determinants of library funding support, respondents' perceptions of the public librarian have a strong influence on funding support. Survey respondents rated the librarians at their local public libraries across a number of attributes. Analysis of the responses shows that a strong positive rating for the librarian across five of these attributes has a strong influence on library funding support. These five attributes can be combined to describe the 'passionate librarian':

- True advocate for lifelong learning
- Passionate about making the library relevant again
- Knowledgeable about every aspect of the library
- Well-educated
- Knowledgeable about the community.

Perceptions of the public librarian have a strong influence on funding support.

The 'passionate librarian' and *definite* library support
Total Voting Respondents

Please rate the librarians at the public library in your community on the following traits using a 10-point scale, where a 10 means 'Describes them extremely well' and a 1 means 'Doesn't describe them at all.'

If there was a referendum, ballot initiative or bond measure for your local public library on the ballot, how do you think you would vote?

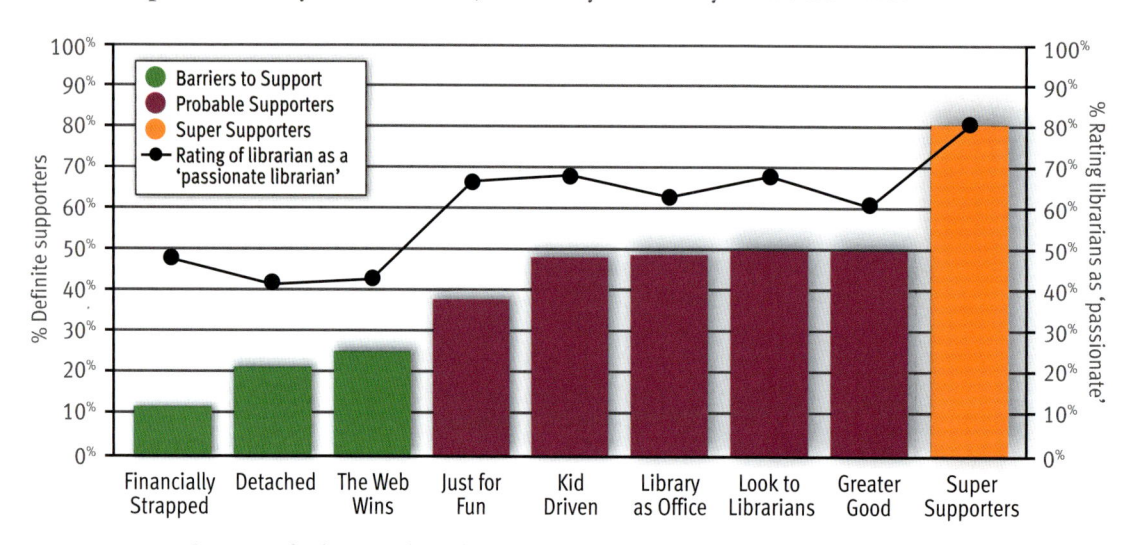

Percentage of voting respondents who would *definitely* vote 'yes' for a library referendum
Percentage of voting respondents who rated their librarian as a 'Passionate Librarian' with an agreement rating of 8, 9 or 10
Source: *From Awareness to Funding*, OCLC, 2008

4-8   From Awareness to Funding: A study of library support in America

Voters who rate the librarian highly on the traits that comprise the 'passionate librarian' are more likely to say they would *definitely* vote yes for a library referendum, ballot initiative or bond measure.

Super Supporters have the highest percentage of respondents (81%) who rate the librarians at their local public libraries highly on the attributes that make up the 'passionate librarian.' The percentage of voters who fall into the Barriers to Support tier of the segmentation pyramid who rate their local librarians highly against the 'passionate librarian' attributes is significantly less at just 45%.

5. The library occupies a very clear position in people's minds as a provider of practical answers and information. This is a very crowded space, and to remain relevant in today's information landscape, repositioning will be required.

The research survey explored how voters perceive the library relative to other brands, categories and activities that could potentially provide similar services, intellectual experiences or emotional benefits. The goal was to understand the emotional and intellectual rewards attributed to the library and analyze the position the library holds in the mind of potential voters relative to possible alternatives.

Respondents rated their local public libraries in terms of how well they provided a number of different intellectual and emotional rewards. For example, respondents rated the library's ability to 'help you make informed decisions,' 'provide an escape from your own world' or 'make you feel safe and secure.'

Respondents also rated other brands, categories and activities that could potentially provide the same rewards, e.g., *Encyclopedia Britannica*, watching a documentary, reading blogs, traveling to a foreign country, Wikipedia.com, or visiting a museum or an art gallery.

Using a correspondence analysis technique, data across all the emotional and intellectual rewards were analyzed to understand how public libraries performed and how they compared to alternatives. Responses were analyzed and mapped on a two-dimensional framework, the Emotional and Intellectual Rewards Framework.

The axes that define the Emotional and Intellectual Rewards Framework were not predetermined, just as the segmentation pyramid tiers and segments were not predetermined but were driven by the survey data.

Library funding support is an attitude, not a demographic

The Emotional and Intellectual Rewards Framework

Correspondence analysis provides a framework for understanding the intellectual and emotional rewards provided by the U.S. public library relative to possible alternative brands, categories or activities. The data analysis resulted in a two-by-two framework with four defining axis points—'Transformation,' 'Information,' 'Purpose' and 'Escape.'

The x axis—the range of intellectual and emotional rewards perceived to be provided by a service relative to its ability to transform, 'Transformation,' or its ability to inform, 'Information.'

- Emotional and intellectual rewards most closely related to **Transformation** are plotted on the left half of the framework. These include such attributes as 'helps you create who you are' and 'enables you to be a more creative person.'
- Emotional and intellectual rewards most closely related to **Information** are plotted on the right half of the framework. These include such attributes as 'provides do-it-yourself information' and 'helps you be the first one to know things.'

The y axis—the range of intellectual and emotional rewards perceived to be provided by a service relative to its ability to support a practical goal, 'Purpose,' or its ability to provide an escape from everyday life, 'Escape.'

- Emotional and intellectual rewards most closely related to **Purpose** are plotted on the bottom half of the framework. These include such attributes as 'helps you make informed decisions' and 'helps you become an authority in your field.'
- Emotional and intellectual rewards most closely related to **Escape** are plotted on the top half of the framework. These include such attributes as 'dramatic and exciting' and 'an oasis from hectic lifestyles.'

Emotional and Intellectual Rewards Framework
Total Voting Respondents

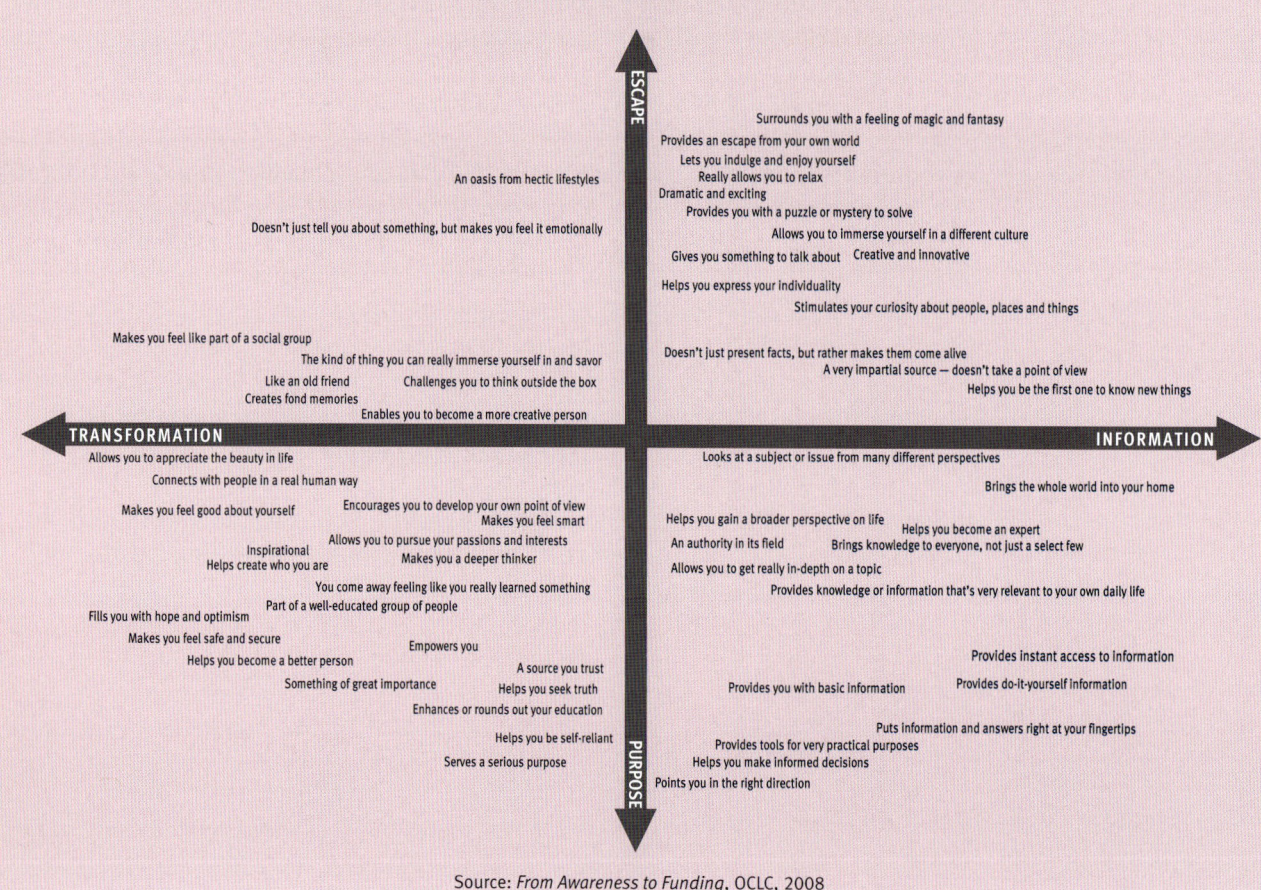

Source: *From Awareness to Funding*, OCLC, 2008

Library funding support is an attitude, not a demographic

All brands, categories and activities rated by the survey respondents were plotted on the Emotional and Intellectual Rewards Framework. These brands and categories included Starbucks, The History Channel, YouTube.com, attending theater/ballet/symphony, getting a college degree and visiting the public library. Their relative position on the framework below corresponds to the emotional and intellectual rewards derived from performing that activity or using that service. For example, 'watching a documentary' is associated by respondents with the rewards 'makes you feel smart,' 'helps you gain a broader perspective on life' and 'helps you become an expert.' 'Playing video/computer games' is associated by respondents with 'surrounds you with a feeling of magic and fantasy.' And the brand 'Starbucks' is associated with emotional rewards of 'enables you to become a more creative person' and 'challenges you to think outside the box.'

Emotional and Intellectual Rewards for the Public Library
Total Voting Respondents

Please rate how well the words or phrases describe the selected brands/categories/activities using a 10-point scale, where a 10 means 'Describes it very well' and a 1 means 'Doesn't describe it at all.'

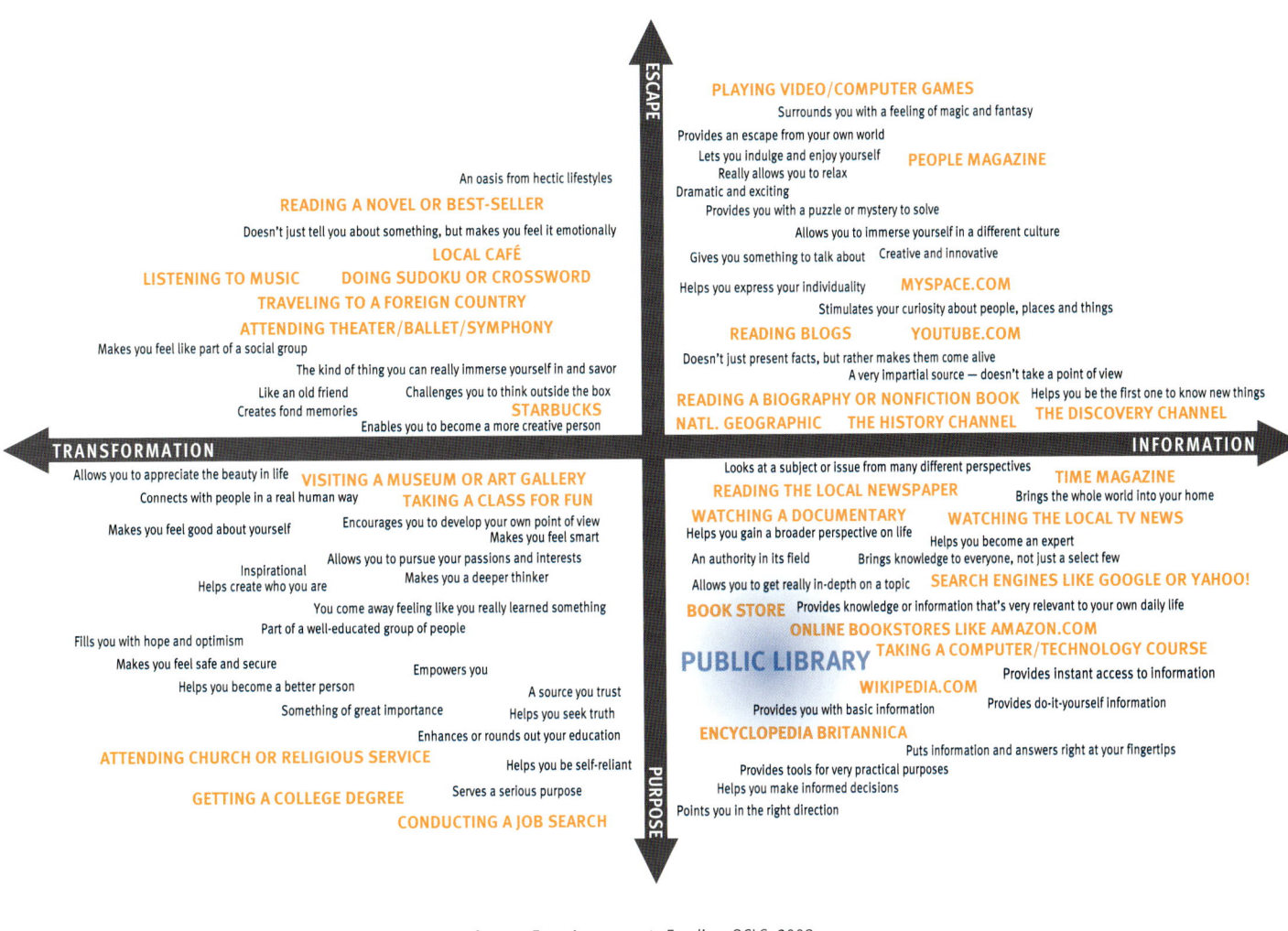

[Four-quadrant framework chart with axes: ESCAPE (top), PURPOSE (bottom), TRANSFORMATION (left), INFORMATION (right)]

Escape/Transformation quadrant (upper left):
- An oasis from hectic lifestyles
- READING A NOVEL OR BEST-SELLER
- Doesn't just tell you about something, but makes you feel it emotionally
- LOCAL CAFÉ
- LISTENING TO MUSIC   DOING SUDOKU OR CROSSWORD
- TRAVELING TO A FOREIGN COUNTRY
- ATTENDING THEATER/BALLET/SYMPHONY
- Makes you feel like part of a social group
- The kind of thing you can really immerse yourself in and savor
- Like an old friend   Challenges you to think outside the box
- Creates fond memories   STARBUCKS
- Enables you to become a more creative person

Escape/Information quadrant (upper right):
- PLAYING VIDEO/COMPUTER GAMES
- Surrounds you with a feeling of magic and fantasy
- Provides an escape from your own world
- Lets you indulge and enjoy yourself   PEOPLE MAGAZINE
- Really allows you to relax
- Dramatic and exciting
- Provides you with a puzzle or mystery to solve
- Allows you to immerse yourself in a different culture
- Gives you something to talk about   Creative and innovative
- Helps you express your individuality   MYSPACE.COM
- Stimulates your curiosity about people, places and things
- READING BLOGS   YOUTUBE.COM
- Doesn't just present facts, but rather makes them come alive
- A very impartial source — doesn't take a point of view
- READING A BIOGRAPHY OR NONFICTION BOOK   Helps you be the first one to know new things
- NATL. GEOGRAPHIC   THE HISTORY CHANNEL   THE DISCOVERY CHANNEL

Transformation/Purpose quadrant (lower left):
- Allows you to appreciate the beauty in life   VISITING A MUSEUM OR ART GALLERY
- Connects with people in a real human way   TAKING A CLASS FOR FUN
- Encourages you to develop your own point of view
- Makes you feel good about yourself   Makes you feel smart
- Allows you to pursue your passions and interests
- Inspirational   Makes you a deeper thinker
- Helps create who you are
- You come away feeling like you really learned something
- Part of a well-educated group of people
- Fills you with hope and optimism
- Makes you feel safe and secure   Empowers you
- Helps you become a better person   A source you trust
- Something of great importance   Helps you seek truth
- Enhances or rounds out your education
- ATTENDING CHURCH OR RELIGIOUS SERVICE   Helps you be self-reliant
- GETTING A COLLEGE DEGREE   Serves a serious purpose
- CONDUCTING A JOB SEARCH

Information/Purpose quadrant (lower right):
- Looks at a subject or issue from many different perspectives   TIME MAGAZINE
- READING THE LOCAL NEWSPAPER   Brings the whole world into your home
- WATCHING A DOCUMENTARY   WATCHING THE LOCAL TV NEWS
- Helps you gain a broader perspective on life   Helps you become an expert
- An authority in its field   Brings knowledge to everyone, not just a select few
- Allows you to get really in-depth on a topic   SEARCH ENGINES LIKE GOOGLE OR YAHOO!
- BOOK STORE   Provides knowledge or information that's very relevant to your own daily life
- ONLINE BOOKSTORES LIKE AMAZON.COM
- **PUBLIC LIBRARY**   TAKING A COMPUTER/TECHNOLOGY COURSE
- WIKIPEDIA.COM   Provides instant access to information
- Provides you with basic information   Provides do-it-yourself information
- ENCYCLOPEDIA BRITANNICA
- Puts information and answers right at your fingertips
- Provides tools for very practical purposes
- Helps you make informed decisions
- Points you in the right direction

Source: *From Awareness to Funding*, OCLC, 2008

Library funding support is an attitude, not a demographic

The public library is associated by respondents with the intellectual and emotional rewards represented in the lower-right-hand quadrant. The library is perceived as a service that provides 'information with a purpose.' As the framework illustrates, this perceptual territory, 'information with a purpose,' is a very crowded space. There are many other information and learning services located in the same quadrant including Wikipedia.com, online bookstores like Amazon.com, search engines and bookstores. These brands and services are redefining the role and definition of information.

The public library historically 'owned' the emotional and intellectual dimension of purposeful information, sharing the perceptual space with relatively few alternatives. But since the advent of the Internet, this is no longer the case. Competition for the information seeker's business and loyalty is intense. The public library now shares its 'information with a purpose' quadrant with many alternatives. And many of these alternatives are spending significant financial resources to solidify their positioning.

The research suggests that the public library's strong associations as a 'place for information' may not only limit the library's ability to gain mindshare and marketshare with information seekers, but the current positioning may also be one of the factors hampering the success of library funding initiatives.

The research indicates that transformation, not information, drives financial support.

The library is perceived as a service that provides 'information with a purpose,' a very crowded space.

6. Belief that the library is a transformational force in people's lives is directly related to their level of funding support.

Aggregation of results across all survey respondents indicates that the public library is viewed as a service that provides the emotional and intellectual rewards of 'purposeful information.' But a review of results of those voters who said they would *definitely* vote in favor of a library referendum provides a very important distinction.

The degree to which the public library was perceived as transformational is significantly higher among the most committed funding supporters (voters who said they would *definitely* vote yes for a library referendum, ballot initiative or bond measure). There are 16 emotional or intellectual rewards that the most committed funding supporters associate with the public library. Of this list of 16 attributes, half are in the 'purposeful transformation' quadrant of the Emotional and Intellectual Rewards Framework:

- Helps create who you are
- Makes you feel good about yourself
- Allows you to appreciate the beauty in life
- You come away feeling like you really learned something
- Fills you with hope and optimism
- Empowers you
- Helps you seek truth
- Serves a serious purpose.

Belief that the library is a self-actualization tool is directly related to level of funding support.

Perceptions of the public library held by people who will *definitely* vote in support of library funding

Respondents who would definitely vote yes for a library referendum

Please rate how well the words or phrases describe the selected brands/categories/activities using a 10-point scale, where a 10 means 'Describes it very well' and a 1 means 'Doesn't describe it at all.'

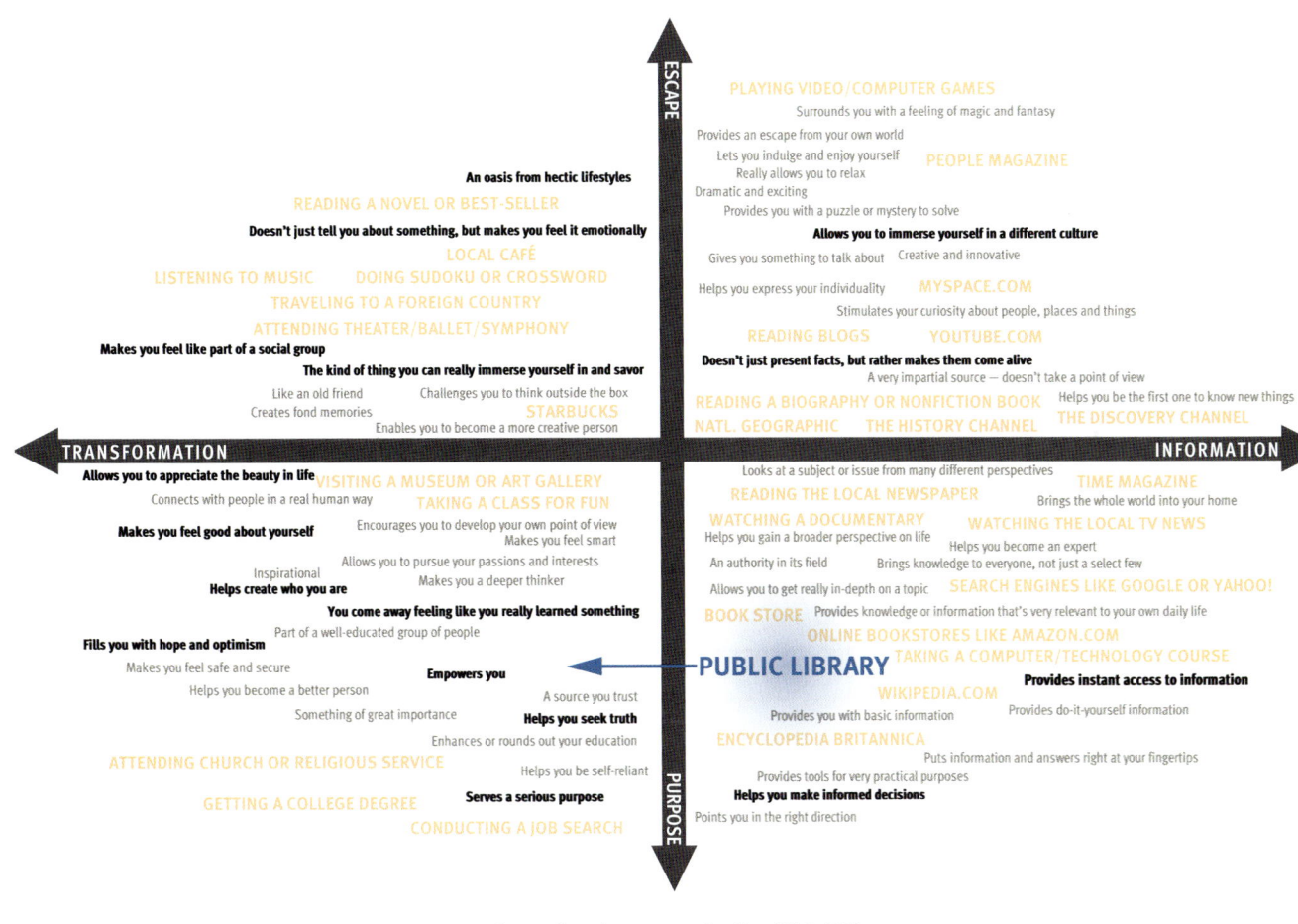

ESCAPE (upper axis)
- PLAYING VIDEO/COMPUTER GAMES
- Surrounds you with a feeling of magic and fantasy
- Provides an escape from your own world
- Lets you indulge and enjoy yourself
- Really allows you to relax
- PEOPLE MAGAZINE
- Dramatic and exciting
- Provides you with a puzzle or mystery to solve
- An oasis from hectic lifestyles
- READING A NOVEL OR BEST-SELLER
- Allows you to immerse yourself in a different culture
- Doesn't just tell you about something, but makes you feel it emotionally
- LOCAL CAFÉ
- Gives you something to talk about   Creative and innovative
- LISTENING TO MUSIC   DOING SUDOKU OR CROSSWORD
- Helps you express your individuality   MYSPACE.COM
- TRAVELING TO A FOREIGN COUNTRY
- Stimulates your curiosity about people, places and things
- ATTENDING THEATER/BALLET/SYMPHONY
- READING BLOGS   YOUTUBE.COM
- Makes you feel like part of a social group
- Doesn't just present facts, but rather makes them come alive
- The kind of thing you can really immerse yourself in and savor
- A very impartial source — doesn't take a point of view
- Like an old friend   Challenges you to think outside the box
- Helps you be the first one to know new things
- Creates fond memories   STARBUCKS
- READING A BIOGRAPHY OR NONFICTION BOOK   THE DISCOVERY CHANNEL
- Enables you to become a more creative person
- NATL. GEOGRAPHIC   THE HISTORY CHANNEL

TRANSFORMATION ← → INFORMATION

- Allows you to appreciate the beauty in life
- Looks at a subject or issue from many different perspectives
- TIME MAGAZINE
- Connects with people in a real human way   VISITING A MUSEUM OR ART GALLERY
- READING THE LOCAL NEWSPAPER
- Brings the whole world into your home
- TAKING A CLASS FOR FUN   WATCHING A DOCUMENTARY   WATCHING THE LOCAL TV NEWS
- Makes you feel good about yourself
- Encourages you to develop your own point of view
- Helps you gain a broader perspective on life
- Makes you feel smart   Helps you become an expert
- An authority in its field   Brings knowledge to everyone, not just a select few
- Allows you to pursue your passions and interests
- Inspirational   Makes you a deeper thinker
- Allows you to get really in-depth on a topic   SEARCH ENGINES LIKE GOOGLE OR YAHOO!
- Helps create who you are
- You come away feeling like you really learned something
- BOOK STORE   Provides knowledge or information that's very relevant to your own daily life
- Part of a well-educated group of people
- ONLINE BOOKSTORES LIKE AMAZON.COM
- Fills you with hope and optimism
- **PUBLIC LIBRARY**   TAKING A COMPUTER/TECHNOLOGY COURSE
- Makes you feel safe and secure
- Empowers you   WIKIPEDIA.COM   Provides instant access to information
- Helps you become a better person
- A source you trust   Provides do-it-yourself information
- Something of great importance   Helps you seek truth
- Provides you with basic information
- Enhances or rounds out your education
- ENCYCLOPEDIA BRITANNICA
- ATTENDING CHURCH OR RELIGIOUS SERVICE
- Puts information and answers right at your fingertips
- Helps you be self-reliant
- Provides tools for very practical purposes
- GETTING A COLLEGE DEGREE   Serves a serious purpose
- Helps you make informed decisions
- CONDUCTING A JOB SEARCH
- Points you in the right direction

PURPOSE (lower axis)

Source: *From Awareness to Funding*, OCLC, 2008

The most likely library funding supporters do not view the library as a source of information, but rather as a source for transformation. Even the rewards identified by *definite* library supporters that are more associated with information, such as 'allows you to immerse yourself in another culture' and 'doesn't just present facts, but rather helps them come alive,' provide useful insights into the mindset held by this group.

The associations held by the stronger financial supporters are connections that are both personal and community-oriented. Leveraging the perception of the library as a transformational force for both individuals and the community is a powerful motivator. A library support campaign must aim to reposition the library as a transformational influence in the minds of Probable Supporters and elected officials. More will be discussed about this connection in "Chapter 6: Mobilizing Probable and Super Supporters—what makes the difference."

Library funding support is an attitude, not a demographic

7. Increasing support for libraries may not necessarily mean a trade-off of financial support for other public services.

Analysis of local funding for public libraries and other public services shows that the public library receives just under 1% of the total local operating budget (source: U.S. Census Bureau). This percentage has remained relatively constant over the last several years. The question arises, then, whether it is appropriate or advisable to mount a concerted effort to increase library funding and, if successful, will such an increase take dollars away from other local services? The research suggests that a funding trade-off may not be necessary.

2004 local government expenditure

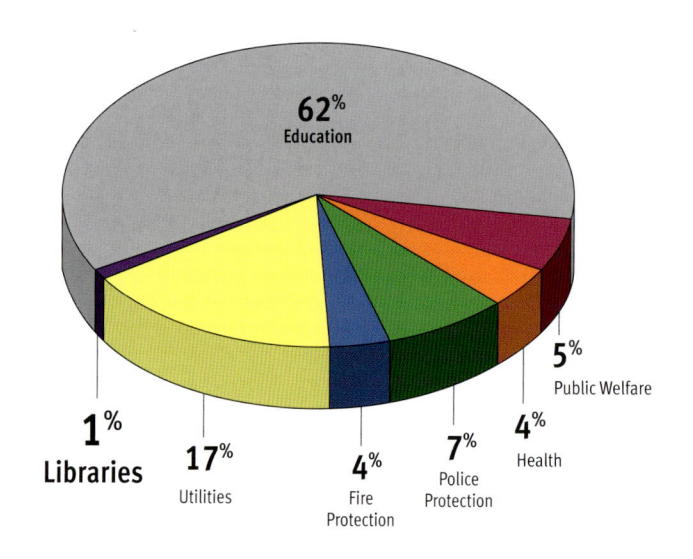

- 62% Education
- 1% Libraries
- 17% Utilities
- 4% Fire Protection
- 7% Police Protection
- 4% Health
- 5% Public Welfare

Source: U.S. Census Bureau

The public library receives just under 1% of the total local operating budget.

Source: U.S. Census Bureau

Voting respondents who say they will *definitely* vote yes in support of a library referendum often indicate that they are also willing to support an increase in taxes to fund other local public services as well.

A side-by-side comparison of the willingness of a voter segment to increase taxes to fund local public services, including the public library, shows that a willingness to fund one service is often similar to their willingness to support other local services.

The most committed library funding supporters, Super Supporters, show a strong intent to vote yes in support of library referenda: 83% agreed strongly that they would be willing to raise their taxes to fund the public library. Community support from Super Supporters does not just include support for the public library. In fact, Super Supporters of libraries are also 'super' in their financial support of other locally funded public services. Eighty-six percent (86%) of Super Supporters agree they are willing to increase taxes in support of the fire department with the same rating; 78% are willing to increase taxes for public schools; and 75% will support a tax increase for police. In fact, over half of all Super Supporters indicated they would support a tax increase for each of the public services surveyed.

Super Supporters

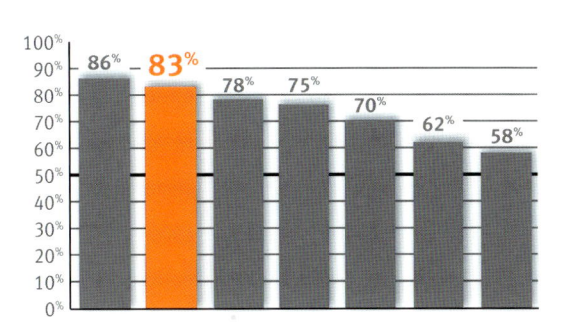

[Bar chart showing: 86%, 83% (highlighted), 78%, 75%, 70%, 62%, 58%]

Source: *From Awareness to Funding*, OCLC, 2008

While Probable Supporters' willingness to support tax increases does not match the level of Super Supporters, many Probable Supporters agree that they are willing to increase taxes for their public library. As with library Super Supporters, many Probable Supporters are also willing to increase taxes for other public services. For example, over 55% of the Look to Librarians segment of Probable Supporters indicate agreement with an increase in taxes for library funding; 45% would also support an increase in taxes for police, fire, schools, public health and parks.

Probable Supporters show a generally consistent attitude toward supporting tax increases across many local public services.

Greater Good
[Bar chart: 63%, 57%, 52%, 42% (highlighted), 41%, 31%, 26%]

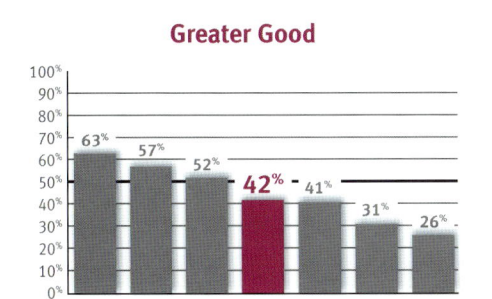

Kid Driven
[Bar chart: 65%, 62%, 61%, 51% (highlighted), 39%, 36%, 30%]

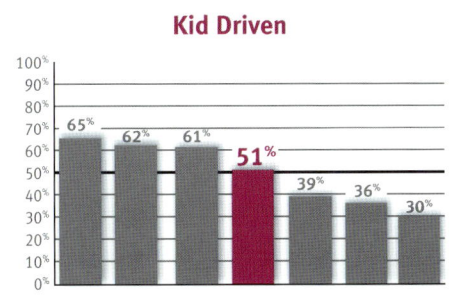

Look to Librarians
[Bar chart: 55% (highlighted), 46%, 46%, 45%, 45%, 45%, 26%]

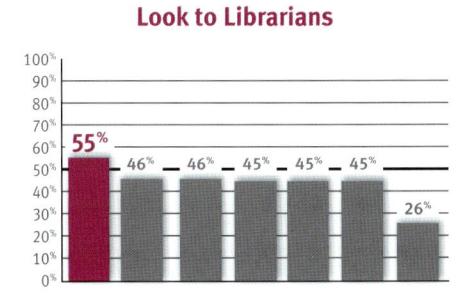

Just for Fun
[Bar chart: 52%, 50%, 49% (highlighted), 44%, 37%, 26%, 21%]

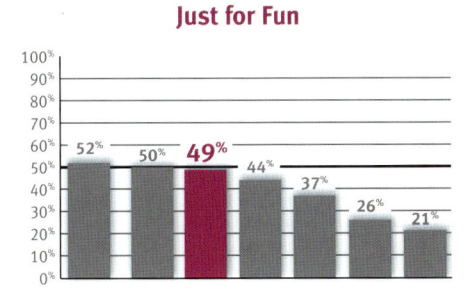

Library as Office
[Bar chart: 48%, 47%, 45%, 39%, 31% (highlighted), 21%, 18%]

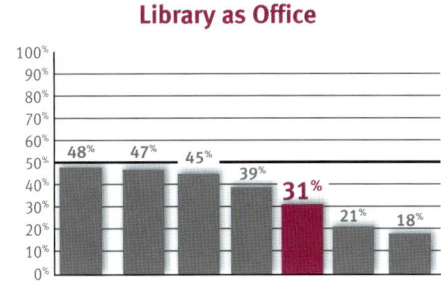

Source: *From Awareness to Funding*, OCLC, 2008

Library funding support is an attitude, not a demographic

The tier of voters with significant barriers to supporting funding for the public library, the Barriers to Support tier, also indicates a lower overall support for tax increases for other local services. While 51% of the Detached segment respondents agree that they would support a tax increase for the fire department, no other local service received majority support from any segment on this tier. In general, respondents across all Barriers to Support segments are less likely than Super Supporters and Probable Supporters to be in favor of tax increases for community services.

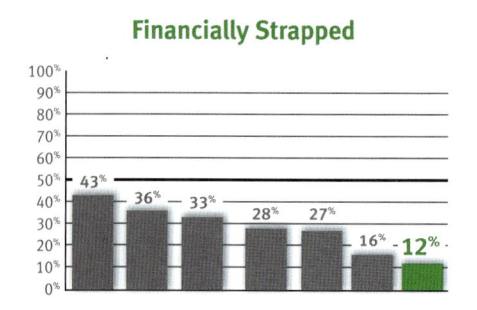

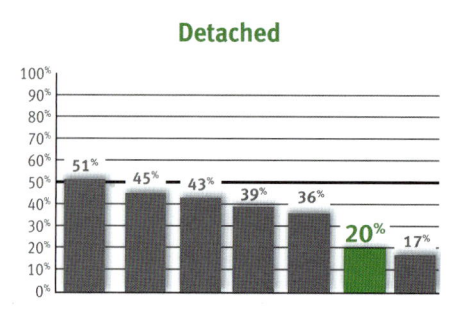

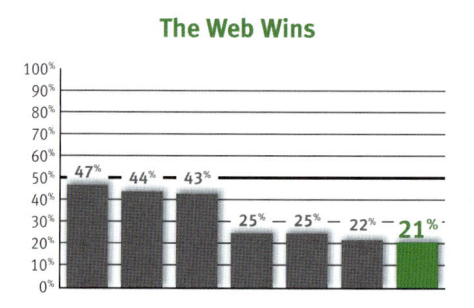

Financially Strapped: 43%, 36%, 33%, 28%, 27%, 16%, 12%

Detached: 51%, 45%, 43%, 39%, 36%, 20%, 17%

The Web Wins: 47%, 44%, 43%, 25%, 25%, 22%, 21%

Source: *From Awareness to Funding*, OCLC, 2008

The willingness to provide financial support across a wide range of public services by Super Supporters and Probable Supporters was reinforced during qualitative field research. Focus group participants did not consider that raising awareness of the library funding meant a decrease in importance of other local services. In fact, many focus group respondents spoke passionately about the need to ensure that the library was considered alongside safety and education in the context of all local funding discussions. Many noted that the relationship between schools and the library as partners in a child's education made it important for both services to receive funding.

A targeted campaign aimed at increasing funding support for libraries in the Super Supporters and Probable Supporters segments does not necessarily call for a decrease in support for other locally funded public services. In fact, placing the library in the consideration set along with other key local services can increase the level of awareness and importance of the interrelationship with other local services.

8. Elected officials are supportive of the library—but not fully committed to increasing funding. Engaging Super Supporters and Probable Supporters to help elevate library funding needs is required.

As outlined in Chapter 3, elected officials hold many of the same views about their public libraries as do the voting population. Overall, they are more committed to the success of their libraries. They visit the library more frequently and rate it higher than most voters. Elected officials are similar to Probable Supporters in their overall attitudes about public library support and funding.

However, positive associations do not necessarily translate into support for funding increases. Elected officials value the public library and sympathize with its financial situation. Sixty (60%) percent of elected officials say they would *definitely* support putting a library referendum, ballot initiative or bond measure on the ballot. Still, the majority of elected officials (73%) think their library has enough day-to-day operating funds.

A comparison of the willingness of elected officials to increase taxes for the public library and for other public services shows that when asked about funding across the board, the elected officials are not likely to pay more in taxes.

It is important to note how similarly elected officials viewed funding increases across most local services. Just nine percentage points separate the level of funding support across the top five services. Police (49%), fire (46%), schools (42%), road maintenance (42%) and the public library (40%) are all in a similar percentage range. Convincing local elected officials to increase taxes for any of these services is not an easy task.

The library places in the bottom half of the list of public services that elected officials are willing to support with a tax increase

Elected officials

For each service, please rate how much you agree with the phrase "I'd be willing to pay more in local taxes to better fund this service." Please use a 10-point scale, where a 10 means you 'Completely Agree' and a 1 means you 'Completely Disagree.'

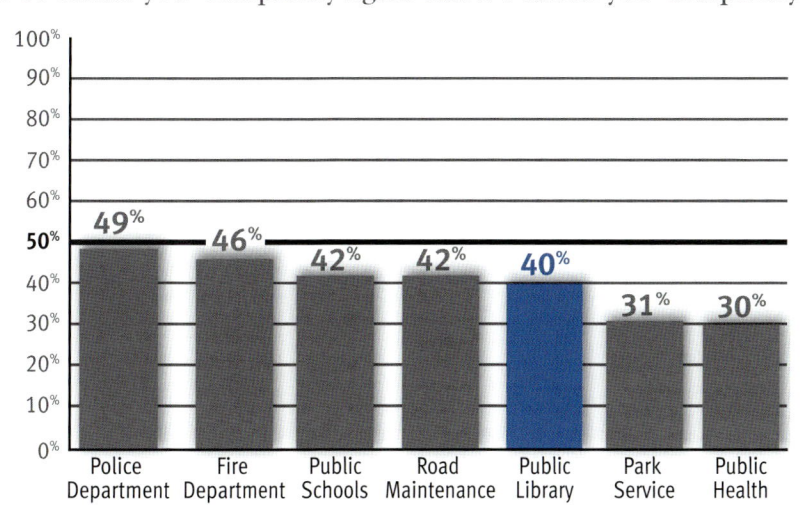

Service	Percentage
Police Department	49%
Fire Department	46%
Public Schools	42%
Road Maintenance	42%
Public Library	40%
Park Service	31%
Public Health	30%

Percentage of elected officials with an agreement rating of 8, 9 or 10
Source: *From Awareness to Funding*, OCLC, 2008

The library is often not a top priority for elected officials. They are managing a long list of important public services that are in need of financial support and many face strong pressure by their constituencies to limit local tax increases.

Library funding support is an attitude, not a demographic

Elevating the financial needs of the library by positioning it as vital community infrastructure, rather than a 'nice to have' service, is required. As local officials weigh the costs and benefits of increasing taxes or allocating funds, the profile and value of the library relative to other services must be increased. Engaging community support from the most likely library financial supporters can be an important factor in elevating this discussion. Engaging the support of Super Supporters and Probable Supporters to increase the attention of their elected officials on tax support for libraries is essential.

Chapter 5

Motivating Probable and Super Supporters—testing the facts in the field

The quantitative research provided a new framework for understanding the dynamics that drive, or limit, library funding in the United States. The research suggests that the U.S. voting population can be segmented into three tiers of library funding supporters: voters with significant barriers to support, probable funding supporters and supporters whose funding support is virtually guaranteed. The attitudes, perceptions and behaviors of the Probable Supporters and the Super Supporters are differentiated and identifiable. A thorough understanding of the attitudes, perceptions and behaviors that define these two groups, and those that separate these two groups, will be essential for creating an advocacy program capable of turning the tide of declining support for public library funding.

While Super Supporters and Probable Supporters share many common attributes, a comparison of these two groups highlights an intensity difference in the commitment to library support. Super Supporters do not question the need to provide ongoing or increased funding support for the library. Probable Supporters see the library as important, but important relative to a set of other local services.

Super Supporters have an emotional connection to the library that transcends the practical function of the library. They do not view the library as simply a place to learn, but instead, see the library as a place that transforms them; a place where they become the person they've always wanted to be. Probable Supporters share the belief that the library can change lives and see the library's role in bringing the community together but are more likely to see the library's role in practical, less transformational terms.

The following chart compares the market size, demographics, attitudes and behaviors of the Super Supporters and the Probable Supporters.

Motivating Probable and Super Supporters—testing the facts in the field

Comparing Super Supporters and Probable Supporters

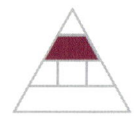

Super Supporters

Statistics
- Comprise 7.1% of the population
- Comprise approximately 12% of *local* election voters
- 80% would *definitely* vote favorably for a library levy
- 14% would *probably* vote favorably for a library levy

Attitudinal/behavioral characteristics
- Demographically average
- Most likely to express their opinions vocally and at the ballot box
- Avid readers who have a long-standing relationship with the library
- Library was important to them as a child

Involvement in community
- They are the most involved and influential in their communities
- Recognize the library's importance to the community and children's education
- View the library as a place that can bring a community together

Emotional connection to the library
- Their emotional connection to the library transcends the practicality—it's a place where they can better themselves intellectually and become the person they've always wanted to be
- Believe the library maintains its relevance to people through all stages of life
- 81% value the 'passionate librarian' as a true advocate for lifelong learning
- Only the fire department (86%) outscored the public library (83%) in definite support of increased local taxes

In their own words...
"To live in a community without a library would be similar to living in a community without air."
Super Supporter

Probable Supporters

Statistics
- Comprise 32.3% of the population
- Comprise approximately 45% of *local* election voters
- 47% would *definitely* vote favorably for a library levy
- 39% would *probably* vote favorably for a library levy

Attitudinal/behavioral characteristics
- A few demographic tendencies, identifiable by segment
- Appreciate the library's contribution to the 'greater good'
- Recognize that the research/information the library provides is superior to the Web
- Believe the library is a key partner in a child's education

Involvement in community
- Feel the library is an important asset to the community
- Often use the library to attend meetings
- Some are local business owners who use the library as their office
- Many are parents of school-age children

Emotional connection to the library
- Believe the library can change the world by turning people into thinkers and achievers, rather than passive participants in life
- Not always personally connected to the library, but believe the library is a noble place; important and relevant to their community
- 66% value the 'passionate librarian' as a true advocate for lifelong learning
- The library ranks comparably with the fire department, police and schools in definite support of increased local taxes

In their own words...
"If the library closed, it would deny many people access to basic information and Internet, as well as shutting down a valuable tool for intensive research."
Probable Supporter

5-2   From Awareness to Funding: A study of library support in America

So, what most motivates Super Supporters to hold, and maintain, their solid and elevated level of support for the public library? The quantitative research indicates that it is not frequency of library visits or knowledge of library services. Can the factors and messages that drive this strong support be identified and then applied to increase the commitment of Probable Supporters? What factors can most influence both Super Supporters and Probable Supporters to increase their library funding support?

Testing the facts in the field

Qualitative round one

Phase two of the advocacy research project was aimed at learning more about the motivations and attitudes that guide, and separate, the library's Super Supporters and the library's Probable Supporters using a variety of qualitative field research techniques.

Ten focus groups of Super Supporters and Probable Supporters were conducted in April 2007 in Huntsville, Alabama; McPherson, Kansas; Medford, Oregon; Minneapolis, Minnesota; and Pittsburgh, Pennsylvania.
Source: U.S. Census Bureau, 2006

Ten focus groups composed of Super Supporters and Probable Supporters were conducted in five towns and cities across the United States. (Two focus groups were held in each location.) The field research explored a variety of attitudes, beliefs and motivations. The focus groups studied the perceived relevance of the library in this time of increased access to information via the Internet and more fully explored the motivations, and the barriers, that impact library funding support. The research explored reactions to 'life without the library' and aimed to better understand how perceptions of the library as a place for information, or a place for transformation, influence attitudes toward library funding.

Field research included the following three primary areas of exploration:

- **Early memories.** Past associations with the library were explored through a 'first memory of the library' exercise.
- **Current perceptions of the library.** Current associations with the library were explored through the development of individual collages.
- **Life without the library.** The importance of the library in the community was explored through futuring scenarios. Focus group participants were asked to envision their community if the library was permanently closed and to discuss the impact to themselves and to their community.

Early memories

The quantitative survey indicated that voters who perceive that the library has the ability to transform their lives and their communities are more likely to vote in favor of a library funding measure. During the focus groups, the Super Supporters and Probable Supporters spoke in more detail about how their perceptions of the library were formed.

Early memories, the library as a transformative force

There was a core emotional imprint of the library formed in early childhood that was shared by most or all participants. This early imprint formed the basis for the belief that the library is a transformative place.

While Super Supporters' and Probable Supporters' first memories of visiting the library were highly individual, there were important consistencies. Focus group participants typically attributed special significance to the person who accompanied them to the library, whether that person was a parent, grandparent, aunt or older sibling. Friends were also often present in early library memories.

The librarian, often remembered by name, also played a key role. Focus group participants noted that the librarian was a person who encouraged and guided, but who also let them find their own way and make their own decisions. The ability to select the books they wanted, not guided by an adult, was often noted as one of the first acts of independence in early childhood. A library card represented a rite of passage to adulthood and independence. A sense of individuality came with the ability to choose a topic and book for oneself. The responsibility of taking library books home made an impression on early memories. For some, this experience launched a love of reading and/or inspired an interest or even a career in a specific area. All shared a sense of the possibilities available at the library.

The library as a transformational place can be associated to this early act of responsibility and choice for many of the Super and Probable Supporters.

The library itself, the physical place, also made a strong and lasting impression on both Super Supporters and Probable Supporters. Memories associated with the physical senses—sight, smell, sound, touch—were vibrant across most all focus group participants. The scale of the library building, both outside and inside, and the sheer volume of books sometimes inspired awe and sometimes ignited memories of the library as overwhelming. The need to be quiet in the library generated memories of responsibility, tension and respect.

Participants remembered a range of experiences at the library, including detailed memories of summer reading programs, puppet shows, story time and specific books they read or checked out. Reactions to these first library experiences were not always positive. Some focus group members recounted being intimidated by the size, seriousness and solemnity of the library. Others were excited by the fun, the adventure and the welcoming comfort of the children's area. Many noted that their first library experiences introduced them to a sense of opportunity and fantasy that books can provide.

> *"The inside was warm; the chairs were the right height. You felt safe. It was quiet and happy. I had a favorite book I would check out over and over again. I remember being excited about being in the library, the potential there, the books and all the things you could look at. Being able to go into yourself and not worry about other people, but just be in your world and everyone else was okay with that."*
> (Probable Supporter, Medford, Oregon)

> *"From outside, the building was like the White House—that's what it reminded me of. Then going in and walking through these big doors. They seemed so big."*
> (Super Supporter, Minneapolis, Minnesota)

> *"I had already started my love of reading. It was a good place to be. That would be the first time I ever got to check out a book. I was feeling so individual ... this is the one thing I'm doing for myself that no one else is involved in. My decision. It's a big part of growing up; that opportunity to be independent."*
> (Super Supporter, Huntsville, Alabama)

The emotional impact of early library experiences was strong for both Super Supporters and Probable Supporters. The lasting impressions of these early associations with their libraries and librarians were reflected in their current perceptions of the library.

Current perceptions of the library

Current associations and perceptions of the public library reveal that the imprint left by early memories of the library still affects a deeply held, lasting belief that the library is a transformative place where anyone can realize their potential.

Current beliefs and attitudes about the library were revealed through a set of projective exercises. The research was constructed to ensure that findings identified current and future-looking attitudes about the library, not simply past associations or top-of-mind perceptions.

The focus group discussions revealed that current associations with the library can be best described by reviewing perceptions and beliefs across three dimensions: the resources offered by the library, the context in which the resources are offered (i.e., the place) and the benefits of the resources.

The resources

Focus group participants described the library as a place of rich resources. Libraries are seen by both Super Supporters and Probable Supporters as a community service providing almost unlimited resources and inspiration, from access to computers, research support, books for story time, art and music. Participants viewed the library as a source of knowledge to explore and learn about almost any topic, from travel destinations to hobbies like gardening and music, to medical conditions and treatments.

The place

The library is seen by most focus group participants as a physical place that provides residents with an oasis and a sanctuary. The environment, which they described as quiet, calm and orderly, makes a great place for relaxation, a place to renew the body, mind and soul. The library provides an opportunity for mental escape from daily concerns or activities.

The public library is also seen as a neutral territory where anyone can feel safe. Probable Supporters and Super Supporters recognize that the library plays a role in building the social fabric of the community. Participants repeatedly note that the public library serves as a community gathering place. Families spend quality time reading together and participating in library programs. Community groups come together at the library. All walks of life meet and interact in the natural process of sharing the library resources and facilities.

The benefits

Participants perceived that the benefit of the library and its resources is a broadened world view. The library was described as a place that 'opens up windows to the world,' a place to gain perspectives on other cultures, places and people. For many participants, this broader view provides an ability to broaden their own personal perspectives. The benefits of library services include providing a sense of enlightenment—the ability to grow beyond the reaches of one's day-to-day reality. Many described the ability to expand their horizons as the heart of the library's value.

Independence to explore and develop individual beliefs, values and priorities without intervention or judgment was often described as another benefit derived from the library and its resources. Reflections on early childhood experiences of choosing books without following a curriculum or direction from an adult create the basis for the belief that the library offers independence. Participants noted that as they grew, the library provided exposure to topics or perspectives they had not previously considered or imagined.

Participants recounted how they discovered a passion for a topic that formed the start of a new career or hobby and ultimately helped them achieve their potential. They discussed how they were able to access resources otherwise unavailable to them that broadened their world view or helped them set their sights on a specific goal. They credited the library with helping form who they are and what they have achieved as adults. Many credited poignant interactions with their childhood librarians as impacting the direction of their lives. Some indicated that the library gave them the vision to do better and go further than they might otherwise have been destined for.

"People who've been exposed to libraries realize that there are a lot of other cultures and things out there that a small town of 4,000 doesn't provide access to. The library is literally a window on the world."
(Super Supporter, McPherson, Kansas)

Current associations with the library

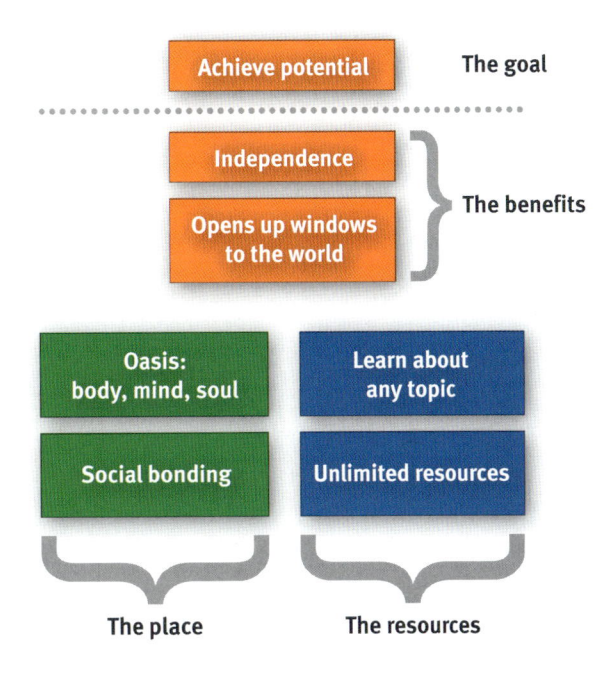

- Achieve potential — The goal
- Independence
- Opens up windows to the world — The benefits
- Oasis: body, mind, soul
- Social bonding — The place
- Learn about any topic
- Unlimited resources — The resources

Ten focus groups of Super Supporters and Probable Supporters were conducted in April 2007 in Huntsville, Alabama; McPherson, Kansas; Medford, Oregon; Minneapolis, Minnesota; and Pittsburgh, Pennsylvania.
Source: *From Awareness to Funding*, OCLC, 2008

Motivating Probable and Super Supporters—testing the facts in the field

Life without the library

Super Supporters consistently expressed the transformational power of the library throughout the focus group exercises. Probable Supporters articulated these same beliefs and perceptions, but often with less intensity. Although both groups were active and engaged research participants, it was not until the discussion moved to an exercise that considered the loss of the library that their real passion for libraries surfaced.

Focus group participants were asked to consider a hypothetical loss of public libraries. Descriptions and attitudes about the impact on the community and members of that community allowed focus group participants to explore their associations with the library beyond their own personal experiences.

Participants were asked to imagine ten years into the future and think what their community would be like if the public library had closed. Participants imagined a range of consequences to their personal lives, to the lives of their children and to their communities if their library had shut down. The exercise revealed significant levels of passion from participants, and two important new findings:

- A belief, held by even the most ardent library supporters, that the library is losing relevance in today's world; and
- A realization that the Probable Supporters' passion for the library is latent and does not fully surface until they are made aware of the real possibility of a decline of library services.

This research activity surfaced two very distinct camps of thought about the future if the library were to close:

- Pragmatic acceptance of the emerging digital tide; and
- Passionate predictions of disaster.

Pragmatic acceptance of the emerging digital tide

The first group of Super and Probable Supporters were emotional about their relationship with the library but pragmatic when it came down to the possibility that the public library could be closed in their community, or ultimately cease to exist as an entity at all. Questions were raised about the relevance and necessity of the public library in an age of technology. During the course of discussion it surfaced that, even for the most passionate lovers of the library, the library is becoming less relevant. Access to information from other sources, often the Internet, is changing the relative importance of the library. Many assumed that usage of the public library is down as 'other' people are increasingly turning to the Internet for information.

Even when focus group members did not see a decline in relevance of the public library in their own lives, they perceived that their children or their grandchildren were using the library and its resources less. There was a sense that as the availability of information in digital form increases, the public library would become less and less necessary. They wondered if, as the digital world continues to evolve, the library might ultimately evolve to become a purely virtual experience.

The pragmatic library supporters were disappointed, but ultimately comfortable, with the fact that the public library could potentially be replaced by other sources of information.

A view of the library as an 'institution' of 'information' more important to residents in the 'past' than into the 'future' was at the heart of the relevancy question for this group of library supporters.

"I don't think the library means the same to my children or grandchildren as it did to me. My son goes on the Internet and gets all the information that he wants. A library was a different time ... a slower pace."
(Probable Supporter, Pittsburgh, Pennsylvania)

"Something in my mind just thought, 'Will that become a thing of the past?' With the availability of the Internet, will they just go to an Internet café that has nice seating and it will take the place of the library because they will be connected. Kids don't seem to mind that. It scares me."
(Probable Supporter, Minneapolis, Minnesota)

Visits to U.S. public libraries increased 19% from 2000 to 2005.

Source: National Center for Education Statistics [NCES]

Motivating Probable and Super Supporters—testing the facts in the field

Passionate predictions of disaster

The second group of supporters had a very different and emotional point of view. For the most passionate library supporters in the focus groups, life without the library was described as a series of losses that would create a domino effect, ultimately leading to the dissolution of the residential community as we now know it. The group cited many specific losses that would lead to weaker communities if libraries closed.

They believed that children would be most adversely affected by the closing of the library and participants imagined a community of less-educated youth. This fiercely passionate group feared that without a public library, children would never acquire a love of reading or the sense of adventure that provides a broadened world perspective. Older children would lose a valuable research resource that the school system would be unable to replicate.

This group was not only concerned about the loss of educational opportunities to children if the public library closes but to all community residents. Focus group members from smaller communities were particularly concerned and felt that their entire communities would begin to slip into what they described as a community with a lower IQ. They reasoned that a less-educated population is less intelligent and that community intellect would decrease over time.

The loss of the community gathering place or social center was also cited as a critical loss if the library were to close. The result, they feared, would be an increase in isolation within their communities. Participants perceived that a world without the library would suffer from a reduction in social interaction, a trend they attributed to the rise in use of the Internet. Focus group members articulated concerns that their community would lose a safe, neutral and open meeting place if the library were closed. This loss would lead to a reduction in the community's moral and social values. The elderly and the youth would be particularly impacted. Many imagined that the loss of the library would result in an increase in crime.

> *"If they close off the libraries, you don't have to worry about a Brain Drain. You'll close off the mental capabilities of the people."*
> (Super Supporter, McPherson, Kansas)

> *"The library shows that a town is better off. That hurts the town's image ... that we don't care about how much we know or the children if we let the library close."*
> (Super Supporter, McPherson, Kansas)

> *"I have this picture of everyone on their computers at home alone. There is a real lack in community. That's very scary."*
> (Probable Supporter, Medford, Oregon)

These library supporters also envisioned that the divide between the 'haves' and the 'have nots' would widen without a library. The loss of universal access to the library's resources would create an even greater disadvantage for those without money to purchase information elsewhere. Participants were especially concerned about reduced access to the Internet, a resource they felt is crucial for success in today's world.

Ultimately, the group projected, the fabric of their communities would disintegrate because the heart of the community, the library, would be gone. Discussion often followed that this loss would lead to a decline of their community's relative stature to other towns and cities with a library. "Who would want to live in a place without a public library?" "Are we backwoods?"

Pragmatically, this group was also convinced that the domino effects that would result from the closing of the library would eventually result in a negative economic impact to their community.

> *"It would hurt most as a separating factor. Lots of people don't have home computers. It would be a real disadvantage to have anything less than wealthy parents. There would be a dumbing down for the lower class."*
> (Super Supporter, Minneapolis, Minnesota)

> *"I'm suspicious of a community that won't fund intellectual or cultural pursuits."*
> (Probable Supporter, Pittsburgh, Pennsylvania)

The belief that closing the library would impact everyone in a community, or just certain residents of a community, varied between smaller communities and large metro areas. In smaller towns and rural areas, participants focused more on the 'we' of their community. They believed the potential negative consequences of closing the library would be shared by all, their neighbors and friends, and that the reputation of the entire community would be diminished. In large metro areas, participants were more tuned into concerns about losses to 'others' in their community than themselves. The loss of the library would impact the children, the elderly and the 'have nots.' They typically stopped short of imagining that the entire community would fall apart. Their top community-wide concerns were the potential negative impact on children and the danger of increased crime.

Would an alternative to the library emerge? The focus group participants were not consistent on this view. In certain geographies, the focus group members could not envision an alternative. In other geographies, in Minneapolis and Pittsburgh particularly, residents assumed that ultimately the lost benefits provided by the library would be replaced by new services that would evolve.

Motivating Probable and Super Supporters—testing the facts in the field

The library's relevance was questioned

A belief that the library may no longer be relevant to many residents was expressed in the field research. There was a fear, even among the greatest library supporters, that the library's place in the community is becoming more nostalgic than essential. Concern about the library's relevance was expressed across a range of perceptions about the library.

Information

Institution

Nice to have

Past

Altruism for others

Information: The library is one of many sources of information. It could potentially be replaced by a combination of bookstores, schools, coffee shops and the Internet.

Institution: The library is an institution sometimes associated with an out-of-date building, aged materials and limited accessibility. (The library has limited hours, the Internet is available 24/7.)

Nice to have: Availability of so many other options for information and learning make the library a 'nice to have' service, rather than a necessity.

Past: The library is an important part of supporters' lives, but they question whether it is still relevant for their children and grandchildren.

Altruism for others: The library is less important to them, but it is important for 'other people' in the community.

Motivating Probable and Super Supporters—testing the facts in the field

Supporters' love for the library is latent

The field research findings from the ten focus groups reinforced and amplified what was discovered about Super Supporters and Probable Supporters during the quantitative research. Both Super Supporters and Probable Supporters appreciate the library's contribution to the greater good. They believe that a strong library is good for them and good for their communities. Their core emotional imprint of the library was formed in early childhood and that imprint continues to reinforce their belief that the library offers a rich set of resources and services. It is a place where people can realize their potential.

Even for some of the most committed library supporters, the library is becoming less relevant.

While Super Supporters and Probable Supporters share many characteristics, the level of intensity of support divides them. Super Supporters are proactive in articulating their support of libraries. Probable Supporters hold a shared belief in the power of the library, but their views are not top-of-mind. Their love of the library is latent and must be activated through conversation and awareness.

The qualititive research revealed another important finding: even for some of the most committed library supporters, the library is becoming less relevant. Many supporters are concerned that the library is being used less and will be even less important for their children and their grandchildren. As vital as the library was, and is, for Probable Supporters and Super Supporters, they know that the library must continue to keep pace. The library cannot be allowed to be seen as an institution of the past. It must be viewed as a vital place for community and personal transformation.

There is a core group of supporters whose 'latent passion' for the library is powerful, once ignited. This group was dismayed at the thought of the loss of the local public library and its members were vocal about their fears of what society would become should that eventuality come to pass. The question is whether this group can be moved to action.

Motivating Probable and Super Supporters—testing the facts in the field

Chapter 6

Mobilizing Probable and Super Supporters—what makes the difference

Research is important, but action is essential. To increase and sustain funding for public libraries in the United States, the qualitative and quantitative research must shape advocacy and marketing initiatives to raise awareness of the important role the library plays in the community and to increase support. More voters must vote yes at the polls for library referenda. More elected officials must be convinced that it is good for the community to put library referenda on the ballot or increase the library's share of the local public purse. And the library must be more visible and connected within the community, in the offices of local elected officials and on the minds of the library's most likely supporters.

The quantitative research identified that a sizable segment of library funding supporters exists—the library's Super Supporters and Probable Supporters. They can be identified and differentiated from U.S. residents less likely to support library funding. Their perceptions, attitudes and beliefs about the library can be documented and profiled. But can these two groups be moved to action?

Can more Probable Supporters be moved to vote yes at the ballot box? Can more Super Supporters be moved to act as catalysts within their communities to increase awareness of the role the library plays and the need for increased funding? What is required to motivate supporters to appeal to their public officials or to engage with their neighbors in dialogue about support for the libraries in their local communities?

How far will the 'latent passion' for the U.S. public library carry Super Supporters and Probable Supporters when it comes down to putting their hands in their pockets and persuading others in their communities to do likewise? Translating 'library love' into library funding support was tested during the ten focus group sessions.

A strange thing happens on the way to the voting booth

As detailed in Chapter 5, both Super Supporters and Probable Supporters exhibit strong, often passionate, appreciation for their public libraries. Projective research exercises with Super Supporters and Probable Supporters identified the foundation for that appreciation by exploring the group's early memories of the library. They discussed the group's current perceptions of the library and uncovered the 'latent passion' supporters hold for the library by asking what it might be like to live in their communities if the public library were to close.

Passion for the library was particularly strong when supporters were asked to consider a future without their libraries. The focus groups supported the insights from the quantitative research; for a subset of the U.S. population, belief in the unique value of the library is strong.

But a strange thing happens on the way to the voting booth.

When the focus group discussions moved from the passion for the U.S. public library as an "American right" critical to the health of the local community to the need for increased tax dollars, the mood changed. Tone of voice and body language shifted perceptibly within the group. The passion held by focus group members quickly went underground as the conversation shifted to the question of increasing taxes, their taxes, to fund the library.

Focus group participants spoke in very practical and logical terms about the political and economic barriers that exist to increasing local funding for the public libraries. The quantitative research phase of this study indicated that Probable Supporters and Super Supporters have a commitment and willingness to vote in favor of library funding increases. Super Supporter commitment was particularly strong, with 80% indicating that they would *definitely* vote 'yes' to a library referendum, ballot initiative or bond measure. Probable Supporter votes were not as certain, but still strong. On average, **47%** of Probable Supporters indicate they would *definitely* vote 'yes' for a library funding initiative. During the focus group sessions, the concerns felt by Probable Supporters that led to hesitation in committing to a positive vote became clear.

Some of the barriers that were raised were ones that had been raised during the quantitative survey. For some Probable Supporters the issue was financial, and some members of the groups indicated that they simply did not wish to pay more in taxes. This was either due to an economic strain they felt personally, or due to a perception that local government was not fiscally responsible with the funds they already had at their disposal.

In some cases, the Probable Supporters knew very little about the current state of funding for their local public libraries and simply assumed that even if there was a funding problem "the funding would come from somewhere." The situation in Medford, Oregon, was particularly interesting. Even though the libraries in that town were closed at the time of the focus group research, the Probable Supporters were planning to vote 'no' at a pending library levy to raise the operational funds that would allow the library to open. This was not because they were against the library,

"Feeling good doesn't equate to voting 'yes' for a library referendum."

but they saw it as a personal statement against the local city council who they felt had mishandled funds that had previously been raised for the library and then placed into the general fund. Even in that situation, the residents believed that ultimately the funding situation would be resolved and the libraries would reopen.

> *"I am naïve to the funding and I feel there is a way to still have the library run well, but as a whole we need to be more responsible with our money so I was looking at it that way. Not sure more money is the answer, maybe better management."*
> (Probable Supporter, Minneapolis, Minnesota)

> *"I am just not in general for a tax increase. I don't know that most people are. I like the idea of funding the library but don't know if I want to increase my taxes to do it. I would have to know more."*
> (Probable Supporter, Pittsburgh, Pennsylvania)

Some members of the groups claimed that the library was less relevant today with the advent of the Internet and that, even though the library was a 'nice to have,' it was not necessary for the community to thrive. There was also some discussion about the relative community need for the public library in comparison to other public services. Some supporters simply did not think that the library should be considered in the same category as police, fire and schools and this would limit their commitment to increased funding.

In contrast, other focus group members felt that communities should not see safety as the only community necessity and that the library was equally critical to a healthy community infrastructure. They also did not want the library to be put into the same category as police and fire, but for a different reason. They spoke of the vital role that the library plays in education and in bringing the community together and did not want to be asked to choose between safety and the educational and social fabric of the community. A small number of people in each group pointed out that the library played a unique role in making the Internet and other important resources available to members of the community who did not have that access themselves.

> *"I think it is unfair to put library with fire, police and schools. Life wouldn't be as good without the library but we could make it work if we had to. The others you have to have. The library is a luxury—not something in the same category."*
> (Probable Supporter, McPherson, Kansas)

> *"[If the library goes away] Not much will change—if you look at the way our society is going, and computers, the world is geared more towards high technology, as far as computers, etc."*
> (Probable Supporter, Huntsville, Alabama)

Turning passion into dollars will take more than discussions of the many benefits of the local public library. A national library support campaign would need to create a bridge between the love of the library shared by both Super Supporters and Probable Supporters and the political and economic realities of the world that voters are living in today.

Messages that make a difference

Focus group members participated in an exercise aimed at uncovering the messages that could potentially move both Super Supporters and Probable Supporters to increase their commitment to financial library support and to enlist the support of others in their communities.

Focus group members were asked to create a set of compelling arguments they felt they could use to encourage citizens in their communities to support the public library. For the purposes of this exercise, support was not defined purely in terms of voting for an increase in taxes, but was left open to a broader interpretation (participate in meetings, e-mail local elected officials, etc.).

Several consistent support themes surfaced in the discussion across all five locations. Probable Supporters and Super Supporters felt that support for libraries can be improved by increasing the public's attention to four essential community benefits that the public library uniquely delivers:

- Equal access
- Shared community values (or teaches values)
- A sacred place
- Community stature.

Equal access

The focus groups were unanimous in their belief that the most compelling argument in support of funding increases for public libraries is the important truth that U.S. public libraries provide equal access to valuable information resources for all residents. The firm belief that 'equal access for all' to information and technology is a fundamental American right was shared by all focus group participants. This opinion was consistent regardless of participants' demography, location or political leaning.

Interestingly, the value proposition respondents agreed was the most compelling, 'equal access for all,' was not top-of-mind for Probable and Super Supporters. While incredibly powerful when articulated, this essential library value was not readily cited, but came out only after two hours of discussion and the use of projective research exercises. This important value was most often surfaced when respondents considered the consequences should their libraries become vulnerable.

Once it arose this topic typically generated significant discussion as people became passionate about the importance of 'equal access for all.' In several groups, access to information was seen as vitally important and the discussions turned to concerns about the technology readiness of their communities and their residents. The groups often came to a realization that many communities—often their own—were falling behind (the world or the country) in what was required to survive in today's information age. Participants also came to the realization that there were no other affordable ways to get access to electronic information without the public library.

Equal access to information and technology was an important benefit that only the public library was firmly committed to delivering.

'Equal access to all' was expressed as both a local and a national benefit. Several members noted that equal access meant that the library was a catalyst and caretaker for equality across all parts of society, giving anyone the opportunity for self-improvement or conversely, giving them no excuse not to improve. Without the 'free' public library, access to information, history, perspectives, technology and self-improvement would be limited to only certain members of society. This argument also swayed the subset of focus group participants who expressed relatively less concern about a possible future loss of the public library. They were particularly convinced by discussions that helped them realize that access to the Internet might be available for certain members of the community only at the public library.

The groups often came together in agreement that the library and its resources, specifically access to the Internet, was vital for every member of the community to realize their potential. Access to information was expressed as fundamental to American democracy.

> *"No kid should have an excuse for not having a book or knowing how to do research. If you don't have a computer at home, you can go to the public library."*
> *(Probable Supporter, Huntsville, Alabama)*

> *"It's a great promoter of equality and democracy. Anyone can go, anyone can read what they want and make whatever use they want of it for whatever they want to pursue—cooking, science, crafts, entertainment."*
> *(Probable Supporter, Minneapolis, Minnesota)*

Shared community values

In addition to providing equal access to information and technology, focus group participants agreed that the library plays a unique role in teaching important community values and responsibilities. This benefit was important enough to activate discussions that could lead to increased library funding support in their communities. Participants pointed out that the library teaches and reinforces important social values, particularly to children. The groups often questioned where else these values might be learned or practiced if the library went away.

The teaching of shared community values included such activities as:

- **Sharing community assets:** The idea of borrowing, using, caring for and returning something that is a shared public resource is considered valuable and unique to public libraries.

- **Respect for the community:** By caring for community resources at the library, residents exhibit respect for others in their community. The act of taking turns (checking out books, using computers) and remaining quiet in certain areas of the library builds and develops a sense of community belonging and respect.

- **Self-reliance:** The idea that a child (or adult) can investigate, explore and ultimately make personal decisions is a core benefit of the library and of a society.

> *"It's one of the few things that truly can provide a sense of community. It doesn't belong to anyone but to all of us. It's a good lesson in respect, being quiet, signing up for Internet time, returning books on time. It's kind of a good building block in respect."*
> (Super Supporter, Minneapolis, Minnesota)

A sacred place

For many Super Supporters and Probable Supporters, the library is seen as a 'sacred place' that has distinct and unique qualities that make it worthy of increased financial support. Focus group members described the 'transformational' qualities of the library in this context:

- **Quiet:** a place where anyone can think, escape and relax
- **Order:** a place of predictable organization and processes
- **Freedom:** an opportunity to think and read about almost anything
- **Safety:** compared to other public places, the library is a safe place—a safe physical location and a safe mental space, a place of open and forward thinking
- **Social bonding:** a location that brings together individuals, groups, friends, family and future families.

> *"It's a gathering place where lots of different people can listen to someone else's ideas, whether spoken or written."*
> (Super Supporter, Medford, Oregon)

Community stature

The library's importance to community stature was the fourth fundamental reason supporters cited to support the library. Focus group participants voiced a firm belief that a community that was not willing to support a library was abandoning its core values, sending a negative signal to the world about what the community does and doesn't believe in. The library is a community's public symbol of intellectual curiosity and respect for learning. It conveys the message that the community seeks knowledge and advancement. Focus group participants were concerned that residents might be inclined to leave a community that didn't value the public enough to keep the library open. They also expressed concern that potential residents might not consider a community that had allowed its library to close.

By its presence, the public library signaled a community commitment to forward progress. The best communities were seen to have a flourishing public library. No library was equivalent to no future—to stagnation.

Supporters felt it is the responsibility of the library to help individuals reach their fullest potential and it is the residents' responsibility to ensure that the community, as a whole, reaches its full potential. Focus group members felt that supporting the public library is equivalent to supporting every community member's right to equal access to information, technology and learning.

There was concern that without a library, the divide between a community's 'haves' and its 'have-nots' would grow wider. The public library was one of the few places that could directly serve to close that gap.

And finally, the focus groups believed that considering the library as having equal community status to other local services was an important and powerful message. The library is as important a part of the community infrastructure as the fire department, the police department and public schools. Economics shouldn't determine which service to fund—all should be funded.

> *"It represents a commitment by the community to cultural and intellectual activities."*
> (Probable Supporter, Pittsburgh, Pennsylvania)

> *"It's necessary for us to continue growing as a society and have ideas for the future. To always be developing in a positive, creative way. We always have to be open to knowledge and I see the library as one place to help us gain that knowledge."*
> (Super Supporter, Medford, Oregon)

Messages that drive library funding support

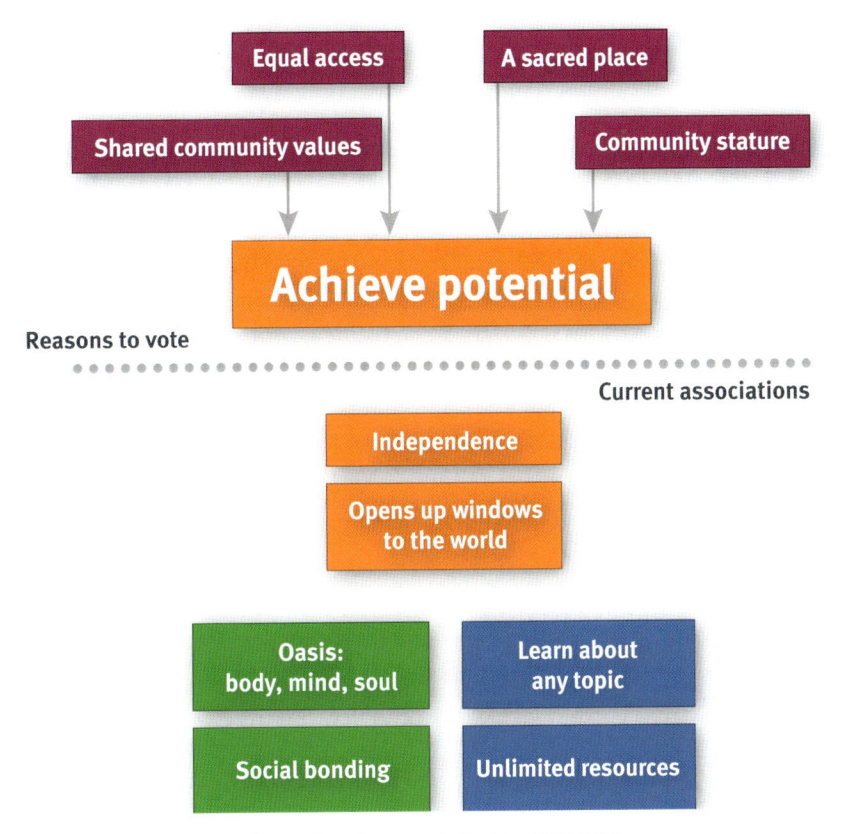

- Equal access
- A sacred place
- Shared community values
- Community stature

→ **Achieve potential**

Reasons to vote

Current associations

- Independence
- Opens up windows to the world

- Oasis: body, mind, soul
- Learn about any topic
- Social bonding
- Unlimited resources

Source: *From Awareness to Funding*, OCLC, 2008

Mobilizing Probable and Super Supporters—what makes the difference

In summary, Super Supporters and Probable Supporters identified four compelling arguments that can drive support for public libraries and public library funding: (1) The library provides equal access. (2) The library teaches important and shared community values. (3) The library holds an important, even sacred, place in the community. (4) The library is a community symbol of freedom of thought and progress; the library creates status for its community.

The focus group research reinforced the quantitative findings that the library's most likely funding supporters view their library, and the librarian, as an essential, transformational community asset. It is important to note that Probable Supporters and Super Supporters did not primarily discuss the library's value in terms of individual or specific library services. They did not equate the library's value to the library's book collection or materials. The objects themselves were not seen as the compelling reason to financially support the library. The impact and value of the library to individual lives and communities are what matters most to library funders.

It is also important to note that while the transformational powers of the library are the defining values to the most adamant supporters, these emotions and beliefs are 'below the surface.' It was not until the focus groups were engaged in discussion that these library values surfaced. These emotions and beliefs are latent even with the most ardent library supporters. Outside the focus group room, these beliefs will easily remain latent when other community issues are pressing or when a funding request is simply that, a request for more dollars, not more value.

The findings of the focus groups strongly suggest that any marketing and advocacy program aimed at increasing library funding will need to frame library funding in both 'value' and 'economic' (i.e., tax) terms. The programs will need to awaken the latent passion that the top library supporters feel about the essential and unique role of the public library in their community, in all communities. Any potential program must reach both the hearts and the economic minds of Probable and Super Supporter voters.

> "If you weren't a cattleman or a farmhand, there wasn't much in the future. I realized at an early age that the library was the ticket out of there. Knowledge is truly power. The more you have, the better off you're going to be.
>
> "We are well behind the curve in the Internet age. These people are thinking about what's happening. If we can't think and adapt to a changing environment, we're going to be left behind. The days of a strong back and weak mind are over.
>
> "People who've been exposed to libraries realize that there are a lot of other cultures and things out there that a small town of 4,000 doesn't provide access to. The library is literally a window on the world."
>
> (Super Supporter, McPherson, Kansas)

Testing campaign messages

Creating a library support brand

The problem a library support campaign strategy must consider is how to turn the tide of dwindling library funding support in an environment where people think libraries are becoming less relevant, where we can anticipate tougher tax choices and where market-specific conditions vary widely.

The proposed solution is to create and promote a brand—not a library product brand focused on marketing library consumption (i.e., usage) but a library *support* brand. The brand must do more than position the library as relevant—it must activate citizen participation and positive funding behavior.

Based on the research findings, the OCLC and Leo Burnett team developed a library support brand strategy and outlined options for messaging and specific marketing tactics for a library support campaign to move the most likely voters from *probable* support of library referenda to *definite* support.

The brand strategy and campaign messaging options were based on the following communications objectives:

Make the library relevant for the 21st century.

Instill a sense of urgency by putting the library in the consideration set for local funding with other public services, like police, parks and fire.

Activate a conversation about how the library is a vital part of the community's infrastructure and future.

Several creative concepts were developed based on these communications objectives. Each creative idea was embodied in the form of an image and a messaging narrative that could form the basis for a library support brand and associated campaign.

Qualitative round two

A second round of field research was conducted to test potential messages and message platforms. The research aimed to identify the most compelling articulation of potential messages that would drive Super Supporters and Probable Supporters to refresh their core beliefs in the library, engage in discussions with elected officials and others members of their communities, and ultimately act in support of increased library funding.

Mobilizing Probable and Super Supporters—what makes the difference

Campaign development and field test

Creative concepts were developed based on the findings from the quantitative and qualitative research. Five concepts were developed for testing. Each concept was embodied in a messaging narrative and a supporting visual image. The goal was not to test potential advertisements but rather to generate reactions, impressions and feedback to messaging and imagery that could guide the further development of an effective messaging platform for a national library support campaign.

The creative directions were evaluated by five focus groups of Probable Supporters and one focus group of Super Supporters in a subset of the same geographies where the initial focus groups were conducted (McPherson, Kansas; Huntsville, Alabama; and Minneapolis, Minnesota). Phone review sessions were also conducted with elected officials using the same creative concepts.

Participants were exposed to the five concepts individually and asked a series of questions regarding their interpretations and reactions. The Probable Supporters, Super Supporters and elected officials were asked to react to the concepts without any previous discussion about libraries or their perceptions or usage of the library. The concepts were randomly selected and rotated to avoid order bias. Groups were not asked to come to a consensus on the best creative direction, but instead to evaluate the concepts individually.

For each concept, participants were asked what they perceived the concept was asking them to do (i.e., use the library, support the library, etc.). After all the concepts had been exposed, they were asked a number of 'compare and contrast' questions to gauge the effectiveness of each concept along the following evaluation dimensions:

- Which concepts, if any, make you see the library differently?
- Which concepts make the library seem more important to your community?
- Which concepts would you talk about with your friends, family and neighbors?
- Which concepts would incite you to take some action to support the library?
- Which concepts, if any, would motivate you to vote yes on a library levy?

The efficacy of a concept to generate active conversation was also observed and asked directly. The goal was to evaluate the concept's ability to generate reactions and impressions that had the power to refresh core beliefs in the library, engage elected officials and ultimately be the foundation of marketing and advocacy programs with the potential to increase library funding.

An effective creative concept must not only appeal to one or more of the four unique, essential values of the library (equal access, shared community values, a sacred place and community stature), but it must also reposition the library to be seen as an essential part of the community infrastructure for the 21st century. As discussed in Chapter 5, for many of the most ardent supporters, the Internet has changed the landscape and the library was seen as losing relevance to themselves and to their children and grandchildren. To respond to this reality, concepts were presented that addressed the issue of the Internet head-on, accepting the fact that for many Probable Supporters, a discussion of the Internet's impact on the library was essential to effectively positioning the library as a critical part of the community's infrastructure.

An effective library advocacy and marketing campaign in support of increased library funding must ensure that the library is positioned or, if necessary, repositioned as both a unique and essential part of the community infrastructure. The library cannot be viewed as a place of information, an institution that is 'nice to have' but not essential, or more important to the past than to the future. Instead, an effective messaging platform must present today's library as a place of transformation.
The library is a vital part of the community infrastructure, as vital as fire, police, schools and parks. It is a necessity, not a 'nice to have,' for a community prepared to compete in the future. The library offers a return to individuals as well as to the community. The value of the library speaks to both the hearts and the economic minds of the target groups, the library Probable Supporters and Super Supporters.

Overall, the feedback to the concepts from Probable Supporters, Super Supporters and elected officials provided important information. Each of the creative concepts satisfied at least some of the evaluation criteria for building a compelling message platform that could refresh the core beliefs of Super Supporters and Probable Supporters, and had the power to drive some level of increased community discussion and support for library funding.

The concepts tested all resonated against one or more aspects supporters believed to be true about the library. Each concept tapped into the latent passion supporters feel about the role of the library. When asked to compare and contrast concepts, the outcome from focus groups varied. Interestingly, each concept was selected as a 'favorite' of one or more respondents in all focus groups. Respondents often wanted to combine concepts.

The library needs to be positioned as a vital part of the community infrastructure

The library must be repositioned. The library can no longer be viewed as a historical institution that is nice to have, but rather as a vital part of the community infrastructure.

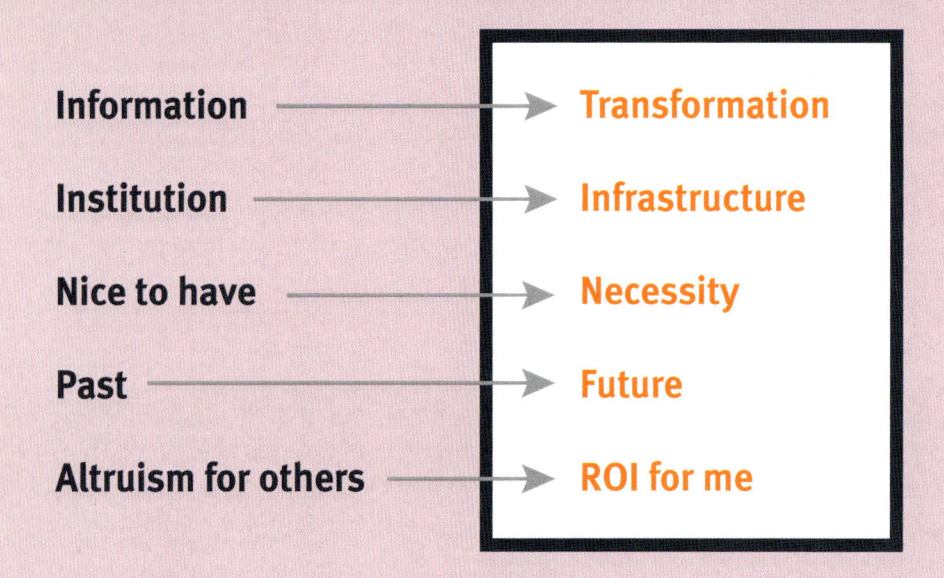

From	To
Information	Transformation
Institution	Infrastructure
Nice to have	Necessity
Past	Future
Altruism for others	ROI for me

Information: The library is one of many sources of information. It could potentially be replaced by a combination of bookstores, schools, coffee shops and the Internet.

Transformation: The library is not about 'information,' it is about 'transformation,' for people and my community.

Institution: The library is an institution sometimes associated with an out-of-date building, aged materials and limited accessibility. (The library has limited hours, the Internet is available 24/7.)

Infrastructure: The library is not an outdated institution. It is a vital part of community infrastructure.

Nice to have: Availability of so many other options for information and learning make the library a 'nice to have' service, rather than a necessity.

Necessity: The library is not simply a 'nice to have' service—it is a necessity. It provides equal access to technology, helping bridge the digital divide.

Past: The library is an important part of supporters' lives, but they question whether it is still relevant for their children and grandchildren.

Future: The library is not a nostalgic building or set of programs. The library provides services and infrastructure for the future.

Altruism for others: The library is less important to them, but it is important for 'other people' in the community.

Return on investment: Library funding support is not based only on a vague sense of altruism, but based on a real economic return for individuals, families and communities.

The feedback to the creative directions indicated strongly that the right campaign can generate the desired response from our target voter segments, repositioning the library as relevant for the 21st century, instilling a sense of urgency to support the library in various ways, and activating conversation with their friends and families. With only a small amount of suggestion, the respondents expressed a desire to find out more and specifically find out what their local elected officials thought about funding the library.

The participants preferred concepts they believed most clearly embodied the role of the library in providing 'equal access for all,' linking the library to the resources that everyone needs to live and succeed in today's society. In particular, the favored concepts were often linked to the importance of access to technology that is provided uniquely at the public library. Several respondents spoke about the library as a right—not a privilege—that should be available to all Americans. They talked about the 'American right to freedom of thought'; 'equal access for the haves and have nots'; and 'one of the American freedoms in the land of opportunity.'

The Probable Supporters and Super Supporters did not need much prompting to move them to a discussion of the library support problem and they did not respond negatively when the issue was raised. Merely saying 'support the library' in the messaging concepts made participants discuss whether the libraries in their communities were vulnerable and they began to suggest ways that they might respond in support.

The concepts generated similar responses in both small and urban markets. Although the three cities included in the research were experiencing different economic and civic dynamics, the creative concept evaluations were consistent and positive, indicating that the right campaign message could bridge a variety of market environments.

The most effective ideas generated a lot of conversation. An effective library support campaign will need to generate conversation and mobilize library supporters to carry the message to others in the community as part of a grassroots component to the campaign, so the ability to generate debate is a critical element of any campaign message. Participants often took the discussion to other relevant topics, inciting a sense of urgency around the idea that in a time of change and new ideas, "we have to keep up." This notion was expressed both in terms of keeping up with technology and keeping up as a nation generally. The most effective concepts connected to both the latent passion Probable Supporters and Super Supporters have for the library and to the economic conversation required to change voting or funding behavior.

Elected officials gravitated to the same concepts and messages as the Probable Supporters and Super Supporters. They believed that an effective library support campaign would have the ability to motivate them in support of the library in their official roles and as members of their local communities. Support for the library was considered to be a platform that they could easily talk about and that their constituents could understand.

Mobilizing Probable and Super Supporters—what makes the difference

Achieving sufficient voting support

The quantitative and qualitative research indicates that is it possible to create an effective messaging platform with the potential to motivate the Probable Supporters and Super Supporters to increase their involvement and voting support of library funding initiatives. But a key question remains: Will a focus on these two market segments provide sufficient increase in the number of committed favorable votes to increase the passage rate of public library levies? Is the target market large enough to achieve the needed result?

A sample of public library levy results

The following list provides a brief sample of 2007/2008 public library operating levies, illustrating that library levies are often decided by narrow, sometimes very narrow, margins. It is not at all unusual for a library referendum to pass or fail by only a few votes. Levies are often placed on the ballot more than once before passing.

2007

Library	Result	Vote
Douglas County Libraries, CO	Failed	49.8% / 50.2%
Sugar Grove Public Library, IL	Failed	47% / 53%
Kingston Public Library, MA	Failed	48% / 52%
Pataskala Public Library, OH	Failed	49.9% / 50.1%
Jackson County Library, OR	Failed	42% / 58%
Edith Wheeler Memorial Library, CT	Passed	52% / 48%
Midlothian Public Library, IL	Passed	51% / 49%
Bay City Library System, MI	Passed	51% / 49%
Wickliffe Public Library, OH	Passed	51% / 49%
Tillamook County Library, OR	Passed	56% / 44%

2008

Library	Result	Vote
Mahomet Public Library District, IL	Failed	44% / 56%
John Mosser Public Library District, IL	Failed	46% / 54%
Wayne County Public Library, OH	Failed	48% / 52%
St. Paris Public Library, OH	Failed	49.8% / 50.2%
Stayton Public Library, OR	Passed	53% / 47%

Sources: Library Referenda 2007: A Mixed Ballot Bag. *Library Journal*, 3/15/2008 (all 2007 results)
Champaign County, Illinois February 5, 2008 General Primary Election Official Results (Mahomet Public Library District)
Knox County Clerk Election Results 2008 General Primary Proposition for John Mosser Library District
Ohio Secretary of State, Report of Votes Cast on Tax Questions for the Primary Election Held on March 4, 2008 (Wayne County Public Library, St Paris Public Library)
Marion County, Oregon, May 20, 2008 Primary Election Final Official Results (Stayton Public Library)

Could a library support campaign targeted at Probable Supporters and Super Supporters make a difference?

The segmentation research findings were applied to create a model of a hypothetical voting scenario using information known about current library levy results.

The model assumes a community with a total population of 50,000 and an eligible voting population of 37,500 (75% of the total population), reflecting the average U.S. eligible voting population.

The model assumes a 30% voter turnout rate to reflect a typical local election.

The model assumes the hypothetical levy failed by a narrow margin, with 48% of votes for and 52% of votes against. The percentage of votes required to pass the levy is assumed to be 50.1%.

The advocacy research provided the following information:

- Together, Probable Supporters and Super Supporters represent 57% of people who vote in local elections:
    - Super Supporters = 12% of *local* election voters
    - Probable Supporters = 45% of *local* election voters

- While a positive vote by the Super Supporters (80%) is almost guaranteed, far fewer Probable Supporters (47%) are *definitely* committed to voting in favor of a library referendum, ballot initiative or bond measure.

- The combined voting patterns of the two target market segments are as follows:
    - Together, 54% of Probable and Super Supporters are expected to '*definitely* vote yes' on a local library referendum **(Definite Supporters)**
    - 13% '*might/would* vote no' on a local library referendum **(Unlikely Supporters)**
    - 33% will '*probably* vote yes' on a local library referendum **(Leverageable Supporters)**

The voting statistics provided by the market segmentation were applied to the hypothetical community to create the model and evaluate the potential impact of a library support campaign.

Mobilizing Probable and Super Supporters—what makes the difference

Hypothetical library levy model
How to read the chart on page 6-17

The model quantifies the potential impact of a library support campaign targeted at Probable Supporters and Super Supporters by applying voting statistics from the market segmentation research to a hypothetical library levy.

- The community modeled has a population of 50,000 residents.

- Seventy-five percent (75%) of the population (37,500) are eligible to vote. This percentage is based on historical U.S. voting statistics.

- Similar to many local elections, only 30% of eligible voters (11,250) turn out to vote.

- Based on the advocacy research, 57% of actual voters are Super Supporters or Probable Supporters (6,413). The research suggests that this target group can be divided as follows:

    - 54% of the target segment (3,463) are expected to *definitely* vote yes **(Definite Supporters)**

    - 13% of the target segment (834) are expected to vote no **(Unlikely Supporters)**

    - 33% of the target segment (2,116) say they will '*probably* vote yes,' meaning that some will vote yes and some will vote no **(Leverageable Supporters).**

- In order to change the result of the failed levy to pass, an additional 236 votes are needed for a majority of 5,636 yes votes (50.1%).

- An additional 236 votes would require 11% of Leverageable Supporters (2,116) to vote yes. 236 votes is 2.1% of the total number of votes cast.

- Therefore, in order to be successful, the library support campaign would need to persuade 11% of Leverageable Supporters to vote yes when they would have otherwise voted no.

Like many failed referenda, this hypothetical levy failed by a relatively small margin. While it is likely that an effective library support campaign would increase the number of favorable votes across all voting segments (Barriers to Support, Probable Supporters and Super Supporters) the voting scenario applies a conservative approach and assesses the outcome based on increasing the commitment of only the most likely 'movable' voters in the target market. The model analyzes a campaign's impact on only 'Leverageable Supporters'—voters in the Probable Supporters and Super Supporters tiers who indicate they will *probably* vote yes on a local library referendum.

It is also realistic to assume that an effective library support campaign would increase the number of favorable votes from the 'Unlikely Supporters' (Probable and Super Supporters who indicated they 'might/would vote no' on a local library referendum). The impact of moving this group was not included in the conservative voter scenario.

Mobilizing Probable and Super Supporters—what makes the difference

Hypothetical library levy model

11,250 VOTES

5,400 YES votes (48%)   5,850 NO votes (52%)
— 236 ADDITIONAL VOTES NEEDED —

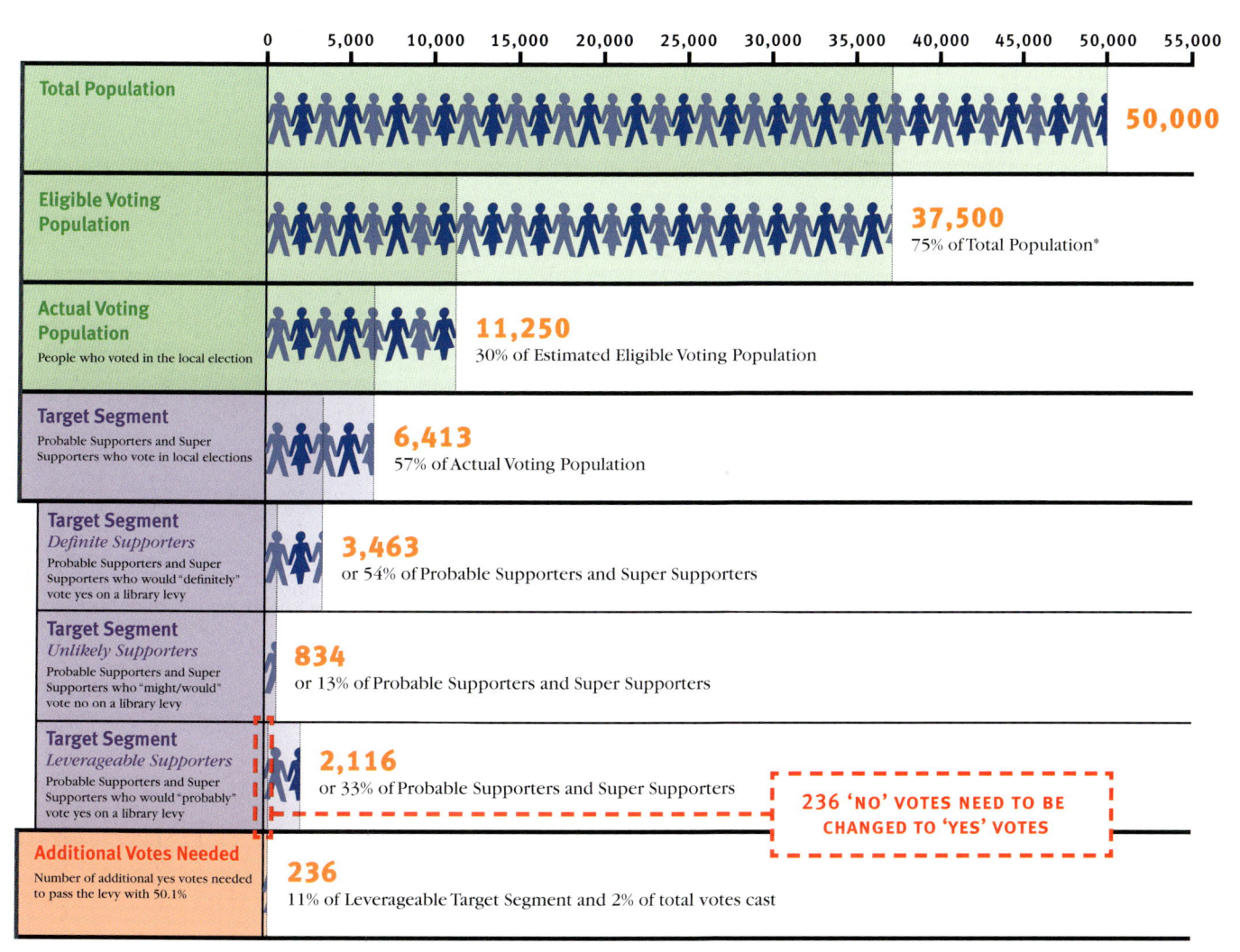

Total Population	50,000	
Eligible Voting Population	37,500	75% of Total Population*
Actual Voting Population — People who voted in the local election	11,250	30% of Estimated Eligible Voting Population
Target Segment — Probable Supporters and Super Supporters who vote in local elections	6,413	57% of Actual Voting Population
Target Segment *Definite Supporters* — Probable Supporters and Super Supporters who would "definitely" vote yes on a library levy	3,463	or 54% of Probable Supporters and Super Supporters
Target Segment *Unlikely Supporters* — Probable Supporters and Super Supporters who "might/would" vote no on a library levy	834	or 13% of Probable Supporters and Super Supporters
Target Segment *Leverageable Supporters* — Probable Supporters and Super Supporters who would "probably" vote yes on a library levy	2,116	or 33% of Probable Supporters and Super Supporters
Additional Votes Needed — Number of additional yes votes needed to pass the levy with 50.1%	236	11% of Leverageable Target Segment and 2% of total votes cast

236 'NO' VOTES NEED TO BE CHANGED TO 'YES' VOTES

*Based on national average as calculated from the U.S. Census Bureau's annual American Community Survey

Source: *From Awareness to Funding*, OCLC, 2008

How achievable is it to change the outcome of a levy by 2–5% or more by targeting Probable and Super Supporters? Based on consultation with political consultants who work specifically with public service funding initiatives, shifts in voter behavior or market share in these ranges are realistically achievable.

The research suggests that a large-scale library support campaign targeted to Probable Supporters and Super Supporters could provide a large enough increase in 'yes' votes to improve the success rate of library levies in many communities across the United States.

Mobilizing Probable and Super Supporters—what makes the difference

Chapter 7

Conclusion

From awareness …

The public's awareness of libraries is based on yesterday.

The research provides important insights into what U.S. voters and their elected officials know, and what they don't know, about public libraries and public library funding.

Most U.S. residents are aware of the traditional 'informational' library services, such as books, newspapers, magazines and Internet access. Far fewer know about the many value-added and 'transformational' services provided by their libraries, such as teen programs, computer training and 'English as a second language' (ESL) classes.

But this is not news to many in the library community. Other surveys have reported similar findings. Libraries have responded by launching marketing efforts focused on increasing awareness of the library and its services. Yet, despite numerous marketing and communications efforts across the country, the perception of the library as 'a physical place offering traditional information services (books and information)' remains well-entrenched in the minds of library users. And while the perceptions of the library may remain fixed, the information landscape is anything but stable. The knowledge landscape is expanding rapidly and the library's once unique position as the 'place that provides books and information' is increasingly crowded. Powerful rivals with deeper pockets—think Google and Barnes & Noble—are able to mount far stronger marketing initiatives in pursuit of the information consumer, claiming more of their mindshare and redefining their expectations of information access. Without action, it is almost certain that the library's brand will continue to be seen as a legacy service, a 'nice to have' but not critical institution, more relevant in the past than for the future.

Residents are not aware that their public libraries are under financial stress.

The advocacy research also revealed that while the majority of residents have visited their public library, most are not aware of how the library facility or its services are funded. Most residents are not aware that their library is largely funded by local taxes—the same community purse that funds their schools, fire, police and public health services.

And of greatest concern, the advocacy research identified that residents are not aware that libraries are under financial stress. Most residents do not realize that libraries—maybe even their local library—have cut services, reduced hours or limited

Conclusion

new material acquisitions due to reductions in their operating budgets or increases in operating costs, such as healthcare, collections and utilities.

Residents are not aware that funding pressures will likely lead to further service trade-offs in the future. It was not until the topic of library financing was explicitly addressed in focus group discussions that residents voiced concerns or opinions about library funding. Even in situations where the focus group members had complained about the reduction in hours of their local libraries, they did not connect that inconvenience with a funding problem. In Medford, Oregon, where the library doors had closed due to a recently failed levy, focus group participants voiced a reluctance to increase taxes, believing that the money to reopen the libraries would come from 'somewhere.'

Elected officials are supportive and aware of the financial needs of the library. Those surveyed report that they are aware of the varied and important services offered by their libraries and recognize their importance to their communities. But the research also revealed that despite their appreciation for the library, local elected officials are not necessarily inclined to increase library funding. The majority felt that their libraries have sufficient operating funds.

So how do we close these perceptual and funding gaps? If, despite the efforts of existing marketing campaigns, the library brand is still about 'books and information,' how can the library be positioned as a 'transformational force' in the minds of more voters? If current library marketing campaigns are focused mainly on driving usage of libraries and awareness of their services, what is needed to increase awareness of the state of library funding to inspire, and activate, residents and local elected officials to increase funding for libraries?

This is not an easy task. Building awareness for any topic, brand or service in a world increasingly blanketed with marketing messages and sophisticated marketing techniques is not easy; nor is it inexpensive. And changing, or stretching, the perceptions of an established brand—a brand as universal in people's minds as the public library—is the most difficult of all marketing activities. But many organizations and brands have successfully increased awareness, revitalized their brands and increased revenues. The research suggests that public libraries can do the same—if they focus on the right target markets.

From awareness ... to funding

Today's support comes from those who believe libraries transform lives.

The research revealed an important distinction between the public library user and the public library funder. Not every library user is a library funder; not every library funder is a library user. A voter's willingness to support increased library funding is not driven, or limited, by library use. In fact, the advocacy research found that there is little correlation between frequency of library visits and willingness to increase funding for libraries.

Conclusion

Not all residents in a community are equal when marketing or advocating for increased funding for libraries.

Not all residents in a community are equal when marketing or advocating for increased funding for libraries. This inequality is not unexpected or unusual. In fact, understanding, accepting and leveraging the differences among different groups of consumers is the premise underpinning successful marketing and branding strategies. Understanding market segments and delivering the right value to the right target segment(s) is the top determinant of market success. As described by our market research partner, Leo Burnett:

"Not everyone is alike and different people want different things from the category. They evaluate, perceive and use brands differently. No brand has 'universal appeal' and the more brands there are in a category, the more this is true.

"For every brand, there is greater chance to build business [funding] among some segments of consumers than others. If these segments can be identified, the brand has a 'roadmap for growth' and can customize marketing efforts to the most likely prospects."

There are many ways to segment a market, including the library funding market. Unlike many research studies and surveys that assume a segmentation construct at the outset of market research (age, gender, income level, education level, etc.), no assumptions were made about which constructs could potentially drive the segmentation of the library funding market; but instead, the constructs were revealed through analysis of the research data. Utilizing the trademarked BrandProspect™ segmentation approach developed by Leo Burnett, the quantitative research data informed the construction of the Library Supporter Segmentation Pyramid.

Library funding support is an attitude, not a demographic.

A crucial and somewhat unexpected finding from the segmentation analysis was that demographics and lifestage were not important constructs in the library supporter segmentation. In fact, demographics are irrelevant to library funding support. The factors that determine residents' willingness to increase their taxes to support their local library are their perceptions and attitudes about the library and the librarian, not their age, gender, education level or household income. Library funding support is an attitude, not a demographic.

The Library Supporter Segmentation Pyramid identified four market tiers: residents who are not registered or do not typically vote in elections (Chronic Non Voters); voters with high barriers to supporting the library (Barriers to Support); voters who are probable library funding supporters (Probable Supporters); and voters who are definite library funding supporters (Super Supporters). Within these four market tiers are 10 distinct market segments, named to reflect their distinctive characteristics: 'Chronic Non Voters,' 'Financially Strapped,' the 'Detached,' 'The Web Wins,' 'Just for Fun,' 'Kid Driven,' 'Library as Office,' 'Look to Librarians,' 'Greater Good' and the 'Super Supporters.' Each of these segments can be profiled according to its unique attitudes and beliefs, as well as its willingness to increase taxes to fund the local library.

Conclusion

Two tiers of the pyramid provide the greatest opportunity for a campaign to increase library funding, the Probable Supporters and the Super Supporters. Together these target market tiers represent roughly 40% of U.S. residents ages 18–69 in communities of 200,000 or less. The market segmentation suggests that a library funding campaign should be targeted at less than half of residents in any community. And because the most likely library funders are not the most frequent library users, the target segments will exclude a large number of regular library users.

The research identified several important shared values and beliefs across the target market segments, the Probable Supporters and the Super Supporters:

- They are involved in their communities
- They recognize the library's importance to the community and to a child's education
- They are not always heavy users of the library, but believe the library is a noble place, important and relevant to the community
- They recognize the value of a 'passionate librarian' as a true advocate for lifelong learning
- They see the library as a vital community resource like public schools, fire and police, and are willing to increase their taxes to support the library.

For the target supporters, the library is not perceived as just a provider of practical answers and information; the most committed supporters hold the belief that the library is a transformational force.

These findings were reinforced during focus groups with Probable Supporters and Super Supporters. Field research in five U.S. communities explored the factors and messages most likely to drive, and to limit, increased funding support for libraries within the target segments.

Awakening and reinforcing the transformational value of the library is the most important factor in increasing library funding support. Several messages made a difference and several messages did not matter.

When Probable Supporters and Super Supporters were asked why they believe the library is a relevant and critical resource for their local community that deserved to be funded, these supporters did not talk about the books or about the information the library provides. They were not swayed to invest in the library because of its products, but rather by the role it plays in helping form the people they are today. Supporters do not believe that the library's value to the community is simply as a source of information, but rather as a 'window to the world' that allows them, and every resident in their community, to achieve their potential. Library funding supporters are not swayed by messages that detail library services delivered, but rather by messages that remind them of the library's impact on their community.

During lively discussions, several themes emerged that supporters felt could articulate the value of the library in ways that could convince them and others in their community to vote for an increase in taxes. Armed with these themes, the

Awakening and reinforcing the transformational value of the library is the most important factor in increasing library funding support.

Conclusion

research team developed and tested a number of potential library support campaign concepts with Probable Supporters, Super Supporters and elected officials. Across all three groups, the most effective campaign concepts addressed the challenges communities face and the positive impact the library can have on alleviating those problems.

A successful library funding support campaign must:

- **Make the library relevant for the 21st century**
- **Instill a sense of urgency by putting the library in a competitive context for funding, alongside the public schools, fire department and police department**
- **Activate conversations about the library's importance in community infrastructure and its role in the community's future.**

The research suggests a large-scale library support campaign targeted at Probable Supporters and Super Supporters, with the right messages and programs, will increase support for the public library. But, of course, this will not happen without library community action. The love that even the most ardent supporters have for the library is latent; their awareness of the funding issues faced by libraries is minimal; and competition for the local community purse is likely to increase. As public libraries face increasing economic strains, Probable Supporters and Super Supporters must be reached, motivated and mobilized to support library funding.

To thrive tomorrow, libraries must translate belief to awareness, and awareness to action.

Next steps

So what are potential next steps?

While the research results are promising, additional field testing and learning are needed before a library support campaign can be constructed. By design, the research and the resulting library supporter segmentation are national in nature; the results therefore represent national averages. Likewise, while we know that Probable Supporters and Super Supporters represent roughly 40% of residents nationally, we do not know how those percentages might vary from community to community.

During the qualitative field research phase, the attitudes and perceptions expressed by Super Supporters and Probable Supporters were consistent from community to community. However, there were differences in the market conditions across the five research locations that could impact the efficacy of a large-scale campaign. From community to community, we found differences in library funding models (levy funding or allocations of a shared local government budget), economic conditions and population changes.

As library funding faces increasing economic strains, Probable Supporters and Super Supporters must be reached, motivated and mobilized to support library funding.

Conclusion

Local library market differences must be studied to determine how local or regional factors can be incorporated into a possible library support campaign. We are happy to report that a 'market-typing' research project is currently planned for summer 2008. This research is the first step in identifying a small number of test markets where a library support campaign could potentially be fielded and evaluated.

OCLC will continue the dialogue with the library community, the Bill & Melinda Gates Foundation and other possible library supporters to evaluate the potential for a library support campaign aimed at turning the tide on public library funding in America.

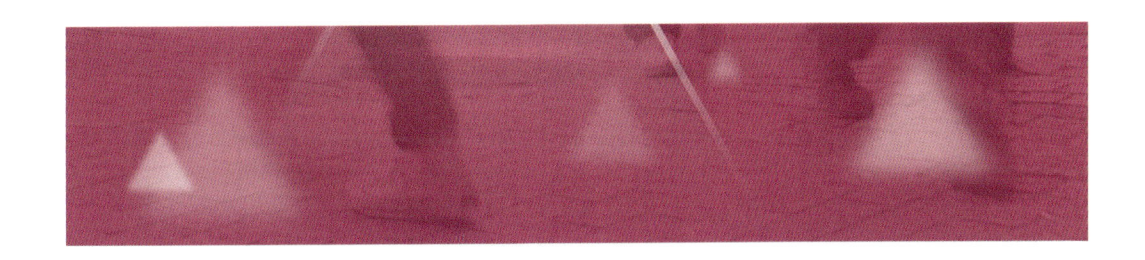

Appendices

A: Glossary — A-1

B: About the Bill & Melinda Gates Foundation and Leo Burnett USA — B-1

C: About OCLC — C-1

Appendices

Appendix: A

Glossary

Advocacy—Active support of a cause, idea or policy.

Barriers to Support—Second-lowest tier of the Library Supporter Segmentation Pyramid. Voters who, for a variety of reasons, have significant barriers to voting for increased library funding.

Bond measure—An initiative to sell bonds for the purpose of acquiring funds for various public works projects.

Brand—The cumulative perceptions about an organization, company or product. A name, term, sign, symbol or design to identify a company, product or service.

Chronic Non Voters—Bottom tier of the Library Supporter Segmentation Pyramid. People who have not registered to vote or have a track record of choosing not to vote.

Convenience sample—Data drawn from a population that has been selected because it is accessible and appropriate; not necessarily a statistically significant sample.

Creative concept—The core idea and framework of a marketing tactic or campaign.

Detached segment—Second segment of the Barriers to Support tier on the Library Supporter Segmentation Pyramid. Characterized by a lack of involvement with local public libraries and their communities as a whole.

Emotional and Intellectual Rewards Framework—Framework that represents a variety of brands, categories and activities, including the public library, based on: 1) the range of emotional ('Transformation') and intellectual ('Information') rewards provided; and 2) the ability to support a practical goal ('Purpose') or to provide an escape from everyday life ('Escape').

Financially Strapped segment—First segment of the Barriers to Support tier on the Library Supporter Segmentation Pyramid. Financial strains are the chief barrier to library support for this segment.

Focus group—A form of qualitative research in which a group of people is asked about attitudes and opinions on a particular topic. Typically held in an interactive setting where participants are free to talk with other group members.

Grassroots—A grassroots movement is driven by forces from within a community. Grassroots activities are ones that can be taken on by members of a group. These movements are often local.

Greater Good segment—Fifth segment of the Probable Supporters tier on the Library Supporter Segmentation Pyramid. Believes that the library plays an important role in serving the needs of the community and can be a great source of pride, given proper funding.

Just for Fun segment—First segment of the Probable Supporters tier on the Library Supporter Segmentation Pyramid. The heaviest users of the library, particularly of recreational activities and services.

Kid Driven segment—Second segment of the Probable Supporters tier on the Library Supporter Segmentation Pyramid. Willing to support the library financially because of the role it plays in educating and inspiring children.

Levy—An imposition of a tax.

Appendix A: Glossary

Library as Office segment—Third segment of the Probable Supporters tier on the Library Supporter Segmentation Pyramid. Uses the library primarily as an extension of the workplace, taking advantage of the library's technology and other resources to conduct work.

Library Supporter Segmentation Pyramid—Market segmentation of library supporters, based on the key drivers of library funding attitudes and behaviors.

Library Support Index—A measure of a segment's willingness to definitely support a library referendum, ballot initiative or bond measure relative to the size of the segment.

$$\text{Library Support Index} = \frac{\%\ \text{Definite Library Supporters}}{\%\ \text{population ages 18-69 in communities} < 200{,}000} \times 100$$

Library Use Index—A measure of a segment's relative frequency of library visitation relative to the size of the segment.

$$\text{Library Use Index} = \frac{\%\ \text{Library Visits}}{\%\ \text{population ages 18-69 in communities} < 200{,}000} \times 100$$

Local public services—For the purposes of this report: the public library, fire department, police department, public health, public schools, road maintenance and park service.

Look to Librarians segment—Fourth segment of the Probable Supporters tier on the Library Supporter Segmentation Pyramid. Has a deep appreciation of the value of the librarian in providing services and research expertise. Also believes that the librarian is a passionate advocate for the library within the community.

Marketing campaign—A series of marketing programs sharing a specific goal and a similar theme.

Marketing tactics—Specific communications vehicles such as paid advertising (TV, radio, newspapers, billboards, direct mail, paid search), earned media (news stories, events, editorials) and social marketing (blogs, wikis, online outreach).

Market segmentation—Dividing a market into distinct groups of buyers on the basis of needs, characteristics or behaviors, who might require separate products or marketing mixes.

Mindshare—Consumer awareness of specific products, companies or institutions within a particular category or field.

Positioning—Arranging for a product to occupy a clear, distinctive and desirable place relative to competing products in the minds of target consumers.

Probable Supporters—Second highest tier of the Library Supporter Segmentation Pyramid. Voters who are likely to support library funding initiatives but are not fully committed.

Qualitative research—Qualitative research aims to gather an in-depth understanding of human behavior and the reasons that govern human behavior. Qualitative research looks for the reasons behind various aspects of behavior, investigating the why and how of decision making, not just what, where and when.

Quantitative research—Quantitative research aims to investigate a human or social issue or behavior based on measurement with numbers and analysis with statistical procedures. The process of measurement is central to quantitative research because it provides the fundamental connection between empirical observation and mathematical expression of quantitative relationships.

Referendum—A direct vote in which an entire electorate is asked to either accept or reject a particular proposal.

Super Supporters—Top tier of the Library Supporter Segmentation Pyramid. People most firmly committed to supporting a library funding initiative.

The Web Wins segment—Third segment of the Barriers to Support tier on the Library Supporter Segmentation Pyramid. Characterized by a heavy reliance on the Internet as information source and a belief that the library provides little added value.

Appendix: B

About the Bill & Melinda Gates Foundation and Leo Burnett USA

Bill & Melinda Gates Foundation

Guided by the belief that every life has equal value, the Bill & Melinda Gates Foundation works to help all people lead healthy, productive lives. In developing countries, it focuses on improving people's health and giving them the chance to lift themselves out of hunger and extreme poverty. In the United States, it seeks to ensure that all people—especially those with the fewest resources—have access to the opportunities they need to succeed in school and life. Based in Seattle, Washington, the foundation is led by CEO Patty Stonesifer and co-chair William H. Gates Sr., under the direction of Bill and Melinda Gates and Warren Buffett.

Leo Burnett USA

Leo Burnett USA, comprising the Leo Burnett brand agency and marketing partner Arc Worldwide, is one of the world's largest agency networks and a subsidiary of Publicis Groupe, the world's fourth-largest communications company. Leo Burnett holds people at the center of its strategic thinking, technological innovation and creative ideas, focusing first and foremost on human behavior before attempting to tell a brand's story. At the core of understanding human insight is Leo Burnett's own quantitative Research Services group. This group is integral to the strategic team and is responsible for handling all types of custom quantitative market research, providing upfront insights into human behavior—the foundation for Burnett's brand work.

With this approach, Leo Burnett ensures that people who buy into client brands believe in them all the more. With expertise in mass advertising and digital, promotional and retail marketing, Leo Burnett partners with blue-chip clients such as The Coca-Cola Company, Diageo, Kellogg, McDonald's, Procter & Gamble and Samsung. The company has won more advertising awards for campaign effectiveness than any other agency in the last six years in the U.S., has been heralded as a "pioneer on the frontier of marketing," and continues to be ranked as one of the world's top-five creatively awarded networks worldwide.

Appendix B: About the Bill & Melinda Gates foundation and Leo Burnett

Appendix: C

About OCLC

OCLC is a nonprofit membership organization that promotes cooperation among libraries worldwide. More than 60,000 libraries in 112 countries have used OCLC services to locate, acquire, catalog, lend and preserve print and electronic library materials.

OCLC was established in Ohio in 1967 by a small group of libraries whose leaders believed that by working together they could find practical solutions to some of the day's most challenging issues. Working together, OCLC and its member libraries cooperatively produce and maintain WorldCat, which now contains over 100 million bibliographic records and more than 1.2 billion library holdings.

Collaboration among librarians and OCLC solved the practical problem of automated cataloging. Ongoing collaboration led to additional OCLC services, including services that help libraries build e-content collections and provide online access to special library collections like maps, newspapers, photographs and local histories. It also led to the creation of the largest interlibrary loan system in the world for exchange of more than 9.7 million items annually to information consumers and scholars around the world.

WorldCat.org continues OCLC's efforts to make library resources more visible to Web users and to increase awareness of libraries as a primary source of reliable information and helpful personal assistance.

In addition to the many services offered, OCLC funds library research programs, library advocacy efforts, scholarships, market research and professional development opportunities.

OCLC Programs and Research incubates new technologies; sponsors the work of library scientists; represents libraries on a range of international standards bodies; and is also actively engaged with the world's information community to further the science of librarianship.

OCLC library advocacy programs are part of a long-term initiative to champion libraries to increase their visibility and viability within their communities. Programs include advertising and marketing materials to reinforce the idea of the library as relevant, and market research reports that identify and communicate trends of importance to the library profession. Several of the reports are noted on page C-3.

Appendix C: About OCLC

OCLC provides financial support for those beginning their library careers and for established professionals who excel in their endeavors through a series of annual awards and scholarships.

OCLC also participates in WebJunction, an online community of libraries and other agencies that share knowledge and experience to provide the broadest public access to information technology. A service created by the Bill & Melinda Gates Foundation's U.S. Library Program, OCLC and other partners, WebJunction addresses real issues that librarians and library staff face every day.

OCLC's vision is to be the leading global library cooperative, helping libraries serve people by providing economical access to knowledge through innovation and collaboration. OCLC is headquartered in Dublin, Ohio, U.S. and has offices throughout the world.

Appendix C: About OCLC

OCLC research and reports

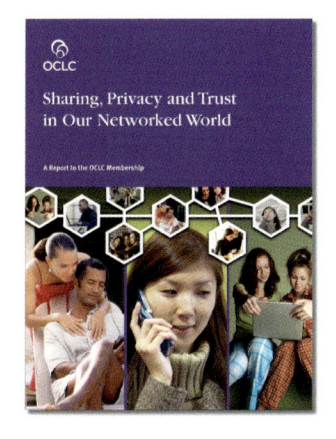

The *Sharing, Privacy and Trust in Our Networked World* (2007) report is based on a survey (by Harris Interactive on behalf of OCLC) of the general public from six countries—Canada, France, Germany, Japan, the U.K. and the U.S.—and of library directors from the U.S. The research provides insights into the values and social-networking habits of library users and explores the web of social participation and cooperation on the Internet and how it may impact the library's role. To access the report, visit the OCLC Web site at: **www.oclc.org/reports/sharing/.**

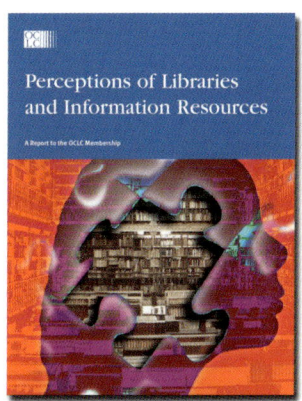

The *Perceptions of Libraries and Information Resources* (2005) report summarizes findings of an international study on information-seeking habits and preferences. The study was conducted to help us learn more about: library use; awareness and use of library electronic resources and Internet search engines; use of free vs. for-fee information; and the 'Library' brand. The report was based on the survey results from 3,348 respondents from six countries: Australia, Canada, India, Singapore, the U.K. and the U.S. To access the report, visit the OCLC Web site at: **www.oclc.org/reports/2005perceptions.htm.**

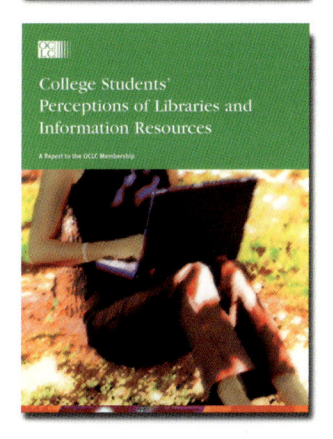

The *College Students' Perceptions of Libraries and Information Resources* (2006) report presents a subset of the *Perceptions of Libraries and Information Resources* report, and focuses on the perceptions and behaviors of 396 undergraduate or graduate students ranging in age from 15 to 57. The study was conducted to help us learn more about: library use; awareness and use of library electronic resources and Internet search engines; use of free vs. for-fee information; and the 'Library' brand. To access the report, visit the OCLC Web site at: **www.oclc.org/reports/perceptionscollege.htm.**

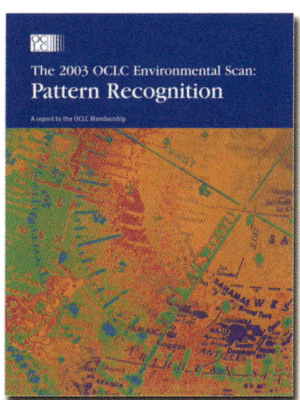

The 2003 OCLC Environmental Scan: Pattern Recognition report was published in January 2004 for OCLC's worldwide membership to examine the significant issues and trends impacting OCLC, libraries, museums, archives and other allied organizations, both now and in the future. The *Scan* provides a high-level view of the information landscape, intended both to inform and stimulate discussion about future strategic directions. To access the *Scan*, visit the OCLC Web site at: **www.oclc.org/reports/2003escan.htm.**